THE ROMANTIC NOVEL
IN ENGLAND

THE ROMANTIC NOVEL
IN ENGLAND

Robert Kiely

Harvard University Press
Cambridge, Massachusetts
1972

© Copyright 1972 by the President and Fellows of Harvard College

All rights reserved

Publication of this book has been aided by a grant from the
Hyder Edward Rollins Fund

Library of Congress Catalog Card Number 79–186677

SBN 674–77935–5

Printed in the United States of America

For
Mary Cecilia
and
John Vincent
Kiely

PREFACE

During the second half of the eighteenth century and the first decades of the nineteenth — that period which we think of as pre-romantic and romantic — some odd things happened to the English novel. The genre which had borrowed successfully from the methods of history and journalism, and derived so much of its strength from a relatively straightforward reporting of ordinary events, became, in some hands, wild and flamboyant, grotesque and luxuriously artificial, by turns. Some of the experiments were silly and artless, attempts merely to cater to a popular taste for the sensational. Others, however awkward their techniques may seem today, were deeply serious efforts to stretch or break through old conventions and to probe areas of experience not approached by Defoe or Fielding.

These narratives, for better or worse, are part of the romantic phenomenon and of the history of the novel. The most interesting are worth examining not only for what they can tell us about Romanticism and the development of prose fiction, but also because of their intrinsic merit as works of art. This book is not intended to be a broadly inclusive survey of the English romantic novel. It is an attempt to define the intellectual context — the premises of taste, the philosophical and psychological preoccupations — in which the romantic novel flourished; and it is a detailed study of particular works. I have chosen books that I like and that are, in some way, representative. *Northanger Abbey* and *Nightmare Abbey* are not, in the strict sense, romantic novels. But, as I

PREFACE

show, they are not simple anti-romances either. In any case, they both shed so much light on the phenomenon of romantic fiction that it seemed a good idea to include them in a book on the subject. I have omitted *Jane Eyre* partly to give the place of honor exclusively to *Wuthering Heights*, but also because the latter epitomizes the encounter between Romanticism and the novel, while the former, with its stress on morality and education, looks to the great themes of Victorian fiction.

Anyone writing in this field quickly becomes aware of his indebtedness to a number of scholars and provocative critics. In addition to the specific citations in the text, I wish to note, in the area of Romanticism, the importance of the work of M. H. Abrams, Harold Bloom, and Northrop Frye; in the area of Gothicism, that of Edith Birkhead, Maurice Lévy, Mario Praz, Eino Railo, Montague Summers, and D. P. Varma; and in the area of prose fiction, that of Albert J. Guerard, J. Hillis Miller, and Ian Watt.

More personally, I would like to express my gratitude to Walter Jackson Bate and David Perkins, the two colleagues and friends who — through their books, lectures and conversation — have taught me more about Romanticism and literature in general than I could ever acknowledge. Both patiently and generously read the manuscript of this book and made suggestions of the most helpful and perceptive kind.

I would also like to thank Martha Johnson Walters for her help in the preparation of the manuscript.

My wife not only listened to the creaks and groans of the book while it was being written, but she demonstrated that proofreading and revising a diabolical text has no power to alter an angelic nature.

R.K.

Cambridge, Massachusetts

CONTENTS

CONTENTS

THE ROMANTIC NOVEL
IN ENGLAND

"Is this the region, this the soil, the clime,"
Said then the lost Archangel, "this the seat
That we must change for Heaven? — this mournful gloom
For that celestial light? Be it so, since He
Who now is sovran can dispose and bid
What shall be right: farthest from Him is best,
Whom reason hath equalled, force hath made supreme
Above His equals. Farewell, happy fields
Where joy forever dwells! Hail, horrors! hail,
Infernal World! and thou, profoundest Hell,
Receive thy new possessor — one who brings
A mind not to be changed by place or time.
The mind is its own place, and in itself
Can make a Heaven of Hell, a Hell of Heaven."

Paradise Lost, Book I

INTRODUCTION

The English romantic novel is, in some ways, an embarrassing subject. There is, first of all, the question of its existence. *Wuthering Heights* exists, but one hardly feels comfortable forming a school or even a loose assemblage of companions around the one novel in English which seems an exception to some of the best literary generalizations. The Waverley novels exist, but persuasive arguments have been made about the strong elements of realism which run through all but the worst of them. Gothic novels exist, but are usually described as pre-romantic rather than romantic, though that designation does not seem very helpful if the phenomenon they were supposedly preliminary to never came into being.

For the sake of convenience it might be enough to say that, within roughly the same period literary historians call "romantic," a number of novels were written which manifest some of the thematic and stylistic characteristics evident in the new poetry and drama of the time. This helps, but it does not eliminate the embarrassment entirely, for there is something calamitous about many of the English novels which fit into this category. They are not all bad; indeed, some are very good. But in nearly every case one has a sense of unresolved struggle, of intelligence and energy at odds. Brontë, Hogg, and Scott are almost alone in finding appropriate terms in which to present and contain this struggle. For most of the others, confrontation and breakdown are not

1

merely fictional themes but structural and stylistic problems. What the narration fails to control takes revenge on the narrative itself. The reader finds himself witness not to an artfully manipulated crisis which will be weathered and resolved, but to moral and psychological ambivalence culminating all too often in a disaster which is *of* the story as well as in it.

Occasionally, as in **Vathek** and *The Monk*, the artist rises above his own earlier contradictions and produces a conclusion which surpasses in power and coherence everything which preceded it. But more often there is a series of minor collisions which the reader learns to anticipate coming pages ahead of time. That may be where much of the embarrassment enters — in watching the inevitable coming about again and again, and then the author picking himself out of the wreckage and going off in search of another unmanageable machine with which to begin the next chapter.

But this may also be where the fascination enters. For though the reader of romantic novels may too often find himself presented with a predictable division of intent, the best romantic fiction does not embrace a frozen antithesis; on the contrary, it releases a dynamic antagonism. This is one reason why speaking of English romantic fiction as a fixed mode is problematical, for although romantic novels do have structural patterns, character types, and situations in common, their primary tendency is to destroy (or, at the very least, undermine) particular narrative conventions. Romantic novels thrive like parasites on structures whose ruin is the source of their life. The result may be a kind of literary sadism which — though it often seems to start in fun — goes beyond parody to a prolonged and serious abuse of the outmoded.

It is true, as Harry Levin has pointed out, that realism often asserts its claim to authenticity by parodying "artifice," as, for example, in Rabelais, Austen, and Thackeray.[1] When the romantic novelist indulges in parody, however, he often finds himself unable to draw a clear distinction between the authentic and the artificial. Either the grounds of his ridicule constantly shift or the supposed artifice is attacked with a vehemence which raises it into significance. One thinks, here, of the works of Beckford and Lewis. But there also may be a squaring off and skirmishing of opposing, equally matched impulses as

2

in the fiction of Godwin. In all romantic novels, aesthetic aims, literary styles, narrative patterns, and themes of utterly different sorts are placed in juxtaposition.

Sometimes such a patchwork method or repudiation of method merely serves to point up the sterility of the fragmented conventions and the ineptitude of the artist. Sometimes it produces the literary counterpart of Frankenstein's monster, a phenomenon not without interest but particularly grotesque when measured against the intention of its creator. But sometimes there are glimpses of a life — and with it, a new idea of art — which the older conventions in their separate contexts did not convey. Insofar as this is true, it is worthwhile to consider some of these conventions and contexts. What were they? And, more important, how were they regarded by those who first experimented with romantic fiction?

2

Nearly a century after Congreve's preface to *Incognita*, English writers were still trying to make a clear distinction between the romance and the novel, and at least some were going about it in much the same way. In 1785 Clara Reeve's *The Progress of Romance* contributed sententiousness if not subtlety to the aging problem: "The Novel is a picture of real life and manners, and of the times in which it was written. The Romance in lofty and elevated language, describes what has never happened nor is likely to." [2] What had been a useful, even necessary, distinction in 1692 had become a nostalgic wish to restore diminishing clarity in 1785. For narrative fiction after the middle of the eighteenth century splintered into a great many more than two parts. And even the two modes which dominated, under the influence of Fielding and Richardson, could hardly be satisfactorily differentiated in Clara Reeve's terms.

Though the old definitions were losing their applicability, they are worth considering, since to know what writers thought they were doing is helpful in determining, with historical hindsight, what they actually seem to have done. Although the novels of the mid-century were rich with variety and innovation, most of their authors would have agreed that they were working in a minor mode, deprived, as if by common consent, of "lofty and elevated language" and marvelous deeds. The major narrative genre, to the eighteenth-century mind, was still the epic. The romance and the novel, as Congreve and Clara Reeve had defined them, were the broken halves of that great form, one retaining its grandeur, the other its truth to life.

Throughout the first half of the eighteenth century, the English romance added its own excesses to the wonders and gallantries treated in the seventeenth-century French *roman* without appreciably altering its formal structure, floridity of style, or pretention to high moral and aesthetic tone. Even Eliza Haywood, one of the most inventive and prolific of English romancers of this period, appealed, as George Whicher has pointed out, to readers "nurtured on French *romans à longue haleine* and heroic plays." [3] In general, whether or not the borrowed convention was technically well handled or applied to serious moral ends, authors defended their romances as "mirrors of all desirable virtues." Defoe, Fielding, and Richardson, on the other hand, while experimenting brilliantly with the conventions of history, drama, journalism, and the picaresque tale, made more modest claims and occasionally even apologized for the frivolous, trifling, and low character of their art. Granted, the apologies became whimsical and politely routine as "realistic" novelists grew confident of their powers to entertain and instruct, yet the fact remains that even the most self-assured did not imagine they were working in a major — and certainly not a "lofty" — literary form.

The memory of epic pervades much of the best eighteenth-century fiction, but that memory is tinged with regret and its effect is more often one of intimidation than inspiration. The uses of epic tend to be ironic or incidentally allusive rather than boldly imitative. One of the most comic, because least appropriate, things Fielding can do with Molly Seagram is compare her with Helen of Troy. By making a joke, he turns the limitations of his subject and style to his advantage, but the sense of limitation persists nonetheless. Richardson, though his epic references are seldom designed to amuse, achieves a mixed effect with them. When he compares Lovelace with Milton's Satan, he may, for a moment, succeed in conveying the extent of Clarissa's fear, but he also portrays a devil of uncertain potency. A Lucifer who wages his war against heaven in a London townhouse is clearly a Lucifer in reduced circumstances.

4

For a time, in the first half of the century, it seemed that for many writers — poets even more than novelists — a primary claim to virtuosity lay in the variety of classical models they were able to allude to humorously or seriously. Originality was not at a premium, and inventiveness consisted not in the avoidance of imitation but in the selection of English models in addition to or in place of Latin and Greek ones. By the middle of the century the number of poetic imitations of early Milton had increased and there was a new interest in Celtic and Scandinavian verse. In his "Ode on the Poetical Character," Collins does not invoke Virgil and Homer, but Shakespeare, Spenser, and Milton. Still, such efforts to expand the affective and thematic range of literature and to find alternatives to neoclassicism were initiated by poets. They seemed to have little applicability to the new realism of the novel or, for that matter, to the rigidities of the prose romance.

Thus, when Horace Walpole confessed in the preface to the second edition of *The Castle of Otranto* that he was attempting "to blend two kinds of romance, the ancient and the modern," the implications of his intention, if not the success with which he carried it out, had considerable importance for English fiction. Walpole had the ambition to try to recapture some of the amplitude of past literature by combining two inferior conventions. His use of the terms "ancient" and "modern" corresponds roughly with the usual neoclassical distinction between romance and novel: "In the former all was imagination and improbability; in the latter, nature is always intended to be, and sometimes has been, copied with success. Invention has not been wanting; but the great resources of fancy have been dammed up, by a strict adherence to common life." [4] Though Walpole's stated aim was to create a "blend," he obviously had it particularly in mind to correct an imbalance by letting fanciful and mysterious deeds flow abundantly over the familiar ground cultivated by novelists of "common life."

It is well known that the result was not a gentle irrigation but a flood, and that *The Castle of Otranto*, despite the presence of a few workaday servants, is a romance of the most excessively improbable sort. Walpole succeeded neither in piecing together the grandeur of epic nor in attaining a Shakespearian mastery of nature, though he claimed Shakespeare as his model. But he did strike the first note for a new magnitude in the novel, an increased reliance upon imagination, and a willingness to combine narrative conventions which had been developing separately. In the same period the only novelist who made a more effective attack on the categorical rigidities which were being imposed upon prose fiction was Sterne. Despite Walpole's opinion that it was "the dregs of nonsense," [5] *Tristram Shandy* was extremely popular in its own time. Nonetheless, it was Walpole's experiment, not Sterne's, which found large numbers of imitators before the close of the eighteenth century.

3

In order to understand the common premises and achievements of the English romantic novelists, we must begin with what Ortega y Gasset calls "the negative influence of the past." What Walpole and his Gothic descendants had most clearly in mind was the kind of novel they did *not* want to write. The first great and seminal works of English Romanticism were poems, and no study of romantic fiction can proceed satisfactorily without considering the influences of poetic innovation. Still, it would be inaccurate to consider the experimental novels of the period as mere prose by-products of a poetic revolution. It must be remembered that whereas Wordsworth reacted against Dryden and Pope, Walpole, and the best of his later imitators, reacted against Richardson and Fielding. Some of the more general motives for rebellion may have been similar, but the powers being opposed were different, and so, of course, was the nature of the new product. The early romantic poets rejected the formal elaborateness of most neoclassical verse; they attacked poetic diction and artificial landscape drawing, and they complained that feeling had yielded to a merely mechanical exercise of wit. The same complaints would scarcely have applied to the kinds of fiction which had prevailed increasingly throughout the century. To the contrary, Lewis, Beckford, Mrs. Radcliffe — all thought, with Walpole, that fiction had become plain. Richardson may have been sentimental and Fielding vulgar, but both were concerned with more or less ordinary people speaking common English and facing familiar problems. "I was so tired," said Walpole of *Sir Charles Grandison*, "of sets of people getting together, and saying, 'Pray, Miss, with whom are you in love?' and of mighty good young

men that convert your Mr. M——'s in the twinkling of a sermon." [6]
And in 1785 he wrote of Fielding that he "had as much humor perhaps
as Addison, but, having no idea of grace, is perpetually disgusting." [7]

Walpole's idea of grace, as his prose style and taste in architecture
attest, was ornate and eclectic. In fact, early romantic novelists, to a
greater extent than their predecessors, made elaborate and often indiscriminate use of other literature. Again, the reason is partly historical. The works of Defoe, Fielding, Smollett, and Richardson, though
obviously derivative, tend to subordinate their sources to the larger
cause of "historical" veracity. The authors, through their fictitious narrators want to seem to be describing and analyzing what they have
actually observed. The early writers of romantic fiction did not merely
turn their attention from contemporary manners and familiar locales;
they wanted to *see* with the eyes of Dante, Shakespeare, Marlowe,
Beaumont and Fletcher, Milton, or the author of the Arabian Nights.
Sometimes, uncertain of everything but this devotion to a literary con-
stellation, they tried on all lenses at once and had kaleidoscopic visions.
The effects are apparent in the echoes of lines, imitations of characters,
and assimilation of whole episodes, and above all in a sometimes confusing, sometimes liberating, uncertainty of form.

From the beginning, romantic novelists demonstrated a dissatisfac-
tion not only with current narrative conventions but with prose narrative convention altogether. Their works often seem about to turn into
plays or poems. Compared with the obtrusive theatricality of the novels
of Walpole and Mrs. Radcliffe, the fiction of Fielding and Dickens
seems only mildly influenced by the stage. If, in the first half of the
eighteenth century, the "new writers of fiction rejected the old tradition
of mixing poetry with their prose," [8] as Ian Watt has said of Defoe,
Richardson, and Fielding, some later "new writers" revived that tradition with interesting results. John Berryman has noted that, in *The
Monk*, M. G. Lewis "helped to recover poetry" for the novel.[9] Whereas
Beckford's *Vathek* has always been considered an anomaly among
novels, Byron — and, later, Mallarmé — regarded it as literary kin.
Hogg's confessional novel has been called a border ballad in prose and
a romantic morality play; Scott let ballads mingle freely with the prosaic
elements of his works; and in *Wuthering Heights* Emily Brontë wrote
a novel with many of the attributes of a lyrical poem.

7

Verisimilitude and moral sentiment were not eschewed altogether, but what was wanted more fervently was the gesture and emotional intensity of drama, the rhythmic and metaphoric possibilities of poetry. The first experimenters, with only this general notion of what they desired and no clear idea of how to attain it, opened the doors of fiction and let in everything — or so it seemed. The first results were like Walpole's Strawberry Hill, a gorgeous clutter; rich in detail but lacking a unifying power, always promising the sublime around the next corner but invariably failing to produce it. The earliest romantic novelists reached for amplitude and struck excess, and, in this respect, might be said to have begun where romantic poetry ended — or paused — more than a hundred years later, in satiety and affectation. When we think of the great achievements of the early romantic poets we tend to think first of those works which restored stylistic purity and natural sentiment to English verse. We place — or at least have the possibility of placing — Songs of Innocence, Lyrical Ballads, the sonnets and odes of Keats and Shelley, before the Book of Urizen, The Excursion, Endymion, or The Cenci. Romantic novelists give us no such choice. If we are to pay attention to them at all, we must pay attention to them as they usually were, flamboyant and extreme.

Even, as in the case of Walpole, where boredom with commonplace themes and impatience with prevailing narrative conventions were of a relatively superficial sort, the introduction of materials and techniques identified with older genres into the general framework of the novel produced some surprising and interesting results. Exotic schemes, however playfully or innocently initiated, did, by implication, challenge some of the basic philosophical assumptions upon which the distinctiveness of the vigorous new genre seemingly depended.

4

The origin of and justification for the novel, as contrasted to other narrative forms, resided in its adherence to "the way things are." [10] Smollett, in his preface to Roderick Random, defended the novel by attacking the inherent falseness of romance: "When the minds of men were debauched, by the imposition of priestcraft, to the most absurd pitch of credulity, the authors of romance arose, and, losing sight of probability, filled their performances with the most monstrous hyperboles. If they could not equal the ancient poets in point of genius, they were resolved to excel them in fiction, and to apply to the wonder rather than the judgment of their readers." [11] To Smollett, the novel was to the romance what the Reformation had been to popery, a purification and return to unadorned truth. But since Locke, investigations into the nature of truth and, above all, man's capacity to perceive reality, had placed greater and greater stress on the importance of the subjective nature of knowledge. Thus, for some eighteenth-century thinkers, the word "judgment" no longer had quite the unshakeable authority it still carried with Smollett, nor did "wonder" seem synonymous with misapprehension, and "fiction" another word for falsehood.

Concepts of reality and therefore of what a serious artist could regard as "probable" had been undergoing enormous changes since the end of the seventeenth century. Reality, rather than being assumed to reside in fixed universal principles which tradition had established and a sound judgment could grasp, was increasingly thought to be located in continually changing concrete particulars perceived through the senses and combined differently by each individual. The novel, which was the first literary genre to grow out of this new intellectual ground, derived its definitive character from a preoccupation with concrete detail and originality.

The essential realism of the novel, as it developed early in the eighteenth century, was not dependent upon subject matter — for example, high life versus low life — but upon method. The novel was presumed to be, as Ian Watt says, "a full and authentic report of human experience," complete with details of time, place, and individual characterization "presented through a more largely referential use of language than is common in other literary forms." [12] The romantic novel cannot be placed in diametric opposition to the realistic novel thus defined since it obviously shared many of its aims and techniques. Watt himself observes that Romanticism "was characterized by the emphasis on individualism and originality which had found its first literary expression in the novel." [13]

The most obvious conclusion would seem to be that the major quarrel the romantic novelists had with Defoe, Richardson, and Fielding was not over method but subject matter, and that it was not, therefore, aesthetically speaking, a serious quarrel. That, initially, was true. Those writers who first turned to Gothic castles and oriental palaces did so because they were tired of the drawing room and the country inn. They turned to demented monks and voluptuous princes because they were bored with sensible ministers and rowdy squires. Certain of the earliest romantic experimenters changed the setting and cast of the novel without substantially altering the narrative procedures established by their predecessors. Neither, in some cases, did they adjust the psychology and moral values of their characters to fit the settings and costumes they had given them. Today, more than one heroine of Mrs. Radcliffe seems the creature of a second-rate Richardson in fancy, foreign, and vaguely antique dress. But in the 1790's that dress was odd enough to appear new, and for many readers new enough to be welcome.

It is not surprising that the premium which the realistic novelists had placed on originality was preserved and extended by romantic novelists, but what is surprising is that the desire to maintain an appearance of historical authenticity was sustained, and in some cases increased, as the subject matter of novels became further removed from the ordinary. Walpole pretended that *The Castle of Otranto* was a translation from a manuscript originally written in "the purest Italian" sometime between 1095 and 1243, later printed in Naples, and only recently discovered "in the library of an ancient Catholic family in the north of England." Mrs. Radcliffe announces in the opening paragraphs of *The Romance of the Forest* that the source is "Guyot de Pitaval, the most faithful of those writers who record the proceedings in the Parliamentary Courts of Paris during the seventeenth century." Hogg's *The Private Memoirs and Confessions of a Justified Sinner* is prefaced by a narrative, nearly as long as the memoir itself, written by an "editor" whose information is said to have come "from tradition, as well as some parish registers still extant." Scott is famous for the prefaces, digressions, footnotes, and appendices with which he seeks to give historical substance to the Waverley novels.

The English romantic novelists seem to have wanted it both ways — to authenticate the incredible, to claim originality without really departing from the familiar. As a result, they have often been accused of having been neither good romantics nor good novelists. What is interesting is the degree to which superficial shifts in theme and setting did gradually bring about significant departures from the technical conventions of formal realism and, by extension, from conventional ideas about the nature of that human experience which it was the novelist's task to report on in detail.

A characteristic of the early realistic novel, as distinct from epic and romance, was its heavy reliance upon language which closely denotes the concrete and particular, language which seems to approximate life unidealized rather than that which conforms to the decorum of a literary convention. Romantic novelists, with characteristic indiscretion, mingled styles as well as genres. They joined Defoe to Milton, with "mixed" results, but they also developed an allusive, euphemistic, and, at best, highly suggestive style which was peculiarly their own. With a bit of research and invention, they could endow their odd settings with a few believable details, but their penchant for placing ordinary characters in extraordinary predicaments put great strain on a denotative style. Phrases like "unspeakable horror" or "indescribable transports of joy" may at first have been little more than trite literary evasions, but they point to an impulse which was ultimately to bring romantic novelists into serious conflict with some of the basic premises of formal realism. The human experience to be reported on was gradually being expanded to include feelings and dreams which seemed to defy — at least before Freud — a referential vocabulary. Richardson had to some extent set the tone, but his repetitious and exhaustively analytical method and his sentimentality seemed to work against the intensity and mystery which most romantic novelists valued.

The relationship between sentimental and romantic fiction is not so direct as is sometimes assumed. True, the pervasive influence of Richardson, Rousseau, and MacKensie cannot be overlooked. Yet the moral value which these writers attached to an indulgence in particular emotions — pity, sorrow, affection — is in sharp contrast to the uneasy fascination with the darker emotions expressed sardonically or with obsessive brutality by many romantic novelists. With the exception of Ann Radcliffe, romantic novelists are among the least sentimental writers of the late eighteenth and early nineteenth centuries precisely because they refused to dissolve ambivalent feelings in an ocean of tears. Moreover, the emotions on which they dwelt were too imperfectly understood or too threatening to be systematically rationalized, except by one as daring as the Marquis de Sade. They explored feelings and

11

compulsions which were not merely impolite to mention but often difficult to label and describe.

Ruined abbeys and dark groves were both stage properties and crude symbols of a kind of experience which seemed no less true because it could not be openly acknowledged, dissected, and particularized. Even while fumbling with the exclamatory clichés and cardboard turrets of high emotion, the early romantic novelists were seeking to evoke what they could not, in any precise sense, name. The trouble was that they tried to introduce the unnamable into a genre which derived much of its strength from an insistence on naming names.

If one follows the debates about the difference between the romance and the novel throughout the eighteenth century, it becomes evident that it was no idle dispute over empty formality, but a continuing inquiry into the nature of reality and its relation to prose narrative. What Smollett calls "monstrous hyperbole" was reintroduced into fiction not on whim alone, but in the hope that it might force uncommon reality somewhat closer to the surface of "things as they are." But if the artist has a responsibility to truth, he has also a responsibility to pleasure. Where the nature of reality is in question, so inevitably is the nature of the beautiful. The realist's claim that truth resides in the clear and the concrete was questioned not only on philosophical grounds, but on aesthetic and psychological grounds as well.

5

"A clear idea is . . . another name for a little idea," wrote Burke in 1756 in his *Philosophical Enquiry into the Origin of Our Ideas of the Sublime and the Beautiful*.[14] Burke's objective was to explore the psychological source and aesthetic role of those human responses which are not clear, reasonable, readily specified, or, in any unmixed sense, pleasurable. Taking pain to be stronger than pleasure, Burke argues that whatever excites a painful idea is a source of astonishment, the sublime passion. The mind becomes so filled with its object that it cannot entertain any other; there is a momentary suspension of rational activity and of unrelated emotion. One is delivered, at least temporarily, from self-consciousness and mixed feelings and therefore, so long as the pain remains imaginary and not actual, the response evoked may be considered desirable.

Behind the apparent morbidity of an aesthetic theory which, like "graveyard" poetry and Gothic fiction, seems obsessed with the fearful, lies a quest for the ultimate. Burke's discussion of the sublime, like most early romantic fiction, is a parade of superlatives. He attempts to describe the *strongest* of emotions, the *most* engrossing of ideas, the *greatest* of pleasures, the *most* dreadful pains, in an effort to ascertain what inventions of the imagination might produce them. The ultimate art should stimulate the ultimate response, but it must first discover images of the ultimate to imitate. Lacking the faith in anthropomorphic ideals and personified absolutes which was so deeply rooted in classical and Christian literature, the precursors of Romanticism found death to be one phenomenon which, despite progress and the advancement of learning, remained both certain and awesome. Since pain carried to its extreme leads to the extinction of life, Burke argues that death or fear of death is the source of all ideas of the sublime.

Some writers, including Burke himself, were tempted to settle the subject by trying to classify those objects and situations which would produce the sublime. Mountains, storms at sea, ruined abbeys, and charnel houses became for some artists the ready-made elements of an emotional shorthand. But the greater effect of the *Enquiry* was to enlarge the possibilities for art rather than to restrict and schematize them. Burke's discussion of language, though brief, points the way to further considerations of words as suggestive and evocative rather than strictly imitative. Extending his own argument that the sublime passions depend, to some degree, on an incompleteness of knowledge, he asserts that the business of poetry and rhetoric is "to affect rather by sympathy than imitation; to display rather the effect of things on the mind of the speaker, or of others, than to present a clear idea of the things themselves." [15]

Like Walpole, who thought Hogarth's *Analysis of Beauty* was "very silly," Burke rejects the neoclassical claim that beauty depends upon proportion and fitness. Burke's own theory of beauty has been the source of amusement and even embarrassment to those who otherwise take the *Enquiry* and its author seriously. Part of the absurdity arises from the humorless manner in which Burke goes about cataloguing and "methodizing" beautiful objects and the sensations they arouse in the observer. "I do not now recollect anything beautiful that is not

13

smooth," [16] he asserts at one point. And, at another, he goes so far as to depict a physical posture which he claims to be the outward sign of love, the emotion excited by beauty: "The head reclines something on one side; the eye-lids are more closed than usual, and the eyes roll gently with an inclination to the object; the mouth is a little opened, and the breath drawn slowly, with now and then a low sigh." [17] Curiously, opinions about the source of the ridiculous in this and similar passages have been derived from quite different, even contradictory, interpretations of Burke's method. Thomas Love Peacock, like Blake, thought that the *Enquiry* "mocked inspiration" by subjecting the imagination to a pseudo-scientific dissection. It attempted to demonstrate a too mechanical relationship between conventional gestures and expressions — the rolling eyes, the sigh — and the highly personal responses of the human heart and mind. Thus, when in *Nightmare Abbey* Peacock shows his despondent hero in an elaborately detailed posture which he calls the "accurate description of a pensive attitude," he is mocking the systematic, theoretical side of Burke.

The post-Freudian reader is more likely to be amused and, eventually, impressed by precisely the opposite tendency in Burke's discussion of the beautiful. Despite his insistence that sexual desire, or what he calls "the passion which belongs to generation," has nothing to do with his subject, it becomes more and more obvious that Burke's "theory" of beauty is based on highly individualistic and masculine assumptions. Not only does he argue that the beautiful must be smooth, but that it must also be small, delicate, and gentle: "We admire what is large and submit to it; we love what is small enough to submit to us." [18] What strikes a modern reader is not Burke's tendency to pigeon-hole, but the number of times he breaks through his framework and talks about his own reactions and predilections: "Observe that part of a beautiful woman, where she is, perhaps, the most beautiful, about the neck and breasts; the smoothness; the softness; the easy and insensible swell; the variety of the surface, which is never for the smallest space, the same; the deceitful maze, through which the unsteady eye slides giddily, without knowing where to fix, or whither it is carried." [19]

Burke might have expressed such sentiments more effectively in a sonnet, but incongruity is at the very heart of the *Enquiry* and of the kind of art it inspired. Philosophically, the incongruity arises out of an effort to bring personal perception into formal theoretical alignment with generally accepted conventions about objective reality. That the results are occasionally ridiculous, grotesque, artificial, and tentative does not detract from the underlying seriousness of the need being expressed. It is in this light that the sexual associations with the sublime and the beautiful may be seen to have more than incidental importance.

Prior to the *Enquiry*, speculations about the sublime had either circumvented the subject of its relationship to beauty or had conceded that the two could somehow exist together in the same object. Burke was the first to admit that, if the distinctions implied by his sexual analogies were valid, it was all but inconceivable that the sublime and the beautiful could be found in the same place: "In short, the ideas of the sublime and the beautiful stand on foundations so different, that it is hard, I had almost said impossible, to think of reconciling them in the same subject, without considerably lessening the effect of the one or the other upon the passions." [20]

Burke's insistence on the essential difference between the sublime and the beautiful and his claims that both are valid and even desirable phenomena in nature and art opened the way for a new breadth in critical theory. Where a work of art did not conform to classical rules of proportion, the critic could search for other, even opposite criteria, before dismissing the achievement. In 1762 Bishop Hurd, in his defense of the literature of chivalry and romance, presented an argument made possible, in part, by Burke's *Enquiry*: "When an architect examines a Gothic structure by Grecian rules, he finds nothing but deformity. But the Gothic architecture has its own rules, by which when it comes to be examined, it is seen to have its own merit." [21] According to Hurd, the "merit" of Gothic architecture as well as of "Gothic fables of chivalry" — indeed their superiority over classical art — lies in their ability to "produce the sublime." As late as 1823, Coleridge, despite the fact that his thinking about the subject had been much refined by his reading of Kant and Schlegel, elaborates on the same point in similar terms: "The principle of Gothic architecture is infinity made imaginable. It is, no doubt, a sublimer effort of genius than the Greek style." [22]

It is worth pausing on Coleridge's reference to infinity because here again it is Burke's floundering between the subjective and objective that helped prepare the way for later, more sophisticated theorists. Despite his suggestive remarks about the "delightful horror" and even the madness which results from an overlong contemplation of the infinite, we tend to remember Burke's discussion of the infinite as bogging down in literal-minded considerations of the difference between vastness and infinity, the degrees of sublimity in a perpendicular versus an inclined plane, the effects of dripping water and the notches on a pole, and so forth. What Burke succeeds in demonstrating, of course, is the enormous difficulty of getting hold of such a subject at all and, more particularly, of representing it in sensuous or concrete terms. It was Kant in 1790 who took up Burke's enquiry and argued that if "the sublime is that in comparison with which everything else is small," it cannot exist in nature but only "in our imagination [where there is] a striving toward infinite progress and in our reason [where there is] a claim for absolute totality." [23] But even in his subjectivism, Kant extends and demonstrates the psychological validity of Burke's claim that the sublime emotion is a feeling of "delightful horror." Where Burke had confronted mortal and limited man with the vastness of the sea or the craggy heights of mountains, Kant confronts man with himself, a creature limited by his senses yet capable of imagining the limitless. For Kant, therefore, the sublime is the "ability to think which shows a faculty of the mind surpassing every standard of sense." [24] The delight comes in awareness of this "supersensible faculty"; the discomfort comes in the inability to realize it in sensuous terms.

Kant's analysis sheds a great deal of light on the role played by pain in romantic aesthetics. Burke had, as we have seen, placed emphasis on pain as arousing stronger emotions than pleasure and, not surprisingly, some writers took this as an excuse to terrify and shock their readers in the name of art. But Burke obviously had much more than this in mind. More than in sensations of sheer pain, he was interested in the extent to which a notion of pain was congenial to and perhaps even productive of pleasure. Once again, it is the interplay of opposites, not the annihilation of the difference, which interests Burke. As Kant later put it:

The quality of the feeling of the sublime is that it is a feeling of pain in reference to the faculty by which we judge aesthetically of an object, which

16

pain, however, is represented at the same time as purposive. This is possible through the fact that the very incapacity in question discovers the consciousness of an unlimited faculty of the same subject.[25]

In other words, the pain comes from a sense of particular incapacity; yet it is only through this sense of incapacity that we can become aware of another faculty in ourselves which transcends it. Thus, "there accompanies the reception of an object as sublime, a pleasure, which is only possible through the medium of pain." [26]

6

The influence of the *Enquiry* was enormous, even upon those who never read it. Theoretical justification, indeed encouragement, had been given to artists to seek inspiration in regions and from objects which earlier in the century might have been regarded as unfit, save for satirists and melancholy poets. Mist-enshrouded mountains, decaying castles, damp caverns, and reeking churchyards seemed, if not instant guarantees of literary greatness, the concrete means by which to escape the confines of drawing room sentimentality. "Richardson had, to me at least, made that kind of writing insupportable," wrote Walpole in 1765. "I thought . . . that a god, at least a ghost, was absolutely necessary to frighten us out of too much senses." [27]

But the *Enquiry*, in addition to its direct influence on writers of the period, provides, in its combination of the new and old, in its earnestness and its sometimes inspired suggestiveness, as well as in its incongruities, a theoretical analogue to the early experiments in romantic fiction. One finds in Walpole, Radcliffe, Reeve, and Lewis not only Burke's ideas but Burke's problems. Whereas the best romantic poetry achieves, indeed embodies, moments of synthesis, the romantic novel, at best and at worst, is an almost continuous display of divisive tension, paradox, and uncertain focus. The dualism of man's nature — of his taste, his impulses, his ambitions — the deep division in his very way of perceiving reality, seemed an inevitable adjunct to the first romantic stirrings in the young genre. Though the conventions of the novel were neither old nor clearly defined by the middle of the eighteenth century, they appeared to be, in several respects, uncongenial to the romantic sensibility.

To describe the novel as a sustained fictitious narrative in prose is to seem to imply that it is the least restrictive and troublesome of genres for writers inclined to experimentation. In a sense, this has always been true. Throughout its history, prose fiction has been subjected to such radical variations that critics have periodically wondered whether the permissive limits of this genre could be exceeded. Still, as Robert Donovan has pointed out, "this looseness of form is only relative." [28] The fact is that the novel, conceived of even in the broadest possible terms, does make certain elementary formal demands. For example, in all the controversies over what a novel is, no one questions the need for length. Though no precise number of pages has ever been or can ever be set, everybody knows that one page or ten pages do not make a novel. Inevitably, then, romantic novelists, like any other novelists, are faced with problems of duration. But their preoccupation with the subjective nature of reality and their increasing commitment to imagination created unique and complex difficulties. The relationship between time as transformed or stopped by the imagination and the world's time of minutes, hours, days, and years, caused even the greatest romantic poets to falter in their long narrative verse. Wordsworth, who retained only a sketchy outline of chronological time in the narrative portions of *The Prelude*, solved the problem by submitting historical time, like everything else, to the rhythm of his own meditations. But even he found it necessary occasionally to apologize for awkward transitions: " 'Tis not my present purpose to retrace / That variegated journey step by step"; "I play the loiterer; 'tis enough to note"; "My drift I fear / is scarcely obvious"; "Here must we pause: this only let me add." Keats was dissatisfied with nearly all of his long narrative verse, and at least one of the reasons for this was the difficulty he encountered in maintaining a coherent linear sequence without sacrificing "intensity." In some moods he strikes out, like Thea, against slow and plodding time: "O aching time! O moments big as years!" In other moods he tries to sustain grandeur and still hurry things along: "Just at the self-same beat of Time's wide wings / Hyperion slid into the rustled air." But even Keats's great technical skill cannot conceal the embarrassment created by a collision of time and eternity. At what rate do the mind's gods move? And how does the artist express a simultaneity of visions without resorting to narrative clichés of the "meanwhile-back-at-the-ranch" variety? In *The Rime of the Ancient Mariner* and *Christabel*, Coleridge creates dream-like states in which conventional time is subdued by the logic of the vision. And in an allegorical poem he pictures imaginary time ever running on ahead while real time, her blind brother, trails behind: "O'er rough and smooth with even step he passed, / And knows not whether he be first or last."

The romantic novelists, ready to experiment with extreme subjective distortion, yet working in a form which owed much to the techniques of historical reporting, found themselves in an even stranger dilemma than the poets. Their admiration for the involved plots of Shakespeare and the Jacobean dramatists only made the problem worse. Often there is a difficulty, for both author and reader, in keeping subjective time (which ordinarily means the connection of events as perceived by a particular character) and historical or chronologically measurable time from utterly confusing each other and making a coherent progression of plot impossible. E. M. Forster states the danger concisely: "The time-sequence cannot be destroyed without carrying in its ruin all that should have taken its place; the novel that would express values only becomes unintelligible and therefore valueless." [29] The romantic novelists usually dealt with the problem in one of two ways: by seeing to it that a major character is literally separated from day and night and from society's reckoning of time (in a prison, a lunatic asylum, a monastery cell) or by depending, even more often than did their realistic predecessors, on the inset story, the plot within a plot which interrupts the chronology of the main narrative and creates a new temporal dimension. But even when these technical difficulties are overcome, more serious questions remain: What have the different versions of time to do with one another? Is one more nearly true than another? Can they be combined in some way that will enlarge man's total comprehension of himself and the universe?

In its earliest stages, romantic fiction either presents unexpectedly subtle and disturbing answers to these questions or else ignores them altogether. In the same way, the technical handling of subjective and historical time can either be crude to the point of absurdity or, as in the case of Beckford, Godwin, and Hogg, astonishingly sophisticated. The point is that, during a period when the novel was still a relatively young and untested genre, romantic novelists confronted some of the

19

most intricate problems fiction can pose. If they were to explore the imaginative possibilities of "spots of time," they had to fit them into a coherent, comprehensible, and sustained narrative. For the novelist there was no retreat to the short form, no equivalent of the sonnet or ode.

The novel's commitment to prose, no less than its traditional length, also created problems for the romantic writer. The ornate formality of English imitations of seventeenth-century French Romance notwithstanding, the eighteenth-century reader regarded prose, in narrative as well as dramatic literature, as a more informal means of expression than verse. Writers seeking to create a reasonable and authentic world of ordinary manners and a comfortable relationship with the reader turned naturally to prose. An initial credibility and intimacy with the reader were not undesirable to the Romantic, but his ambition for sublime heights was much greater. To achieve both extremes involved extraordinary demands on tone. If an author assumed the voice of an omniscient narrator, he had to avoid that kind of reasonable alliance with the reader, so skillfully formed by Fielding, which implies ironic detachment from the lives of the created characters. For once a too sensible, solid, prosaic tone has been successfully established, it is difficult to raise it passionately without sounding inconsistent, unconvincing, or silly. Nearly a century after the first romantic novelists found themselves in this dilemma, Dickens and Thackeray were still struggling with it.

Some early Gothic novelists begin on a high, often hysterical, note; sentences are broken off unfinished, or punctuated with exclamation marks. But that kind of effort cannot be successfully maintained for very many pages, and most writers settled for an occasional awkward diminuendo. Others, particularly after the Gothic revival, chose a first-person narrator, or several narrators, through which some parts of the story could be told. Learning from the epistolary and autobiographical methods of their predecessors, romantic novelists varied and stretched first-person techniques to suit their own purposes. The primary aim in the romantic novel was not, like that of *Clarissa* or *Humphry Clinker*, to present a variety of opinions about events which everyone agreed had occurred and were of sufficient importance to merit discussion. To a greater and greater extent in romantic fiction the sub-

INTRODUCTION

jective vision *became* the crucial event. Where the author was truly successful, external reality paled before it or fused with it, but never dominated it.

The uses of first-person narrative techniques were many and varied in the eighteenth-century novel, and in some superficial ways they all had something in common. But in intention and ultimate effect they split into two major divisions. On the one hand, the speaker is ordinarily a representative type of his social class (even when he is separated from it), relating certain events of his life in an orderly fashion and usually drawing a moral lesson at the conclusion. Here, reason, society, the world, predominate. On the other, the speaker is more likely to be at permanent odds with society, a prisoner or outcast, ordering the events of his life in his own fashion and meeting death or disappointment at the conclusion. The ego absorbs all and temporarily becomes the world.[30]

Novels of the first category may be said to have developed into the *Bildungsroman*, while novels of the second revived the much older tradition of the confession. The heroes of romantic novels usually have nothing to learn and a great deal to tell. Rousseau says of his characters in *Julie, ou la nouvelle Héloïse*: "They talk of everything; they are wrong about everything; they know nothing but themselves; yet . . . their errors are worth more than the knowledge of the wise man." [31] The romantic novel, having begun with an attempt to combine "ancient" and "modern" narrative methods, also brought the penitent's concern with self and the poet's concern with tone of voice into the realm of prose fiction.

But even assuming that the romantic novelist could solve all the problems of continuity and tone inherent in prose fiction, he still had to penetrate, scale, or dismantle an existing wall of subject matter, for there was little chance that he could construct a totally new one by himself. Once again, it may seem surprising that the most amorphous and youngest of genres should present difficulties in this regard, yet to the Romantic it did. For, at its very foundations, the English novel was a social genre, not taking its earliest inspirations from fear of God or love of nature, but from a preoccupation with the structure of society. Whether the protagonist was a picaro making his acrobatic way on a scaffold of class and wealth or a heroine debating with her family about

21

whom she should marry, the communal unit was, for better or worse, the novelist's basis of reality. A sensible character was not expected to repudiate or escape that reality, but rather to learn how to live in harmony with it, the assumption being that through eventual union with society, the picaro improved himself and the virtuous heroine improved the world. Moll Flanders, Joseph Andrews, and Roderick Random do not choose to be homeless wanderers. Though they make merry with bad luck, most of their energy is spent trying to regain a footing in society. Fanny Burney's Evelina wins our affection with her social ineptitude, but the reward for her good intentions is a noble lord. Even Clarissa, though an unusually complicated case, wants reconciliation with her family and friends so much that her chamber of penitent "isolation" witnesses a virtual parade of Harlowes and Howes before the end.

It is not really enough to say that the novel grew with the middle class and therefore took middle-class institutions as its prime subjects. One must add that these institutions, the family, the parish, the profession, became symbols of order, stability, moral purpose — in fact, of a whole concept of objective reality. The institutions might be threatened and the symbols weakened by ignorance, folly and vice, but, like the older institutions of church and court, they were presumed to possess inherent resources of strength and goodness to refresh and preserve them.

Most early romantic novelists were not political or social radicals, yet they had chosen the one genre in which to give free play to private vision and extreme emotion was to come into inevitable conflict with the idea of a well-regulated society. Walpole and Mrs. Radcliffe tried to avoid the issue by setting their stories in other countries and periods. The Middle Ages proved useful. And, if one insisted upon being up to date, there was safety in France or Italy, where native blood ran hot and social institutions had long been corrupted by popery. Only Godwin faced the challenge head on. Beckford escaped into fantasy and tangential satire. Scott could make rebellion and anarchy look glamorous, but he always reared back as if surprised by his own impetuosity. Emily Brontë solved the problem by eliminating the obstacle. She created a private world of such peculiar power that, for the duration of the narrative, nothing else seems to exist. Rousseau had made explicit the link between egocentric literature and social radicalism, but he also set an influential precedent for a kind of fiction in which society at large is not recognized as consequential except in a negative and secondary sense. Defending the naïveté and "unnaturalness" of the characters in *La Nouvelle Héloïse*, he explains that "they do not accept discouraging truths; finding nowhere what they feel, they fall back upon themselves, creating for themselves a little world that differs from ours. There they compose a spectacle which is truly new." [32]

Few English novelists possessed that combination of single-mindedness and extraordinary imagination which characterized Rousseau and Emily Brontë. For most, human relations of any sort, however distant in place or time, however distorted by private vision, bore resemblances to the familiar patterns of organized society and served, therefore, as reminders of an objective and general reality. Two hundred pages of narrative fiction could not be written about a skylark or a butterfly; a novelist was supposed to write about people in community. Even Robinson Crusoe dealt with isolation by recreating the conditions of the society from which he had been separated.

7

The creation of a new world has, to some degree, been the ambition of artists always, but Rousseau's stress on originality, on the value of the unique, is markedly romantic. It is characteristic of the English mentality, however, even in the midst of philosophical upheaval, to shun extremes. For none of the English romantic novelists, except Godwin, was there a tendency as strong as that present in so many American writers of the nineteenth century to identify the "new world" of their art with a social and moral world capable of realization in the future. The difference is not merely one of utopianism versus political realism, but, more broadly, of the degree to which an ideal vision is capable of determining the world of actual event.

It can be argued that because of the sheer accumulation of national events, literary as well as political, the climate of England in the latter half of the eighteenth century was not conducive to undisturbed dreaming. But English literature had nearly always been a literature on which the "world" encroached. And romantic fiction, despite claims to the contrary, was no exception. Even the novels of Godwin and Mary Shelley are deeply marked (and probably thereby delivered from absurdity) by a sense of the way things are. In fact, one might say that the primary problem for the English romantic novelist was not so much to discover how to reconcile his vision to the world as to suppress or transform the world long enough to have any vision at all.

The case for the American romantic novelist appears to have been precisely the reverse. Frank Norris accused Fenimore Cooper of being "saturated with the romance of the contemporary English story-tellers," [33] by which he meant Byron, Scott, and Bulwer-Lytton, but D. H. Lawrence argued more persuasively that, despite a superficial resemblance to British writers, Cooper is a quintessentially American author precisely because he refused to take the world as he found it. His art begins and ends with the "Great Ideal" of democracy, which, according to Lawrence, he pushes like a pin "through the heart of the continent." [34] Melville, too, despite his reputation as a writer obsessed by minute details, drew his dominant inspiration from a transcendent idea of quest and progress, or what Newton Arvin called "physical unrestingness and the forward push." [35] His most immediate literary antecedents were not novelists at all, but the writers of travel books. His America was an undiscovered land. The quality of Hawthorne's fiction is in many ways different from that of Melville, yet his admission to an "inveterate love of allegory" suggests that, as an artist, he too proceeds from ideal conceptions. He insists on calling his works "romances," which he says "need ruin to make them grow," because the term implies temporal and spatial distance. In his preface to *The Marble Faun*, he justifies setting the story in Italy because it afforded "a sort of poetic or fairy precinct, where actualities would not be so terribly insisted upon." [36] Indeed, many American writers of the nineteenth century called themselves romancers and deserve to be called romancers precisely because of the formative role of the ideal in their art.

Most of the English writers who, at an earlier period, raised romantic issues in prose fiction were not idealists by temperament, nor were they working out of a national tradition of idealism. Neither memories of old allegories nor hopes for a luminous future of "political justice" could diminish the down-to-earth presence of Defoe and Fielding and a readership accustomed to thinking of fiction not as moral parable and prophetic romance but as sentimental comedy and palatable history. Even the first writers of Gothic fiction were not romancers in the true sense. They and most of their successors were romantic *novelists* — puzzled and sometimes torn by the contradictions implied by that label.

Partly because of the nature of the genre and partly because of the nature of artists who chose to express their extraordinary sentiments in a genre which had proved itself so well adapted to mundane subjects, the romantic novel became a battleground. Theories, techniques of craft, and moral imperatives related to the cultivation of imagination and the supremacy of the self collided with those associated with reason and the public welfare. Though the essential conflict occurred within the intention and practice of the individual artists, it sometimes also exploded into public debates among writers. To take an early, minor, but characteristic example, one can look at the amusing dispute between Walpole and Clara Reeve over the extent to which the improbable should be introduced into a romantic novel. In her 1772 preface to *The Old English Baron*, an imitation of *The Castle of Otranto*, Miss Reeve suggests that Walpole strains credibility and therefore mars the seriousness of his work by including episodes which have no rational explanation. In a letter to a friend, Walpole commented, "The criticism . . . directly attacks the visionary part, which, says the author . . . makes one laugh . . . The [*Old English Baron*] is a professed imitation of mine, only stripped of the marvellous; and so entirely stripped, except in one awkward attempt at a ghost or two, that it is the most insipid dull nothing you ever saw." [37]

Both the humor and the annoyance of Walpole's response are telling. Walpole, like Beckford, Lewis, and Scott, was self-conscious about his visions. Hoping they might be taken seriously, but not altogether able to do so himself, he anticipates laughter with a half-smile rather than risk being regarded as a too earnest fool. In a letter to Elie de Beaumont, he wrote a little pathetically of *The Castle of Otranto*, "If I make you laugh, for I cannot flatter myself that I shall make you cry, I shall be content." [38] The uncertainty of tone and method as well as the peculiar appeal of much English romantic fiction stems from precisely this inability to follow a Rousseauian extreme in leaving the world behind in pursuit of one's own dreams. Conscientious and humorless ladies like Clara Reeve and Ann Radcliffe take the ghosts out of their ruined castles or explain them with sheets and trapdoors; others leave the ghosts in without explanation, but reveal their doubts in unexpected shifts in tone. But whether the inconsistency is one of substance or tone, it signifies a similar division of purpose and duality of vision.

The English romantic novel is unquestionably a schizoid phenomenon. The reader discovers the expected array of Byronic heroes and persecuted heroines, but he also discovers that they each have their mundane, unimpressive, even comic side. If allusions to Faust, Prometheus, and Lucifer abound, so do repeated, if less explicit, reminders of Robinson Crusoe, Pamela, Joseph Andrews, and Humphrey Clinker. One cannot always be sure whether the demons are plaguing the practical, workaday world or being plagued by it. There certainly is no happy marriage between the romance and what Frye calls the "low-mimetic mode," but there is a juxtaposition which produces its own sparks of originality and life. Walpole's prefatory remarks to *The Castle of Otranto* may be the best key to a definition of the English romantic novel after all. His mistake was not in speaking of combining the ancient with the modern, the romance with the novel, but in assuming that the result would be a simple and harmonious union.

In looking at specific works, one is tempted to focus upon split character types or contradictory ideologies; that is, to bring order to the problem by tracing a single pattern of disjunction. However useful this may be, it raises difficulties. In focusing too narrowly, one risks misrepresenting the breadth and depth of the division and sacrificing rich, though imperfect, texts to abstractions. If anything, romantic fiction has already suffered from too much categorization. It's fate is to have been pigeon-holed more often than read. Some common traits and tendencies have been suggested in the preceding pages, but what the romantic novel deserves more than generalized description is to be taken seriously, text by text, and analyzed in the light of what we know of the romantic mind and the peculiar demands of prose fiction.

I

THE CASTLE OF OTRANTO

Horace Walpole
1764

"I waked one morning, in the beginning of last June, from a dream, of which all I could recover was, that I had thought myself in an ancient castle (a very natural dream for a head filled like mine with Gothic story) and that on the uppermost bannister of a great staircase I saw a gigantic hand in armour. In the evening I sat down, and began to write, without knowing in the least what I intended to say or relate." [1] Thus wrote Horace Walpole in 1765 of the conception of *The Castle of Otranto* and thus began the cult of the Gothic novel in English. Castles and terrifying apparitions had occurred in the literature of Britain and the Continent before, but the peculiar combination of subject and style which Walpole had attempted gave rise to a distinct literary fashion in the second half of the eighteenth century.

Between the end of the seventeenth century and the end of the eighteenth, the term Gothic, like many other terms applied to works of art, underwent a change which almost completely reversed its connotation. Originally it had referred simply to a Germanic tribe; and to an age which revered all things classical, the association with lack of cultivation and taste seemed obvious. In 1695 Dryden explained, "All that hath nothing of the Ancient gust is called a barbarous or Gothic manner." [2] Even those who did not associate the term with barbarian hordes retained the pejorative sense of the word, applying it to whatever seemed in poor taste. Addison, defining a "Gothic" style of writing in 1711, mentions "epigram, forced conceits, turns of wit," [3] having in mind the faults of overelaboration rather than those of underdevelopment. Whatever its own characteristics were thought to be, the Gothic was consistently assumed to be at odds with classical order and restraint. As those qualities were valued less, the Gothic in one shape or another was valued more. Writers in the second half of the eighteenth century were more and more inclined to associate the term with a salutary break with a discipline which had become too mechanical in its application.

The first sustained defense of Gothic art appeared in 1762 in Bishop Hurd's *Letters on Chivalry and Romance*. The *Letters* contain comparisons of medieval and Homeric customs and concepts of heroism, but they bear only the most superficial resemblance to a modern study in comparative social anthropology. Hurd is not really interested in comparing societies but in defending what is English and Christian against what is pagan and Greek. His rallying point is Spenser, though he also proclaims the superiority of Shakespeare and Milton. Hurd's first line of argument is nationalistic. He points out that the spirit and pageantry of the Middle Ages are naturally congenial to the minds of English writers who are at their best when "rapt with the Gothic fables of chivalry." Secondly and more importantly, Hurd defends the technical diversity and thematic excesses of medieval literature as aesthetic virtues and dismisses the notion that they represent a breach of decorum. "The fancies of our modern bards are not only more gallant, but, on a change of the scene, more sublime, more terrible, more alarming, than those of the classic fablers. In a word . . . the manners they paint, and the superstitions they adopt, are the more poetical for being Gothic." [4] What Hurd is suggesting is a new idea of decorum in which extraordinary events and extreme emotions figure as positive factors. If *The Faerie Queene* lacks "unity of action" in the Aristotelian sense, it has its own "unity of design" based on chivalric practices and an overarching moral intent.

Hurd's final and most far-reaching argument appears during his attack on the "exact, but cold Boileau" for prejudicing Addison and other English critics against the fanciful and "artificial" in poetry. "But the source of bad criticism, as universally of bad philosophy, is the abuse of terms. A poet, they say, must follow Nature; and by Nature we are to

28

suppose can only be meant the known and experienced course of affairs in this world. Whereas the poet has a world of his own, where experience has less to do, than consistent imagination." [5] If Nature may be taken to include a "world" of the poet's own to which he has access through the imagination, then the term Gothic may be understood to refer not merely to a historical period or literary convention, but to a state of mind, to a way of seeing.

The Middle Ages were thought to be important primarily because they marked a time of faith and superstition during which the boundaries between religion, poetry, and history were indistinct. One could carp, as Smollett had, saying that the period was one of great ignorance. Or one could see it, as Hurd obviously did, as a time of wider experiential scope than the eighteenth century because conventional ideas of reality were compounded of the imagined as well as the known, of the half-hidden interior as well as of the exterior life. For those who found value in the Gothic, the "darkness" of the Dark Ages was not, aesthetically speaking, a disadvantage.

It is not surprising that a clergyman should defend the art of an age of great faith. For where the modes of expression and inquiry were mixed, the quest for the eternal and the infinite could be found nearly everywhere. One of the curses of neoclassicism was that it made too many distinctions, that it separated things too well: heaven for the divines and earth for the artists, which was all right so long as the artist did not find the earth a tiresome place. But many longed for a new mingling of the transcendent and the mundane, not so much by means of mere imitation of medieval art as by an attempt to understand and translate its spirit into modern terms.

"Grecian is Mathematic Form: Gothic is Living Form," wrote Blake in one of his outbursts against Homer and Virgil. "Mathematic Form is Eternal in the Reasoning Memory: Living Form is Eternal Existence." An inner life, not fully comprehensible to the reason, is what Gothic suggested to Blake, and thus it was transformed, with his own peculiar emphasis, to a positive term of highest praise.

Coleridge, in the first of his 1818 lectures, turned his attention to Gothic art and insisted, as Schlegel had, that its definitive characteristic was a dependence upon "a symbolical expression of the infinite . . . whatever cannot be circumscribed within the limits of actual sensuous being." [6] What is most interesting in Coleridge's remarks is his concern with the effect of such art on the individual viewing it. He does not speak of moral elevation, instruction, or inspiration, but of a loss of separate identity, a kind of metamorphosis: "Gothic architecture impresses the beholder with a sense of self-annihilation; he becomes, as it were, part of the work contemplated." [7] Coleridge's remark is dramatic and Germanic, but it is also profoundly suggestive of the way in which a preoccupation with medieval art, however idiosyncratic its expression was earlier, led to the very heart of serious romantic theory.

Walpole comes chronologically between Dryden and Coleridge and he falls to neither extreme. For him, Gothic meant medieval and, though the Middle Ages were his passion, he tended to regard that fact as a personal eccentricity rather than as justification for an aesthetic revolution. "I am deeper than ever in Gothic antiquities," he wrote to John Chute in 1759. "I pass all my mornings in the thirteenth century, and my evenings in the century that is coming on." [8] For Walpole, "Gothic antiquity" was an intellectual interest, an entertainment, and an admitted escape from the disappointments and tedium of the present. Once it became clear that a career in politics was impossible, he deliberately exercised his intellectual energies on pursuits which he himself called "idle." The Castle of Otranto had for him an importance certainly not greater than his Catalogue of the Royal and Noble Authors of England, his Historical Doubts on the Reign of Richard III, or his unstageable play The Mysterious Mother; and it probably seemed a good deal less important than the construction of Strawberry Hill. Yet there were twenty-one editions of the novel in the eighteenth century alone, and there have been close to a hundred more since then, including translations into every major language.

2

What Walpole had done was to write a prose narrative which evoked medieval Catholic atmosphere, relied upon fear as its primary emotional stimulus, and mixed stylistic and formal conventions borrowed from a wide variety of literary modes. In a broad sense, all later Gothic writers did these same things with variations. Some, indeed, were much better craftsmen than Walpole, but few possessed his cultivated mind or critical sensibility, and none could tell so coherently why this particular narrative mode was so appealing.

In the first place, to Walpole, an interest in the past was essentially a creative avocation. The study of history was in fact a partial release from rationality, because the historian — especially the amateur historian — had to work on the basis of hints and clues rather than on detailed evidence, and was called upon to imagine as often as to deduce. Inasmuch as imagination was associated with curiosity about the distant past, it was regarded by Walpole as the sole realm in which one was safe from the vicissitudes of time as experienced in the present. "Visions . . . have always been my pasture," he wrote in 1766. "I almost think there is no wisdom comparable to that of exchanging what is called the realities of life for dreams. Old castles, old pictures, old histories . . . make one live back in centuries, that cannot disappoint one. One holds fast and surely what is past. The dead have exhausted their power of deceiving; one can trust Catherine of Medicis now." [9] Far from seeing a risk in visions, Walpole considered them an insurance of security, a protective vehicle by means of which one can approach dangers of all sorts without being hurt. And this is precisely what Walpole did in *The Castle of Otranto*. His interest in Catholicism, his preoccupation with fear, and his cavalier mixing of styles, all involved dangers which he expected his Gothic dream to reveal and save him from at the same time.

Walpole's use of Catholicism, like that of most of his imitators, is neither theological nor ecclesiastical in emphasis. For the eighteenth-century English Protestant the trappings of the Roman Church provided an exotic background, but, more than that, they were symbols of superstition, fanaticism, and odd behavior. Thomas Aquinas notwithstanding, the majority of Walpole's readers would have taken it for granted that where Catholicism reigned, reason was deposed. And of this Walpole was perfectly aware, for it was in its aspect as emblem of the irrational that he cultivated the Church as a presence in his novel. It became almost a cliché of Gothic fiction that there was a ratio between religious suppression of reason and emotional extravagance. There are no parallels to Dostoevsky's Grand Inquisitor scene in the English Gothic novel because no representative of the Church could be permitted to reason so coolly. The Church's power was not portrayed as residing in logic, even logic hypocritically employed, but in a madness common to all its members. A penitent bathed in tears, a novice tormented by guilt, an abbess burning with rage — these are the stock religious figures in the Gothic novel. Unlike Diderot in *La Religieuse*, English writers tended to dwell on such figures not in protest against an institution which still had the power to harm them, but precisely because its energy seemed largely a thing of the past. Heightened emotion was the objective for which the Roman Church was a convenient excuse.

The particular emotion in which the Gothic novelist most regularly dealt was fear. But, despite obvious excesses, he was motivated by more than gratuitous sensationalism. Much as the sublime had been defined in sharp contrast to beauty, fear was taken as the antithesis of love. And, since in the eyes of some writers, love had deteriorated in the novel to the level of an insipid sentiment, whatever seemed opposed to it promised to provide a fresh source of vitality to the artist. Of course, such manipulation of opposites has about it much of the mechanical view of human nature which later Romantics so heartily despised. Instead of being frightening, Gothic "horror" is often merely amusing simply because it is so carefully arranged to provide diversionary contrast. Walpole's decorator's temperament did reign over a good deal of later Gothic fiction, but behind the *objets d'art*, the elegant letters, the precious mysteries, one senses a genuine longing for strong emotion. Paradoxically, his antiquarian fictions were meant to guard the emotions from injury and at the same time to shock them back to life.

Consistency is not one of the earmarks of romantic fiction, especially in its earliest stages. Walpole was eager to proclaim his deliberate blending of formal and stylistic conventions in *The Castle of Otranto*. High life and low life, tragedy and comedy, formal discourse and common speech, the miraculous and the mundane, were all to be mingled together with "Shakespearian" abandon. However questionable the result, one cannot deny the bravado of this early defiance of neoclassical decorum. In explaining the success of his novel among his countrymen, Walpole wrote to a French acquaintance:

Whatever good sense we have, we are not yet in any light chained down to precepts and inviolable laws. All that Aristotle or his superior commentators, your authors, have taught us, has not yet subdued us to regularity:

we still prefer the extravagant beauties of Shakespeare and Milton to the cold and well-disciplined merit of Addison, and even to the sober and correct march of Pope.[10]

Extravagance and irregularity in uncertain hands can lead to literary chaos and, though *The Castle of Otranto* is a slight work, it is both in form and content very far along the way to total confusion. Walpole tries to create a kingdom in which reason, love, and order have been overthrown and he tries, as well, to adopt a narrative mode appropriate to his subject. His antiquarian's mentality — his tendency to treat the elements of his own dreams as though they were dead — may have given his fictional experiment an air of static harmlessness which made it acceptable to the public, but it also prompted him to write with the too-inclusive instinct of the collector rather than with the selective imagination of the artist. Madness, death, and riot are at the center of *The Castle of Otranto*, wrapped together with pious sentiment and delicate manners in the parchment of another country and era, and preserved in a conglomeration of styles. Walpole's love of long sentences, balanced periods, personified abstractions, and polite circumlocutions mark him unmistakably as a man of his own century. Two sentences taken from the same page are sufficient to illustrate the point. The first is in the narrator's voice, the second is spoken by the heroine:

Thus jealousy prompted, and at the same time borrowed, an excuse from friendship to justify its curiosity.

"Can I stoop to wish for the affection of a man who rudely and unnecessarily acquainted me with his indifference — and that at the very moment in which common courtesy demanded at least expressions of civility?"

Beside such sentences, sudden outbursts of passion seem empty bombast, as when Manfred cries out to a ghost: "Lead on! I will follow thee to the gulf of perdition." Abruptly, Walpole alters his tone to describe a more modest journey: "The spectre marched sedately, but dejected, to the end of the gallery, and turned into a chamber on the right hand." Not only is there an incongruous change in tone, but an introduction of commonplace detail in a scene of supposed supernatural significance. Again and again, Walpole alternates between contradictory voices: Pope's fondness for litotes and oxymoron might be followed by gruesome

33

detail in an exaggerated Jacobean style and the whole thing concluded with a bland note in the straightforward descriptive manner of Defoe. Thus, we are treated with a servant "foaming at the mouth" at the sight of "the bleeding mangled remains" of his master, then soothed by pages of "pleasing melancholy" and "gentle violence," and presented finally with the cool assertion that "three drops of blood" have fallen from the nose of a miraculous statue.

Like his stylistic borrowings, Walpole's adoption of character-types and episodes from Shakespearian drama is usually taken by critics to show his ineptitude as an artist. More specifically, it illustrates a confusion of aim which stems from a desire to reject current narrative conventions without any clear idea of what to do with the older ones chosen to replace them. The ancestral ghost, for example, is obviously patterned after the ghost of Hamlet's father. It sighs and beckons, but goes "sedately" down its gallery without saying anything because there is nothing to say. Similarly, there are talkative servants, like the nurse in *Romeo and Juliet*, who chatter without coming to the point. But, again, there never is any point for them to come to in the first place. Finally, Walpole attempts to evoke emotional agitation by means of theatrical gesture and movement, but his mind tries to work from the outside in and he succeeds only in putting his characters through frantic exercises which have no correspondence with the pace of human emotion. In a typical passage, a character is discovered by a princess "prostrate on his face before the altar"; the princess shrieks, "concluding him dead." "Rising suddenly, his face bedewed with tears, he would have rushed from her presence," but is prevailed upon to explain his "posture," after which "bursting from her," he hastens to his own apartment where he is "accosted" by the prince, who invites him "to waste some hours of the night in music and revelling." Offended by such levity, he pushes him "rudely" aside, and entering his chamber, flings the door "intemperately" shut and bolts it. Enraged by such treatment, the prince withdraws and as he crosses the court, is met by "the domestic he had planted at the convent as a spy." This man, "almost breathless with the haste he had made," informs his lord that "Theodore and some lady from the castle" are at that instant "in private conference at the tomb of Alfonso in St. Nicholas's church." Aside from the exhausting rate at which the characters are made to dash about the castle, there is a disturbing lack of focus on any single person or event. The plot is part obstacle course, part free-for-all, and part relay race in which the participants run through a cluttered labyrinth passing the baton to whomever they happen to meet.

Just as this accelerated movement is intended to create an atmosphere of emotional excitement, complicated relationships and inscrutable events are to provide the obscurity necessary to all sublime art. The young and sickly son of Manfred, Prince of Otranto, is crushed to death by a huge, mysterious helmet on the morning of his wedding to the beautiful Isabella. Manfred, eager for heirs and full of lust, decides to divorce his own wife and marry Isabella himself. Though warned by an old friar against his "adulterous intention" and "incestuous design," Manfred pursues the frightened Isabella through dark corridors and damp chapels until a mysterious knight appears with an army of one hundred men bearing an enormous sword which seems to belong with the magic helmet. After various turns in the plot, including Manfred's murder of his own daughter and the revelation that a peasant named Theodore is the real Prince of Otranto, the castle collapses, the usurper Manfred retires to a monastery, and Theodore, whose true love had been Matilda, lives gloomily ever after with Isabella.

In speaking of Beddoes' *Death's Jest-Book*, Northrop Frye notes the elaborate and unnatural sequence of events: "The characters are not acting out what they are but are being made to do things, like a social gathering organized into games and charades." [11] This describes equally well the atmosphere of *The Castle of Otranto*. Frye goes on to suggest that in romantic literature mechanically manipulated plots are often signs of the rejection of the social process because external events have ceased to be genuine expressions of character. In works like *The Monk* and *Melmoth the Wanderer*, this is certainly true, and in *The Castle of Otranto* we see the phenomenon emerging in a very early form. The author's impulse to reject the social process is simply not yet matched by a conception of individual character powerful enough to create dramatic tension. The plot *is* an imposition, but resistance to it is more likely to come from the reader than from the fictitious protagonist.

3

Some biographers have pointed out that the curious nature of the plot reflects Walpole's dark feelings about his politically powerful and sexually undisciplined father. The truth of this would be difficult to prove or refute, but though it may explain something about Walpole's own psychology, it does not explain why his artless novel was so enthusiastically received by the English public and imitated by writers for several decades. Discussing the influence of Jacobean drama through *The Castle of Otranto* on the German and English theater at the end of the eighteenth century, Coleridge suggested in his *Biographia Literaria* that the secret of this kind of literature consisted in "the confusion and subversion of the natural order of things in their causes and effects." It is not surprising that Coleridge, writing after the American and French Revolutions, gives, as his primary example of such confusion, a reversal in the social order whereby outlaws and vagabonds are treated sympathetically and even endowed with "qualities of liberality, refined feeling, and a nice sense of honor."

The Gothic novel did eventually encourage large-scale social subversion, but, in its earlier forms, the "natural order" which it disturbed was of a simpler and more fundamental type. The confusion existed not between lawmaker and renegade, but between father and son, brother and sister, lover and mistress. Basic human relationships were thrown into an extreme disorder which was symbolized most commonly in sexual terms — adultery, incest, pederasty. These are ancient means of signifying cultural and moral changes of the most disturbing sort, but the peculiar characteristic of much Gothic fiction is the apparent lack of seriousness with which it treats symbols of such serious potential. One reason for this, as exemplified by Walpole, is that there was neither sufficient fidelity to an old order nor a clear enough conception of a new one to place the vision of disorder in relief. Richardson could build a narrative of tragic proportions around a rape because chastity and its association with the values of a whole society were profoundly real to him. Fielding could make comic use of lustful old women and effeminate *beaux* because he assumed a norm beside which their behavior seemed a foolish deviation. But Gothic fiction was not only *about* confusion, it was written *from* confusion. Its imaginary realm is a purgatory in which tragedy and comedy are not only mixed but mixed up, where hope and despair dilute one another because their objects and causes are equally indistinct.

The uses of the incest theme by Walpole and other Gothic novelists

36

illustrate the ambiguity of their moral and aesthetic position. Though the subject of incest is most often associated with late Renaissance drama and early romantic narrative, it persisted as a theme throughout the Restoration and the eighteenth century. It appears in four of Dryden's plays, *The Spanish Friar, Aureng-Zebe, Don Sebastian,* and *Love Triumphant.* It figures in Aphra Behn's *The Dumb Virgin or the Force of Imagination* as well as in later anonymous romances on the order of *The Illegal Lovers, a True, Secret History, Being an Amour Between a Person of Condition and his Sister,* published in 1728. And, of course, both *Moll Flanders* and *Tom Jones* contain episodes of real and imagined incest. In *Moll Flanders* the episode demonstrates comically the extremes to which a poor girl is sometimes driven; in *Tom Jones* it demonstrates, also comically, the extremes from which a healthy boy can be delivered by good nature and a little bit of luck. In both novels incest stands for something socially and morally unacceptable, but it operates explicitly as a literary convention rather than as an instrument of profound character analysis. It is no more "in character" for Moll Flanders or Tom Jones to be tempted by incestuous love than it is for them to be delivered from it. The whole concept is an external one, a trick of fate or a tired literary joke.

Walpole was aware of the stock conventional uses of incest, but he was also aware that the ancient taboo retained considerable psychological and moral potency. In his play *The Mysterious Mother,* he tries to explore the emotional source of human perversity by showing it not as originating in fatal coincidence but in the deliberations of a deranged mind. A countess, shocked and bereaved by the sudden death of her husband, deliberately assumes the place of her son's mistress and gives herself to him in a darkened chamber. Walpole justifies the incident in a postscript in which he explains that grief and confusion may lead almost anywhere because "a conflict of passions [throws] reason off its guard." [12] Though the psychology is crude, it is not untypical in an age when heightened emotion of any sort (including fear and sorrow) was associated with sexual arousal. Smollett follows a similar line of reasoning in *Ferdinand Count Fathom,* which was published twelve years before *The Castle of Otranto* and is in some respects a precursor of the Gothic novel. While his protagonist prepares to seduce a girl frightened by a supposed onslaught of thieves, Smollett notes: "This is a season, which of all others is most propitious to the attempt of an artful lover . . . There is an affinity and short transition betwixt all the violent passions that agitate the human mind. They are all false perspectives, which, though they magnify, yet perplex and render indistinct every object which they represent." [13]

The important point is that in *The Mysterious Mother* Walpole begins with an act knowingly committed and tries to explore the state of mind in which it is possible. But this is only part of the extremely elaborate plot of the play. For, almost as though frightened by the possibilities of his own investigation, Walpole falls back on ingenious subplots filled with mistaken identity which distract attention from the peculiar and fascinating countess. The question shifts from "Why does she do it?" (and, by implication, why does anyone act irrationally) to "Who did what to whom when?" When the countess discovers that her son, still unaware of her deception, returns from exile years later and marries the girl who was born of the illicit union, she cries:

"Confusion! Phrenzy! blast me, all ye furies!
Edmund and Adeliza! When! Where! How!"

Neither the tone of voice nor the questions asked evoke the dilemma of a guilty and maddened woman. Facts will hardly help at this point, and yet facts are what Walpole and the countess (addressing Edmund) finally provide:

"Lo! where this monster stands! thy mother! mistress!
The mother of thy daughter, sister, wife!"

The lines are like an answer to a riddle. And it is precisely as a solved riddle rather than as a human mystery that Walpole leaves the problem. Despite his love for the Dark Ages, he retreats from the unknown and seeks to present experience, in the true spirit of rationalism, as perfectly explicable when all the parts are arranged in their rightful places. One of the play's noble and righteous characters speaks in part for Walpole when he says menacingly to two scheming friars:

"But day darts on your spells.
Th' enlightened age eschews your vile deceits,
And truth shall do mankind and Edmund justice."

38

4

Rational habits are as difficult to shake off as irrational ones, and that is perhaps why the personifications of those moral and aesthetic extremes so much sought after by the first romantic novelists are curiously wraith-like in *The Castle of Otranto*. The source of fear and the object of love, the sublime as well as the beautiful, are intangible, ineffectual, and unconvincing. Walpole's ghosts, as might be expected, are gratuitous phantoms which serve little purpose other than to arouse the servants from time to time. But, more surprisingly, Manfred himself is a blustering, bungling demon who fails to possess the lovely Isabella, kills his own daughter by mistake, and retires quietly to a religious life at the end. The beautiful characters, male and female, who inspire love are even less substantial, particularly to one another, than the ghosts and villains. The only promise of a mutual and conventional love is that which exists between the young Theodore and Manfred's daughter Matilda. But its fulfillment proves to be a physical impossibility; it can be expressed only when one of the two is absent. Matilda lingeringly pours her adoration upon an ancestral portrait to which Theodore bears a resemblance, but her personal encounters with him are usually hurried and formal. After Matilda's death, Theodore consents to marry Isabella only because she can help him keep alive the memory of Matilda: "Theodore's grief was too fresh to admit the thought of another love; and it was not until after frequent discourses with Isabella of his dear Matilda, that he was persuaded he could know no happiness but in the society of one with whom he could forever indulge the melancholy that had taken possession of his soul."

Where any human contact requiring time, intensity, and reciprocity is called for, whether it be violent or loving, one of the two characters involved is almost certain to evaporate or become someone else. One of the most overused and therefore amusing stock devices in the novel is mistaken identity. A peasant turns out to be a prince, a prince an outlaw, a monk a parent, an orphan a daughter, and so on to a bewildering extreme. Characters are also continuously mistaking one another for ghosts. In one scene, Theodore, assuming himself to be alone in a cave, sees a moving shape, thinks at first it is a demon, then a robber, and eventually discovers it is only Isabella. But Theodore himself casts similar doubts in the minds of others. "What occasioned Manfred to take Theodore for a spectre?" asks Isabella. The cause, it would seem, is in the eyes of the beholder, for, as the mysterious knight later says to Manfred, "It is not the youth's fault if you took him for a spectre."

Indeed it is not the youth's fault. For nearly half of the novel he does not know who or what he is himself. When his shirt slips down and betrays a birthmark in the shape of a bloody arrow on his shoulder, the old monk cries, "Gracious heavens! What do I see? It is my child, my Theodore!" But the revelations in this book are even more pointless and inconsequential than the mysteries. At the beginning, nobody knows who anybody is and, at the end, it no longer makes any difference because identity has been sacrificed to atmosphere. Believable relationships — sexual or otherwise — are impossible, not because the state is tottering with corruption, but because the essence of individual identity has been dislodged from its human centers and diffused in an architectural construct which seems to have more life than the characters who inhabit it.

If anything gives this novel unity and animation, it is the castle. Walpole does not describe the building in great detail, but its presence — dark, confining, labyrinthine — is felt on nearly every page. Even those characters who seem foolish or wraith-like in their behavior with one another, can be relatively credible when pictured alone in some part of the castle. If we can believe little else about them, we can nearly always believe that they are lost. One of the few instances in which we can sympathize with Isabella is when she seeks an underground escape from Manfred:

The lower part of the castle was hollowed into several intricate cloisters; and it was not easy for one under so much anxiety to find the door that opened into the cavern. An awful silence reigned throughout those subterraneous regions, except now and then some blasts of wind that shook the doors she had passed, and which, grating on the rusty hinges, were reechoed through that long labyrinth of darkness.

The place itself seems sufficiently charged with emotion to require little assistance from the characters. In fact, external conditions play a larger part in determining the behavior of the characters than do their own internal motivations.

There is almost no correspondence between human behavior and the demands of soul, mind, heart, and body because of an inability on Walpole's part to assign primary value to one or to establish harmony among all four. What makes *The Castle of Otranto* a novel of historical importance is that this incapacity was not merely the failing of a single writer, but the dilemma of an age. It is one of the pervading characteristics of all Gothic fiction — and initially one of its failings — that individual personality is subordinated to physical setting. Yet it is one of the triumphs of later romantic fiction that this limitation is transformed into an extraordinarily liberating augmentation of the whole concept of individual identity.

Early Gothic fiction succeeded in raising ghosts more effectively than many critics have admitted. Nearly all of its major characters are shadows of the more substantial literary figures whom they vaguely resemble. Unable to think, to feel, to believe, they exist in a frantic whirl of meaningless motion cut off from one another and even from the imaginary world they inhabit. Just as the Church, though possessing an independent emotional value of its own, is empty and inert as a symbol of spirituality, so too the great helmet and sword, if obvious phallic shapes, are not phallic symbols because the characters have no lives to which they can refer. Littered with lifeless images and archaic conventions, Walpole's novel may still strike some as an act of irresponsible vandalism rather than a creative literary experiment. He himself was sure only of his own boredom with the current state of English letters. And it is true that his novel proves him more adept at dismantling the old and presenting it in shambles than in building something truly new.

That the source of much Gothic fiction was boredom rather than righteous anger or scorn or visionary commitment helps to explain its lack of focus and moral seriousness as a literary form. Some defenders of Walpole would like to justify *The Castle of Otranto* by calling it a parody or satire, a long joke at the expense of prose romance. The thought certainly occurred to Walpole, but there is little evidence to support the claim that he intended the whole book as such himself or that many contemporary readers took it in that way. In the first place, it was not much like the romances which were being written at that period, as he himself points out in his preface to the second edition and as most eighteenth-century commentators recognized. Speaking of the English fashion of prose romance during and after the Restoration, Pope wrote in his imitation of *The First Epistle of the Second Book of Horace*: "The soldier breathed the gallantries of France, / And ev'ry flow'ry courtier writ Romance." In the Warburton edition of 1770 the following footnote was attached to this couplet:

Amidst all this nonsense, when things were at their worst, we have been lately entertained with what I will venture to call a Masterpiece in the Fable, and of a new species likewise. The piece I mean is *The Castle of Otranto*. The scene is laid in Gothic Chivalry. Where a beautiful imagination, supported by strength of judgment, has enabled the Author to go beyond his subject, and effect the full purpose of the ancient Tragedy, that is, to purge the passions by pity and terror, in colouring as great and harmonious as in any of the best Dramatic Writers.[14]

Although few readers may have regarded the work as a masterpiece, it did receive a popular applause which pleased Walpole. Though he tried to be detached about it, his letters show that he was offended when people laughed in the wrong places. His repeated invocations of Shakespeare as the literary model and justification for his work have nothing whatever in them of humor or irony.

Boredom and confusion are genuine, and, in some eras more than others, common human responses. Though they do not tend to produce great works of art, they often produce interesting ones which clear the way for better things to come. Beneath the fakery and bombast of *The Castle of Otranto* there is an authentic impulse, which is to throw off the current platitudes and clichés of art in an effort to discover something new and hopefully better. It is a theme repeated many times in Walpole's letters. In his old age he wrote to a young poet: "I have long been weary of the common jargon of poetry. You bards have exhausted all the nature we are acquainted with; you have treated us with the sun, moon, and stars, the earth and the ocean, mountains and valleys, etc., etc., under every possible aspect. In short, I have longed for some American poetry, in which I will find some new appearances of nature, and consequently of art." [15] It is out of this sense of external nature "exhausted" by conventional art that Walpole took to portraying, as an antidote, unnatural acts performed by improbable characters in unlikely places and thereby established the general fare of Gothic fiction for decades to come.

II

VATHEK

William Beckford
1786

Fonthill Abbey notwithstanding, William Beckford did not regard himself as a follower or admirer of the Gothic school of writers. Except as a rival collector, he was not impressed by Walpole, "the cursèd Pest of Strawberry Hill." [1] His distaste for lady romancers, including those who wrote in the Gothic vein, is recorded in his parodic *Modern Novel Writing*. And in 1821 he noted, "It might be as well if instead of weaving historical romances the super-literary ladies of the present period would pass a little more of their time at cross stitch and yabble stitch. We should gain some pretty chair and screen covers and lose little by not being tempted to pore over the mazes of their interminable scribbleations." [2]

The phenomenon of orientalism in eighteenth-century literature provides one of the best proofs that exotic atmosphere alone does not make a narrative romantic. While it is true that many romantic writers chose settings far removed from the immediate environs of London, the significant distinguishing factor was not the foreignness itself but the way in which strange setting was used. Between 1704 and 1712 Galland's French edition of *Mille et une nuits* was translated into English and contributed substantially to an interest in the Near and Far East which hitherto had been more economic than literary in character. Still, for the first three quarters of the century, artistic no less than commercial imports from the Orient were intended to profit and embellish the status quo rather than to provide a departure from it. Oriental settings and characters established the "distance" necessary for a supposedly unprejudiced look at Western society as it was. The moral and religious opinions expressed through oriental tales were occidental and rationalistic in nature, and the views espoused were never so heavily clothed in foreign atmosphere as to be incomprehensible to a European reader. *Lettres Persanes* (1721), *Candide* (1759), *Contes Moraux* (1761–1765) and their English counterparts, *The Vision of Mirzah* (1711), *Rasselas* (1759), and *Citizen of the World* (1760–61), however different in quality and point of view, were alike in their adoption of an oriental disguise which gave freedom and charm to the satiric or didactic Western writer.

Published in 1786, Beckford's *Vathek*, when not dismissed as Asian Gothic, is often regarded as the last remnant of this pseudo-oriental literary fashion which had reached its peak nearly thirty years earlier. Nothing could be less true. And nothing has been more harmful to a fair appraisal of Beckford's novel than to treat it as a decadent *Rasselas*. Beckford's interest in the Orient was obviously made possible by translations and adaptations done earlier in the century, but an equally important factor is the atypical education he received as the only child of one of the richest families in England. He was tutored by Sir William Chambers, who had traveled in China, and was taught drawing by Alexander Cozzens, who had been born in Russia and was a student of Persian. Young Beckford knew more of the Orient than its usefulness as a disguise for Western morality. In addition to *The Arabian Nights*, the sources of *Vathek* include *Persian Tales, Mogul Tales,* and *The Adventures of Abdalla Son of Hanif.*[3] And although these tales had been translated into French and English, Beckford's knowledge of Arabic and Persian appears to have been sufficiently good to enable him to consult them in the original.

But even more important than Beckford's study of the Orient, which at best was fragmentary and unsystematic, is the quality of his mind. Beckford is the first of the romantic novelists whose subject is always and irrevocably himself. The Orient is not a convenient mask through which to criticize the world of London and Paris, but an imaginary region, authentic in some details, but constructed to his own specifications for his own occupancy. Thus, though *Vathek* can stand by itself

44

VATHEK

as a work of originality and peculiar beauty, if we want to understand
it in terms of an appropriate context we must turn not to Montesquieu
or Goldsmith but to Beckford himself.

Like Byron, who admired Beckford's "power of imagination" and
thought that Vathek "surpassed all European imitations" [4] of oriental
literature, Beckford was rich, noble, and handsome, and was forced
because of a sexual scandal at home to spend years in exile abroad.
Though less widely known as an artist than Byron, he too created an
image of himself which became almost inseparable from his literary
achievement. The Caliph of Fonthill, whose weakness was adolescent
boys, was hero, heroine, and villain of his own life and fiction.

2

Of all the roles in which Beckford saw himself, the one which recurs
most often in his writing and which is most important to his concept
of fiction is that of the dreamer. With a fervor and deliberation much
greater than Walpole's, he asserted his intention to dwell in his dreams
of the past and future rather than to be circumscribed by the historical
accidents of the present. It is perhaps only a coincidence that Beckford's
declaration in 1777, "I am filled with futurity," is echoed by Blake in
1803, "My heart is full of futurity." But, despite their differences, few
artists other than Blake have proclaimed with more vigor and conviction, the superiority of their private visions over the realities of the
world. In a letter written in 1778, Beckford anticipates even Blake's
tone:

I refuse to occupy my mind with impertinent society . . . the encroach-
ments of Fashion . . . solemn Idleness and approved Dissipation . . . I
will break my shackles, however splendid, and maintain my Allegiance . . .
I will seclude myself if possible from the world, in the midst of the Empire.
I am determined to enjoy my dreams, my phantasies and all my singularities,
however discordant to the worldlings around. In spite of them, I will be
happy, will employ myself in trifles, according to their estimation; and instead of making myself master of the present political state of America . . .
I will read, talk, dream of the Incas, of their gentle Empire and solemn
worship of the sun, the charms of Quito and the majesty of the Andes . . .
[My attention] shall never be turned toward a Philadelphian Meeting
House.[5]

Beckford's dreams have little in common with Blake's prophetic
visions, and he shows a tendency, quite foreign to Blake, to parade his

45

peculiarities in public, to flaunt them in the face of a disapproving world. Whereas both may commence their programs with similar energy, Blake's anger becomes a divine wrath, while Beckford's hovers indecisively between bitterness and self-indulgence. The important point is that Beckford cultivated a nonrational, impractical, subjective view of the world which became his prime reality. As a student in Geneva, he came under the influence of Rousseau and published an autobiographical journal which his guardians tried to suppress, entitled *Dreams, Waking Thoughts and Incidents.* "Shall I tell you my dreams?" the journal begins. "To give an account of my time is doing, I assure you, but little better. Never did there exist a more ideal being. A frequent mist hovers before my eyes, and through its medium I see objects so faint and hazy, that both their colours and forms are apt to delude me." [6]

Here, it would seem, Beckford reveals another contrast to Blake, who always insisted that the visionary sees with a sharpness and clarity not possible to those who look only with their eyes: "He who does not imagine in stronger and better lineaments, and in stronger and better light than his perishing and mortal eye can see, does not imagine at all." Blake translated his doctrine into drawings and concentrated poetic images which are often so sharply defined and luminous as to appear etched by lightning. Yet, despite his penchant for looking at things through a mist, Beckford admired Blake's art and commissioned drawings from him. What the two dreamers shared was a distaste for those forms of literary and pictorial realism which sought to represent experience as static and commonplace. In his satire, *Biographical Memoirs of Extraordinary Painters,* Beckford mocks a painting of a chair and carpet so realistic that "every man wished to sit down in the one, and every dog to repose on the other." Furthermore, he notes that the fictitious painter in question detested "colossal representations . . . bold limbs . . . woeful countenances; conscious they were out of his reach, he condemned them as out of Nature." [7] The "colossal," the "bold," and the "woeful" were closer to the artistic reach of Blake than of Beckford, but they played major roles in the dreams of both.

In truth, Beckford's dreams and "waking thoughts" are not all so hazy and vague as he claims them to be. The sharpness of some of his images and his relative economy of style come closer to Blake's ideal than they do to the euphemistic practice of Walpole and Mrs. Radcliffe. Beckford's style in his journals and fiction is not circumlocutory or Latinate, but it often does produce a dream-like effect by creating a continuous present in which everything is in perpetual and rhythmic motion and the narrator/protagonist is a passive, somewhat remote observer. Even a country fair can be transformed into a series of pleasantly undulating patterns: The peasants "were scattered over the lawn, some conversing with the monks, others half-drunk sliding off their asses and sprawling upon the ground, others bargaining for silken nets and spangled rings to bestow on their mistresses. We rambled about . . . in perfect incognito." [8] If there is vagueness in such passages, it stems from an evasion of sequential time and completed actions, and an obscurity about the relationship between the observer and what he observes.

A partial explanation for these ambiguities is that, next to his role as a dreamer, Beckford liked to imagine himself as a perpetual child. All in life was to be happy and frivolous, a game without strict requirements and without end. His images of childhood are not those of the divinely wise infant or the uncorrupted heart, but of the lithe and frisky youth engaged in eternal sport. At the age of twenty-seven he wrote: "No child of thirteen ever felt a stronger impulse to race and gambol than I do. My limbs are as supple and elastic as those of a stripling, and it gives me no pain to turn and twist them into the most playful attitudes." [9] The more solemn and restrictive the circumstances, the more tempted Beckford was to play the child. Traveling in Portugal after the death of his wife, still unable to return home and ignored by the British ambassador to the Portuguese Court, he suffered the attentions of tedious guides and attempted without great success to behave himself: "How tired I am of keeping a mask on my countenance. How tight it sticks — it makes me sore. There's metaphor for you. I have all the fancies and levity of a child and would give an estate or two to skip about the galleries of the Patriarchal (Cathedral in Lisbon)." [10]

Beckford's ideal child is the absolute egotist, the central — perhaps even sole — occupant of the universe. He is not without feeling: he cries when he is hurt and laughs when he is gratified. But one could not easily speak of his being moral because other creatures do not exist for

47

him as having minds and hearts like his own, but only as sources of pleasure or pain. He is capable of strong affection and also of committing acts of considerable cruelty without necessarily feeling malice. He is lonely, easily moved, and his predominant characteristic is appetite.

The dreamer and the child was also a sensualist, but always an artistic sensualist, seeking exquisite refinements and, above all, ways to avert satiety and prolong gratification in a state of pleasing delirium. As with his dreams and childish games, he avoids climaxes and chooses to sacrifice intensity to duration. One of his favorite words was "languor," and one of his most characteristic descriptions of pleasure has to do with a kind of Portuguese song which he calls

the most voluptuous and bewitching music that ever existed . . . languid interrupted measures, as if breath was gone with excess of rapture, and the soul panting to fly out to you and incorporate itself with the beloved object. With a childish carelessness they steal into your heart before it has time to arm itself against their ennervating influence. You fancy you are swallowing milk and you are swallowing poison. As to myself, I am a slave to *modinhas*.[11]

Whatever his "subject," Beckford has a way of transporting himself to the center of the picture. In his romance fragment, *The Vision*, his narrator/protagonist climbs a mountain (Beckford's beloved Salève) and, like many wanderers in later romantic poetry, he calls attention to himself. But Beckford's ostentatious narcissism makes Wordsworth and even Shelley appear modest. "See me wantonly treading," he commands like a child performing a stunt. "See how cautiously I measure my steps and poise my body; see how I keep my eyes fixed . . . Now behold me leap exaltingly on a grassy bank . . . Well, give me joy." [12] On recalling an especially beautiful beach in his *Portuguese Journal*, his first thought is to imagine himself on it: "How I should enjoy stretching myself on its sands by moonlight and owning all my frailties and wild imaginations to some love-sick languid youth reclining by my side and thrown by the dubious light and undecided murmurs into a soft delirium." [13]

Nature was not, for Beckford, a symbol of objective order against which he could balance the disorders of his own mind, but a spectrum of possibilities with which to illuminate the ego. Religion seemed to have played much the same role for him and, despite his interest in Roman Catholicism, there is little evidence in the journals to suggest that the Church was more than a convenience. It was pleasant during his travels in Italy, Spain, and Portugal to be thought, especially by influential ecclesiastical and court figures, to be always on the verge of conversion. Since Beckford loved the ceremony, color, and music of the Church, the game was not difficult to play. His descriptions of religious ceremonies are almost entirely devoted to the decorations of church interiors, the texture of vestments, and the quality of the music. On one occasion he mentions hearing a *Libera me, Domine* which "thrilled every nerve in my frame and affected me so deeply that I burst into tears." [14] When the ceremonies lasted too long and the music was not well performed, Beckford's faith weakened. He was once repelled by a procession because it included Negroes and displayed inelegant images. But if he was willing to play the public hypocrite, he rarely seems to have failed being honest with himself:

I hear there is no conversation in Lisbon but of my piety. Really this joke begins to have its inconveniences. I am incessantly plagued with deputations from convents, epistles and holy greetings in Latin, English and Portuguese, invitations to sacred festivals and presents of sweet meats in cut paper from lady abbesses and young virgins.[15]

Beckford's orthodoxy was impeded not only by his thorough-going sensuality, but by his identification of himself with the unredeemable victim — not because he believed in damnation, but because he believed in the implacability of pain. It is not the suffering Christ but the vanquished Lucifer he thinks of when attending a Michaelmas service: "I assisted with apparent devotion (at the mass of St. Michael) but could not help feeling all the while more sympathy for the old Dragon than became a pious Catholic. Alas, we are both fallen angels!" [16] The Christian conception of sin, repentance, and redemption seems to have been wholly foreign to Beckford's temperament. He did not see himself as punished by God for his "sins," but as persecuted by a world jealous of his dreams. All impediments to his childish and sensual visions were instruments of torture fashioned by a hostile society which could not bear to let him escape the limits of mortality and social convention in pleasures fashioned by his imagination.

But even in his role as victim, Beckford assumed the center of the arena. If in church he was the devil in the form of a dragon, at his first bullfight he identified himself so thoroughly with the "patient" and bleeding animals that he "seemed to feel cuts and slashes the rest of the evening." [17] Beckford's was an extraordinary imagination but one almost totally lacking in empathy. He did not lose or extend himself through his contacts with external reality, but ingested all that he was able to and refashioned it after his own image. He may not consciously have attempted to usurp the powers of God calling creation back to himself, but he seemed unable to exercise any others with effectiveness. Thus his fiction, like his journals, has an almost shocking originality and, at the same time, a peculiarly narrow range.

Aside from *Vathek* and his letters, Beckford's main literary output consists of travel journals in which he observes himself against various backgrounds. Even *Vathek* is a kind of travelogue, and the Orient is a region pieced together to suit the author's specifications. What Beckford could imitate most effectively in Eastern literature — because it reinforced a tendency already strong in him — was its un-British immoderation. *The Arabian Nights*, though dotted with homely wisdom, is essentially a hymn to excess. By the standard of Western literature, it is too sweet, too cruel, too erotic, and too silly by turns, and therefore suited Beckford's mentality perfectly.

3

Originally written in French, *Vathek* was translated into English by Beckford's friend, the Reverend Samuel Henley, who worked closely with the author until 1786 when he prematurely published the volume without Beckford's permission and claimed that it was "adapted from the Arabic." Beckford himself then quickly brought out French editions in Lausanne and Paris and made the claim that he had written the whole thing in "three days and two nights." The assertion is not true but it serves the double purpose of suggesting that very little time was wasted on such a literary "trifle" and that, like the first pages of *The Castle of Otranto*, it was composed in a passionate fit of genius. Introduced with exaggerated claims and counterclaims, *Vathek* has been, from the beginning, a novel which defied moderate appraisal and consensus. Byron thought it so authentically oriental "that those who have visited the East will have difficulty in believing it to be more than a translation." [18] Mallarmé found it admirable because, like a poem, it possessed a pure and smoothly flowing style "with a lively limpidity, with a broad undulation of phrases." [19] Sacheverell Sitwell compared it with other works out of the "false East" and regarded it as a prominent member of "a gang of wild and *fauve* romances, the collective appearance of which marked the break-up of classicism." [20]

In one way or another, each of these impressions is justifiable. Like Walpole, Beckford was an eclectic. He constructed his strange novel by weaving into it the conventions of oriental fantasy, lyrical poetry, melodrama, burlesque, and allegory. But as none of these conventions predominates, to attempt interpreting the whole book in terms of any one mode is to encounter hopeless inconsistencies and contradictions. Yet, in contrast to *The Castle of Otranto*, there is integrity, even a peculiar unity, in *Vathek*. There is an organizing energy which shapes the disparate literary conventions to its own end.

Whereas taste and its correspondence to a universal standard of reason had been a major preoccupation of earlier eighteenth-century writers, Beckford's concern, like that of the Caliph Vathek, is his own appetite and how to satisfy it. The subject of the novel and the guiding principle of its composition is the gratification of pleasure, as perceived by a single imagination. Taste, insofar as it is identified with balance, moderation, rational discipline, and a general aesthetic standard, is precisely what *Vathek* lacks.

That rational and benevolent view of life represented by Emily St. Aubert's father in *The Mysteries of Udolpho*, unconsciously challenged but still respected by Mrs. Radcliffe, is pulverized by Beckford. St. Aubert, whose philosophy is based on the Horatian dictum that "all excess is vicious," judges peoples' characters by the way they furnish their houses and arrange their gardens as well as by the way they behave since, for him, "virtue and taste are nearly the same." For Beckford, there is no virtue except in the indulgence of pleasure; and taste is the mere threshold of appetite. It seems a waste of time to attempt, especially by means of abstract logic, to determine what is universally pleasing when a lifetime hardly seems long enough to discover the variety and extent of those things which please one's self. Here again Beckford anticipates one mood of Blake, two of whose *Proverbs of Hell* could serve as mottoes for *Vathek*: "You never know what is enough unless you know what is more than enough"; "The road of excess leads to the palace of wisdom."

Vathek, ninth caliph of the race of the Abassides, grandson of Haroun al Raschid, did not think "that it was necessary to make a hell of this world to enjoy paradise in the next." [21] He is a man who lives for the gratification of his senses and who eventually does, through a great variety of excesses, pursue the road to a subterranean palace where Soliman reposes "surrounded by the talismans that control the world" and which is presided over by the satanic Eblis. At the beginning of the novel, Vathek's pleasures, though exaggerated, are fairly conventional. There are five palaces devoted to the gratification of the five senses where Vathek continually gluts himself on a profusion of everything. Tables are "continually covered" with food, wine flows from "a hundred fountains that were never exhausted," songs are "continually varied," perfumes "perpetually burning," and concubines available "by troops."

In contrast to these artificial, rococo palaces of pleasure, Beckford describes a plain on the summit of a nearby mountain so naturally beautiful "that it might have been taken for the paradise destined for the faithful." Vathek, however, does not repair to this Edenic retreat to meditate on his sins or purify his soul, but to quench his thirst at one of its four natural fountains, frequently prostrating "himself upon the ground to lap the water, of which he could never have enough." In a manner which persists throughout the novel, Beckford sets up contrasts which have so often been used in Western literature to make a moral point that to do it again would seem almost unavoidable. And then he avoids doing it. Thus the implied moral distinction between the sensual palaces and the mountain green which Beckford at first encourages by referring to the paradisal beauty of the natural retreat, is marred by the figure of Vathek lapping water like a dog from one of the pure fountains. The contrast is not between a Bower of Bliss and a Garden of Adonis because the protagonist's behavior is essentially the same in both places. There is no moral statement about artificial and selfish vice versus natural and productive virtue, but a crudely aesthetic statement about two different kinds of pleasure and a disturbing suggestion of human debasement involved in both.

A similar invitation to draw moral inferences which the author proffers and then withholds occurs when Vathek, tiring of the modest pleasures of Samarah, hungers for knowledge beyond the power of ordinary mortals. Beckford here encourages a comparison between Vathek and Faustus. The Caliph consults the stars and his sagest wizards in order to penetrate the deepest secrets of the universe and is warned by an old adviser, "Woe to the rash mortal who seeks to know that of which he should remain ignorant, and to understand that which surpasseth his power!" When all else fails, Vathek sells his soul to a devilish Giaour who makes him "abjure Mahomet" and "adore terrestrial influences." Immediately before committing himself to the Giaour, Vathek sees the "clear blue sky streaked over with streams of blood." Though the striking image signifies only one more marvel which whets Vathek's curiosity, it echoes Marlowe's majestic line, "See, see where Christ's blood streams in the firmament."

Beckford may or may not have been thinking of Marlowe's imagery, but he most assuredly was thinking of Faustus when he created Vathek. Yet Vathek is a character without moral dimension. We are prevented from seeing him as a "fallen" character since, from the beginning, he is just Vathek, always and forever the same, a fantasy sensualist with a few tender traits but without sufficient complexity of character to make us mourn his loss of innocence or regret his unfulfilled promise. Despite superficial parallels, he does not possess Faustus' conscience or intelligence, even at the beginning; we never witness in him the destruction of something valuable. The blood streaking in the sky does not, therefore, belong to Christ or any other redeeming agent. Beckford retains some of the signs and emblems of Christianity to give shape to his fantasy, to point up the irrelevance of the morality which was conventionally attached to them, and to reinterpret them according to his own purposes. Though he did not attempt, like Blake, to create a whole cosmology, he did convert and combine Hebraic, Christian, and Moslem myths to suit himself. Heaven and hell may retain some of their familiar markings, but the context in which they are found undermines any attempt to decipher them in traditional ways.

4

To say that the absolutely debauched Vathek consigns himself to "terrestrial" and "satanic" forces is one way of indicating that he is moving into a new phase of pleasure-seeking, and it is also a bizarre joke. The humor throughout *Vathek* is, in fact, the most disturbing and original element of the book. Like the invention of an irrepressible and half-witted jester, it appears unexpectedly, even at random, distorting and often seeming to spoil "serious" moments. Yet, without it, *Vathek* would not only be a far less original work, but it would have less psychological force. For it is the peculiar humor of the novel, rather than the misleading signs of its pseudo-allegorical landscape, that suggests the nature and the extent of the protagonist's journey into the center of the only pleasure principle which Beckford believed in, the self.

One must distinguish first between the sense of humor which Beckford adopts for himself as the narrator of the tale, and which serves as a kind of bridge between himself and the reader, and that humor which he assigns to characters in the novel. The humor which he adopts for himself is almost entirely literary in nature and derives its effectiveness from stylistic parodies, puns, and incongruous euphemisms. In other words, it is a humor which depends upon artistic, social, and ethical conventions which exist outside the novel and with which Beckford assumes his reader is familiar.[22] Thus, those parodic passages which are at the expense of Vathek's mother Carathis, introduce details common to the sentimental fiction of the period. In the midst of her most depraved excesses, Carathis is endowed with the traits of the stock authoritarian matron, prudish, strong-willed, and ambitious for her son. Before Vathek's departure for the subterranean kingdom of Eblis, Carathis gives him what Beckford calls an "edifying discourse," warning him away from strange women since in his "ambulatory seraglio there are at least three dozen of pretty faces" and reminding him that she would like to follow him eventually to satisfy her own "taste for dead bodies and everything like mummy."

In addition to parodying character types familiar to his readers, Beckford repeatedly resorts to understatement, *double entendre*, and euphemism, especially when commenting on excessive and perverse sexuality. Castration, necrophilia, incest, and sodomy are part of the novel's regular fare; yet Beckford assumes a vague detachment from them all, giving the impression that he is not responsible for the way these people act. He resorts to what Wayne Booth calls "un-earned irony," which, like sentimentality, provides the author with a "substitute for an honest discrimination among his materials." [23] Beckford pretends to ally himself with the reader by means of a Kiplingesque smirk which implies an amused superiority to the curious but gross behavior of the natives, even though these natives, more purely than Kipling's, are the inventions of his own imagination. When intruders in the harem are sent to be castrated, they are consigned "with good commendations to the surgeons of the serail." When Vathek is saved from a fire by one of his Ethiopian wives, she is called "the roughest trotting jade he had hitherto mounted." When the young boy Gulchenrouz is carried off by the chief eunuch, he receives "a thousand unwelcome caresses," a phrase which is at the same time an exaggeration and an evasion. And when Carathis stops in a cemetery to preside over a supper of fresh corpses, her "negresses" form "tender connections with the ghouls."

Through such attempts at humor, Beckford makes mild concessions to the prejudices of his readers, but, as with the Edenic and Faustian parallels, he is also mocking those prejudices. We can never laugh very heartily at Beckford's jokes since the verbal plays are not sufficiently interesting to divert our attention altogether from the forms of moral anarchy to which they refer. Beckford's alliance with us is a fragile bond and one which he reserves the right to break at any moment. In fact, the reader of *Vathek* may have the distasteful sensation of being manipulated at random like most of the characters. Samarah is a region of unfulfilled promises where the author leads the reader by means of flattering language, hints of moral reward, and ironic asides, to the brink of expectation. Yet, always adept at autostimulation, Beckford tricks the reader out of the biggest laugh and keeps it for himself.

For it must finally be assumed that Beckford's real delight comes not from the taut asides or the music hall burlesque of the overbearing matron, but from the same reckless, relentless desire to throw off self-control which he attributes to his main characters. Their laughter often merges into a scream as they respond, like passengers on a roller-coaster, to the thrill of release in competition with the horror of vertigo. Perhaps all situational humor, if interpreted broadly enough, possesses some of the same tension, but what distinguishes Vathek from most English novels is the literal, even physical, way in which it is presented. The most characteristic — almost the only — action of the narrative is that of going over the edge of a precipice. The last scene in the subterranean kingdom has often been called an anomaly in this novel; yet it is only the last and most detailed in a series of similar descents. The main difference is that Vathek, who had previously caused others to go, finally makes the journey himself.

5

The first and most telling of the episodes in which the abandonment of self-restraint concludes literally at the edge of an abyss occurs early in the narrative. Having become irritated by the insolence of the Indian Giaour, who has released him from his mysterious thirst, Vathek begins kicking the stranger down his palace steps. Quickly followed by the members of his court, the Caliph continues as if invigorated by a new sport: "The stranger afforded them no small entertainment; for being both short and plump, he collected himself into a ball and rolled round on all sides at the blows of his assailants." But what had begun as a release of anger and was continued as an amusement becomes a frantic obsession which draws in every beholder. The "fatal ball" is kicked up and down the whole of Samarah by a stumbling and screaming crowd led by their frantic Caliph. Ultimately, it is pursued onto an open plain where it bounds into a deep chasm where Vathek and his people might have followed it "had not an invisible agency" stopped them:

They all gazed at each other with an air of astonishment; and notwithstanding that the loss of veils and turbans, together with torn habits, and dust blended with sweat, presented a most laughable spectacle, yet there was not one smile to be seen. On the contrary, all with looks of confusion and sadness returned in silence to Samarah . . . without ever reflecting that they had been impelled by an invisible power into the extravagance for which they reproached themselves.

Bizarre and strangely prolonged, the whole episode might have been conceived by Céline. Originally presented as more than human, the

Giaour suddenly takes on the inanimate rigidity of something less than human. At first, he seems to have been transformed into an "object" of fun. But the newly created thing, the man-like ball, is pursued with such compulsive energy that the transformation ceases to be a momentary alteration and therefore ceases to be a joke and threatens to become a permanent paralysis. The power of Vathek's unconstrained passion has succeeded in obliterating the free will of his subjects as well as the human traits of the Giaour. When that energy itself is spent or when it no longer has an object on which to feed, there is nothing to do but wait until the next opportunity arises. Vathek's people may return home reproaching themselves for their extravagance, but the Caliph remains at the edge of the chasm hoping the Giaour will emerge with new secrets and new challenges.

Beckford's comment at the end of the episode is both curious and suggestive:

It is but just that men, who so often arrogate to their own merit the good of which they are but instruments, should also attribute to themselves absurdities which they could not prevent.

Though passed off in a casual way, it is a statement of a random determinism. In a world where behavior is beyond the power of the individual to regulate, moral judgments become irrelevant. Though he speaks of the "good" in this passage, Beckford avoids mention of evil and substitutes "extravagance" and "absurdity." In the realm of Beckford's imagination, there are only two kinds of people: those who reproach themselves and place artificial restraints on their behavior and those who give in without regret to the desire of the moment. At bottom, both kinds are driven by the same irrational and impersonal force and both are headed, by different routes and at different speeds, for the same abyss.

The second episode in which victims are forced over the edge of the abyss once again turns on the unleashing of Vathek's passion and his lust for power. Told by the Giaour that he will be given the secret directions to the Kingdom of Eblis only after appeasing the Giaour's thirst for the blood of fifty children, Vathek calls for a festival of games on the plain near the great chasm. At the end of an archery contest,

he calls forth each handsome boy individually to present him with some
part of his own rich dress:

All extolled the liberality of a prince who would thus strip himself for the
amusement of his subjects and the encouragement of the rising generation.
The Caliph in the meanwhile undressed himself by degrees, and, raising
his arm as high as he was able, made each of the prizes glitter in the air;
but, whilst he delivered it, with one hand, to the child, who sprung forward
to receive it, he with the other pushed the poor innocent into the gulf.

Whereas the first episode had been a wild chase, involving at first a
kind of boisterous humor, this is a seduction observed by the narrator
with cynical irony. Yet the basic pattern is the same: Vathek turns
creatures into objects of amusement and ultimately engulfs them. That
his aim is achieved by means of deception rather than by direct and
open pursuit has significance primarily because it demonstrates a refined variation of the means by which appetite can be gratified.

In some ways, Vathek, in this scene, is Beckford's model artist. The
only way in which we can misunderstand the irony with which he
describes Vathek's enchanting "dexterity" is to believe, with the innocents, that it is all for the sake of the audience or the art rather than
for the amusement of the artist himself. It is more than a coincidence
that the one episode in which Vathek gains his point by means of art
rather than by force is also the one with the most prominent homo-
sexual overtones. Art, for Beckford, is a form of exhibitionism in which
performer and audience are aspects of the same self and in which re-
generative union is impossible. Art is a temporary diversion out of
which nothing new can be created. However elaborate and energetic
his exertion, the artist-spectator is left after each episode with an unchanged self, his hunger unsatisfied and yet his desire to satisfy it his
prime reason for continuing to endure life at all.

This episode also provides a clue which helps us understand Beckford's use of other literature. There is the element of parody, of ridicule,
already mentioned, but there is little consistency to it. No particular
convention is singled out for special criticism, nor is the aim the exposure of a particular folly or falsehood. All artifice is a "come-on,"
attractive and pleasurable in itself, but leading nowhere. Fragments of
oriental legend and Biblical parable, of Dante and Marlowe, are like
the gorgeous bits of Vathek's clothing. They do not lead to the exposure

of an old lie or, by implication, to the discovery of a new truth. Like all the highways and byways of Beckford's world, they lead to the abyss. What may sometimes appear to be a frivolous criticism of art is in fact the ultimate criticism of life and the ultimate self-revelation.

The last episode before the final descent into the Kingdom of Eblis, which involves an obsessive release of energy followed by a fall, is perhaps the most frivolous and prodigal of all. The chief eunuch of Vathek's harem is tricked by the playful Nouronihar into sitting on a sofa, really an enormous swing, which she and the other concubines begin to push "with unmerciful jerks" until it is swept "through the whole compass of a very lofty dome," taking "from the poor victim all power of respiration." The louder the eunuch's cries and the more grotesque and "eminently disgusting" his appearance, the more the women laugh and the harder they push. As in the football episode, the sport works up to a frenzied pitch and then suddenly comes to a halt with the victim's collapse. The swing breaks, and the eunuch falls into a pool where he is left to spend the night, "a deplorable animal . . . overwhelmed with darkness."

The joke, like everything else about the book, including its composition, is an act of high-spirited wantonness. The harem girls fondle the beautiful boy Gulchenroz and tease the ugly eunuch, but the important point is that they amuse themselves either way. The beautiful and the bestial are equally good material for toys. Vathek, too, though he varies his tactics accordingly, pursues the ugly Giaour and seduces the handsome innocents with the same vehemence. The young Beckford had vowed to overcome the world with the power of his imagination, with his waking dreams; Vathek tries to overcome it with his appetite. Despite conventional distinctions between good and evil, happiness and misery, beauty and ugliness, the voracious protagonist claims the capacity to transform anything to his own delight.

The closer Vathek gets to the subterranean Kingdom of Eblis, the less he distinguishes one pleasure from another. He does not become worse morally; since he has committed a variety of crimes from the beginning, that is hardly possible. He moves from Samarah and the five palaces of pleasure — a state of excess, artificially organized — toward a condition of complete sensual as well as moral chaos. In the kingdom of the Emir Fakreddin, where he encounters the conventionally beautiful Nouronihar, he is also surrounded and apparently amused by "the blind, the purblind, smarts without noses, damsels without ears . . . a superb corps of cripples," and "others in abundance with hump-backs, wenny necks, and even horns of exquisite polish."

If there is any progress in the narrative of the Caliph Vathek, it is from relatively conventional debauchery to a horrifying sadism, a total anarchy of the senses which stems from an inability to channel conflicting instincts toward a particular region or object. One of the traditions of Western literature is that the collapse of a rational and moral hierarchy of values is accompanied by a collapse of the aesthetic and the sensuous hierarchy. But Vathek does not present a coherent relationship between sensuous and rational values in the first place. If anything, it begins with the assumption that there is no correlation. Nothing is forbidden to Vathek because there is no agent in heaven or in the mind of man which has the power to forbid. He is not therefore a Faustus, but a child's fantasy Everyman who fills the whole world with amusing toys and good things to eat. If he himself is eventually consumed by his own voracity, if he finally descends into the gulf where he has thrown so many others, that is not necessarily a sign of punishment and certainly not of divine judgment, but a statement of how, for everyone, sooner or later, the world ends.

Immediately before his descent into the subterranean kingdom, Vathek is given two opportunities to repent and turn back. The first occasion presents itself in the form of a group of ancient holy men who beg the Caliph to pray with them and visit their city. In gratitude for their concern, Vathek has them tied backwards on their donkeys and then contends with Nouronihar to see "who should most enjoy such a degrading sight. They burst out in peals of laughter to see the old men and their asses fall into the stream. The leg of one was fractured, the shoulder of another dislocated, the teeth of a third dashed out, and the rest suffered still worse." Beckford's irony, not very effective at best, has no power whatsoever to justify this gratuitous bit of sadism. This is not moral satire, but psychic exhibitionism which Beckford seemed no more able to repress than Vathek could his urge to travel. But by this point in the narrative, moral and rational justifications have long since become irrelevant.

The second supposedly moral impediment to Vathek's final plunge is treated with sophistry rather than with sadistic humor. A good genie dressed as a shepherd plays beautiful melodies on his flute and stops Vathek's entourage with a Christian sermon on hope and grace. And, for the last time, Beckford pulls a retort out of his Faustian bag and puts it into Vathek's mouth: "If what I have done be so criminal as thou pretendest, there remains not for me a moment of grace." But these words, uttered by Vathek at this moment, convey neither parodic humor nor pathos. Beckford has succeeded in creating a world in which terms like "grace" have no meaning. Vathek has not newly fallen into debauchery nor is he about to enter a hell which is distinct from the rest of the universe because within its boundaries there is no hope. Samarah is as hopeless a region as the subterranean kingdom, and Vathek's behavior has been from the beginning that of a cynic. He acts from moment to moment, grasping the pleasure at hand, unable to envision the future while gratifying himself in the present. Even his trip to Eblis is a series of sensual digressions, and the only honest thing he says to the good genie is that "it matters not where it may end." That statement is implied in Vathek's actions from the start; it is not a new revelation about his character nor evidence of a moral change.

6

Where, then, *does* such a journey and such a narrative end? The conclusion of *Vathek* has always been considered the most moving and perhaps the best part of the novel, but there has been little critical agreement about its relationship to the episodes which have preceded it. Is the subterranean kingdom one more cynical parody, this time of Dante's *Inferno*, or is it a genuine statement of the suffering and remorse caused by a life of sensual excess? The Caliph and Nouronihar enter the lofty and ornate halls of the underworld where they meet the wise Soliman who lies in anguish repenting his excessive "love of women" and unrestrained "curiosity." They also meet Eblis himself who is not a ferocious demon but "a young man, whose noble and regular features seemed to have been tarnished by malignant vapours . . . in [whose] large eyes appeared both pride and despair . . . [and

61

whose] flowing hair retained some resemblance to that of an angel of light." But their most compelling vision is of a "vast multitude" which they themselves must eventually join,

> incessantly passing, who severally kept their right hands on their hearts, without once regarding anything around them; they had all the livid paleness of death . . . Some stalked slowly on, absorbed in profound reverie; some shrieking with agony, ran furiously like tigers wounded with poisoned arrows; whilst others, grinding their teeth in rage, foamed along more frantic than the wildest maniac. They all avoided each other; and though surrounded by a multitude that no one could number, each wandered at random unheedful of the rest, as if alone on a desert where no foot had trodden.

This is neither parody nor irrelevant moralizing, but a consistent extension of the narrative to its only possible conclusion. Beckford's hell is a state of imaginative and physical exhaustion, where there is nothing new — neither innocence nor brutality — on which to gorge mind and body. In Eblis, Beckford not only paints another portrait of himself but by doing so, confronts Vathek with an image from which he can learn nothing new. In the persons of Soliman and Eblis, and finally in that of Vathek, victims and victimizers become one. Hell is a hall of mirrors with no power to instruct, surprise, or gratify. As the entire narrative has been conducted on the level of the imagination and the flesh rather than on that of reason and the soul, the suffering of the multitude moving in constant agony must also be understood in physical and imaginative terms rather than in metaphysical and rational ones. The hell of the voluptuary is impotence and that of the dreamer is a failure of imagination. The victims in Beckford's hell are not, in any conventional sense, the damned, but the worn out, the used up, for whom the pleasures which made life worth living are nothing more than a memory burning in the heart.

This inferno is not reserved only for criminals. Nouronihar, though not a model of virtue, has not committed any of the atrocities of which Vathek and Carathis are guilty, yet she suffers the same fate. The one character of whose "salvation" Beckford reminds us at the end is the epicene Gulchenrouz who "passed whole ages in undisturbed tranquility, and in the pure happiness of childhood." The only way to escape the punishment, it would seem, is not to grow up at all; but even that, as

Beckford foresaw, demanded a struggle between the imagination and circumstances which the imagination must inevitably lose.

From the beginning of his career as a writer, Beckford saw the pursuit of beauty as inevitably leading the pursuer to the brink of self-destruction. The mountain-climber in *The Vision* finds the plants more fragrant and charming as his own position among them becomes more and more precarious:

Take your eyes off this beautiful spot and let them range along a frightful perspective of steeps, of crags, of impending mountains just admitting the moonlight to shew my path and discover the flowers. But I must own I could not enjoy this delicious vegetation untainted by disagreeable sensations, the ridge was so narrow, that the least false step might have precipitated me to destruction, the very herbs and flowers I trod on, tho' all fair, might give away and put a period to my worldly existence.[24]

As always, the wandering protagonist calls attention to himself. But also, as always, there is an honesty in the self-scrutiny which penetrates even the most fantastic dream:

Behold then in my countenance a strange mixture of pleasure and pain; haste, mark on your tablets that uncertain character.[25]

This passage, like *Vathek*, is a reflection of the artist's sensitivity to the mutability of nature, often most cruelly felt at moments of extreme pleasure. In Beckford's case, the "uncertainty" about pleasure proceeds in part from an ambivalence about his sexuality. But what is more to the point is his uncertainty about his powers as an artist to subdue the earth with his mind. To despair of external reality and turn inward is one thing, but then to despair of the mind must become nearly unbearable. Yet this seems to have been the course of Beckford's artistic life and one which he himself foresaw with extraordinary lucidity in the fantastic adventures of the Caliph Vathek. It is not a legend of allegorical guilt, but the dream of an unrepentant voluptuary coolly conscious that neither the flesh nor the imagination can be, for him, the source of what Blake called "Eternal Existence." Beckford was the prototype of the romantic egotist, without faith in the self he so loved. Swinburne wrote of him:

WILLIAM BECKFORD

I have always pictured Beckford as a most unhappy man, more deeply consumed by malaise, ennui and melancholy than ever his admirer Byron was . . . To be a millionaire and to want to be a poet and only to be half a one! . . . Almost to succeed in finding the path to artistic creation, and then to fall back on one's riches! All of this must make the life of the poet *manqué* something much more gloomy than the Hall of Eblis.[26]

Beckford prefigured how, for some artists, the long romantic dream would end a century later. It is not surprising that Swinburne understood him so well.

III

THE MYSTERIES OF UDOLPHO

Ann Radcliffe
1794

Although the popularity of *The Castle of Otranto* was widespread, Walpole's immediate imitators were few and tended, like Clara Reeve and Charlotte Smith, to show more timidity than their master without displaying a superior literary skill. Not until the last decade of the century did the Gothic novel reach its true depths, and presiding over its subterranean regions was the curiously benign figure whom De Quincey called "the enchantress of that generation," Ann Radcliffe. Despite legends that she was arrested in Paris as a spy, died a raving maniac in a lunatic asylum, and went about haunting her imitators, Mrs. Radcliffe appears to have lived an unexceptional life.

Neither the originator of the Gothic novel nor its most daring advocate, she nevertheless produced works which have come to be counted, with Walpole's novel, among the ancestors of English romantic fiction. Her gently euphemistic prose, her fainting heroines, and explainable ghosts were reproduced by other writers so quickly and on such a large scale that they were clichés before they had time to become conventions. Not only the plots but the titles of her books were borrowed and used with slight variations. *The Bloody Monk of Udolpho* was one among many chapbooks which required no advertisement beyond the obvious one contained on its cover. Some writers thought it would enhance their status to claim Mrs. Radcliffe as an intermediary source of their "ancient" narratives. Hence, there was published in Paris in 1816

L'Hérmite de la tombe mystérieuse; ou, Le Fantome du vieux château, anécdote extraite des annales du treizième siècle, par Mme. Anne Radcliffe. Along with the compliment of imitation, there was the criticism of parody, like Mrs. Patrick's *More Ghosts!* and Maria Edgeworth's *Angelina.*[1]

Imitated, plagiarized, widely read, occasionally ridiculed in their own time, today Mrs. Radcliffe's works are more often classified as "typically Gothic" than studied with an attempt to understand what it is they are and what precisely they typify. Virginia Woolf put the case fairly when she said that *"The Mysteries of Udolpho* have been so much laughed at as the type of Gothic absurdity that it is difficult to come at the book with a fresh eye. We come, expecting to ridicule. Then, when we find beauty, as we do, we go to the other extreme and rhapsodize. But the beauty and absurdity of romance are both present and the book is a good test of the Romantic attitude, since Mrs. Radcliffe pushes the liberties of romance to the extreme." [2]

Like *The Castle of Otranto, The Mysteries of Udolpho* (1794) is set in the past, 1584, and in Catholic Europe, France and Italy; the plot is involved, events are extraordinary and often violent; the cast of characters includes sensitive gentry, talkative servants, and a band of swarthy outlaws; Shakespeare and Milton are frequently invoked, quoted, and paraphrased, along with William Collins and Mrs. Radcliffe's favorite nature poet, James Thomson; and the central image and most commanding physical presence in the novel is a Gothic castle.

Taken against her will to a retreat in the Apennines, the heroine, Emily St. Aubert, first sees the Castle of Udolpho at sunset:

As she gazed, the light died away on its walls, leaving a melancholy purple tint, which spread deeper and deeper as the thin vapour crept up the mountain, while the battlements above were still tipped with splendour. From those, too, the rays soon faded, and the whole edifice was invested with the solemn duskiness of evening. Silent, lonely, and sublime, it seemed to stand the sovereign of the scene, and to frown defiance on all who dared to invade its solitary reign . . . Emily's heart sank, and she seemed as if she was going into her prison.[3]

Although the architecture of the castle is described in considerable detail, one is more aware of it as a random assemblage of ramparts, arches, towers, galleries, and corridors than as an aesthetically unified whole.

But what distinguishes Mrs. Radcliffe's castle (and therefore her book) from Walpole's is not merely the quantity of information, but the kind of information and the manner in which it is presented. The Castle of Udolpho, unlike the Castle of Otranto, is placed in a natural setting and seen primarily through the eyes of a single major character. Ann Radcliffe takes that middle realm of nightmare presented in such hermetic confusion by Walpole and tries to place it in relation to an objective reality and an individual point of view. The fading light of the sun and the fears of Emily St. Aubert give a shape to Udolpho which has little to do with architecture.

Critics have often pointed out that in the writings of Mrs. Radcliffe nature is a stationary backdrop before which pass sentimental heroines of the sort which can be found in a large number of earlier eighteenth-century novels. To some degree this is true. When introducing a place where a major character lives or even stops for a few hours, Mrs. Radcliffe is likely to present a guide-book description. The views, usually encompassing enormous distances, are presented with the distinctness of telescopic vision on an extraordinarily clear day. (Mrs. Radcliffe is said always to have traveled with a "long distance glass.")[4] Presumably, nature is dependable, logical, and it rewards investigation. In order to understand abrupt natural changes or seemingly mysterious phenomena, it is simply necessary to study, to learn from experience, to move in closer and examine in minute detail, as St. Aubert does by collecting various species of plants. In the fiction of Mrs. Radcliffe one is either very close to or very far away from nature; one either "botanizes" like St. Aubert, gaining practical wisdom, or one muses from afar, like his daughter, discovering images of order and harmony everywhere. Emily St. Aubert loves to contemplate mountains, but Mrs. Radcliffe rarely fails, especially in the early chapters of her book, to place "gloomy pine" and "tremendous precipices" in perfect balance with "soft green pastures" and "simple cottages." "On the whole," the author wrote in her travel journal, "I prefer rich beauty to wild beauty."[5] Human beings may become wild, confused, and unbalanced, but nature, if seen from the proper perspective, does not.

In the first chapters of the novel there is a great deal of attention paid to the peaceful landscape of Gascony where Emily St. Aubert lives quietly with her parents. The country, we are told, gives comfort, consolation, and wisdom, while the city fatigues and corrupts. When Mme. St. Aubert dies, Emily takes her father on a journey to Languedoc in order to calm his disturbed spirits, and crossing a part of the Pyrenees, they meet the heroic Valancourt who serves as a moral travel guide for part of the trip. Stopping their carriage every few miles to admire a new vista, Valancourt gives speeches which explicate nature's lessons and reveal his essential goodness of character:

"These scenes . . . soften the heart like the notes of sweet music, and inspire that delicious melancholy which no person, who had felt it once, would resign for the gayest pleasures. They waken our best and purest feeling; disposing us to benevolence, pity, and friendship."

Like much nature poetry of the late eighteenth century, these lines are close to Wordsworth in idea, if not in feeling and expression. Valancourt's view of nature, like that of Emily, is usually from a distant prospect which permits him to harmonize all he sees into moral generalizations. That Mrs. Radcliffe never saw the Pyrenees, nor, for that matter, any part of France or Italy, hardly surprises us since particular impressions are nearly always subordinated to universal philosophical and ethical considerations. Despite the painstaking descriptions, she seems, in the main, to be adhering to a neoclassical tradition rather than introducing new ideals into fiction. But to stop here is to fail the novel by treating its descriptive parts as isolated romantic poems manqué rather than placing them in the context of the whole narrative. For, if Mrs. Radcliffe shows obvious neoclassical influence in subordinating concrete particulars to moral generalizations, she reveals an equally strong inclination in the major section of the novel to subordinate everything — natural vistas, moral lessons, and even art itself — to an individual state of mind.

2

Despite the conventional speeches about the grandeur of nature and its power to convey the presence of what Mrs. Radcliffe calls the "Deity," there are as the narrative progresses a gradually increasing number of instances which reveal the relative impotence of nature beside the projections of the human imagination. The countenance of nature may be improved or worsened by one's state of mind, but landscape itself, though pleasant to a mind in repose, has almost no power to change the temper of a mind already filled with its own sorrows or joys. Valancourt himself admits in a mood of expansive generosity that "every object around him appeared more interesting or beautiful than before." But the gayest vineyards and richest plains of Languedoc cannot cheer the aged and brooding St. Aubert: "As his languid eyes moved over the scene, he considered that they would soon, perhaps, be closed forever on this world." After her father's death, Emily St. Aubert remains for a while on the picturesque Mediterranean coast, "but her thoughts were now occupied by one sad idea; and the features of nature were to her colorless and without form." Orphaned and separated from Valancourt, Emily becomes melancholy and apprehensive. She continues to travel, under the supposed protection of her aunt, through parts of France and Italy which are alternately pleasant and desolate. But only dark forests and lonely ruins match her frame of mind and therefore come alive for her, whereas "her senses were dead to the beautiful country through which she travelled."

Many critics, including Coleridge, have praised Mrs. Radcliffe for her "elegant description and picturesque scenery" [6] while expressing reservations about the stiff conventionality of her characters' sentiments. It is often true that their emotional responses seem automatic and the generalized diction familiar, but there is a note evident in Mrs. Radcliffe's travel journals, as well as in her fiction, of a sadness which is not merely fashionable. Especially after the death of her parents, her thoughts return again and again to death and *intrude upon* rather than derive superficially from scenes of natural beauty. A sunset viewed during a trip to Seaford, rather than inspiring admiration or serenity, creates anxiety in her and prompts a nervously hopeful prayer that "the Creator of that glorious sun, which never fails in its course, will not neglect us . . . nor suffer us to perish." [7] In certain moods, Mrs. Radcliffe is sharply conscious that the more beautiful a scene is, the more melancholy it is to think, as Virginia Woolf observes in *Between the Acts*, that it will continue to be there after the viewer is gone; or, what is perhaps worse, to recognize, as Coleridge does in "Dejection," that one is in the presence of beauty and yet can feel nothing.

It is inaccurate to describe Mrs. Radcliffe's characters, especially her heroines, as passive creatures who merely react emotionally to their immediate environment. On the contrary, there are many environments, meticulously described by the author, to which they cannot react at all, and others, of a more obscure sort, to which they seem constantly to overreact. Mrs. Radcliffe detains Emily St. Aubert in Venice and provides a luxurious and fanciful picture of the place which became part of Byron's boyhood image of that "fairy city of the heart" and prompted him to recall in *Childe Harold* that "Otway, Radcliffe, Schiller, Shakespeare's art, / Had stamped her image in me." But Emily is not a Byronic heroine and she remains unmoved by the splendors of Venice.

While all is relatively calm in her life and her mind, Emily can derive moral edification and a mild *frisson* from a contemplation of the sublime juxtaposed with the beautiful. On the descent from the Pyrenees with Valancourt and her father, she savors a landscape of pastures and vineyards which "with the surrounding Alps, did indeed present a perfect picture of the lovely and the sublime — of "beauty sleeping in the lap of horror." The real nightmare for Emily — the Radcliffean personification of "beauty" — is not that she will wake up and behold a beast, but that she will wake up to a chaotic landscape where the boundaries have become blurred, where the sublime and the beautiful have fused and the integrity of her own role cast into doubt.

Soon after leaving Venice, Emily is imprisoned in Udolpho Castle by the wicked Montoni. The few natural images which attend her during her imprisonment are nearly all of flux and confusion. The wind that roars through the castle's corridors is not only powerful enough to agitate tapestries and slam doors, but to move furniture, including the heavy chair which Emily has braced against her door. And during an interval of "savage discord" among Montoni's men, Emily's mind is thrown into a turmoil not metaphorically different from the one being physically enacted by her captors: "The contending elements seemed to have retired from their natural spheres, and to have collected themselves into the minds of men, for there alone the tempest now reigned."

Mrs. Radcliffe's heroines are not always the simpering puppets which critical tradition has held them to be. They can, at times, be obsessive, implacable, and morbidly excitable women whose moods often make difficult situations worse. One might argue that the ease with which they become frightened is merely a sign of their general silliness and ignorance of the world, or that they are excitable because they have a special faculty for sensing danger, an intuitive ability to pierce through surface reality. Their sensibility may, as Northrop Frye says, "put them closer to superior forms of consciousness and perception, which are reflected in their fragile and exquisite appearance and their affinity with trance and tears." [8] Mrs. Radcliffe does not call Emily silly or clairvoyant, but the properties of her novel — including the labyrinthine Udolpho and its relatively conventional band of outlaws — derive what interest they have from the shadow cast on them by the heroine's prolonged state of panic. She may preach prudence, moderation, and universal harmony, but the potential fertility of that irrational state remains the most original and convincing aspect of Mrs. Radcliffe's art.

In the early chapters of the novel, the human mind, like the natural landscape, is presented as being composed of contrasting, even opposing, parts. Ostensibly, the moral lesson which justifies the telling of Emily St. Aubert's adventures is that of balance: reason against passion, sense against sensibility. "All excess is vicious," says St. Aubert early in Chapter II, and this, in different words, is about all he has to say, though the length at which he expounds upon this simple philosophy casts some doubt on his ability to practice what he preaches. In fact, the incongruity between human behavior and moral principles which increases as the book progresses is strangely prefigured in Emily's philosophical father. After the death of his wife, he warns Emily against an overindulgence in mourning and then is discovered weeping bitterly in his chamber. He recommends nature as the great consoler, but finds himself less and less moved by Gascony and the new countryside through which he travels. He counsels against impetuous reactions, but mistakes Valancourt for a bandit and shoots him in the arm before giving him the opportunity to identify himself. In Fielding or Sterne, such contradictions would have obvious satiric overtones, but there is no irony in the manner in which St. Aubert is presented, and comedy is, of course, restricted to the servants. St. Aubert's deviations from his own rules only show, as he himself points out, the constant need for self-control even on the part of the wisest and most disciplined of persons. He may seem to us a nervous and morbid old man, but that is only because we do not at first share Mrs. Radcliffe's assumptions about the emotional excesses or utter barrenness of feeling which he could give into if he let himself.

71

The path which Mrs. Radcliffe's virtuous characters must try to keep winds literally between the madhouse and the graveyard — that is, between chaotic emotional release and an inhuman absence of feeling. Unguarded passion leads to insanity and, as a consequence, to irrational and vicious acts, but apathy, as St. Aubert tells his daughter from his death bed, "is a vice more hateful than all the errors of sensibility . . . because it leads to positive evil." Sister Agnes, the mad nun, raving, weeping, plagued by nightmares and visions, "a dreadful victim of unresisted passion," personifies the consequence of undisciplined sensibility. "It was the first misfortune of her life, and that which led to all her succeeding misery, that the friends who ought to have restrained her strong passions, and mildly instructed her in the art of governing them, nurtured them by early indulgence." Having been swept by her passions from luxury to adultery and finally to murder, her soul may or may not be salvageable — Mrs. Radcliffe does not seriously concern herself with that — but her reason is permanently lost.

The other extreme is embodied in Montoni, the ruthless Italian who marries Emily's aunt and keeps his wife and her niece prisoners in his castle in an effort to get one and then the other to sign over their property to him. He is repeatedly described as committing acts of cruelty without displaying pity or, for that matter, much feeling of any kind. "Without some object of strong interest, life was to him little more than a sleep." Mrs. Radcliffe remains consistent in treating Montoni's character, and adds to the humiliation of her suffering heroine by allowing her to be a minor victim of a villain preoccupied with more important matters. Much to the irritation of both ladies, Montoni finds neither aunt nor niece an "object" of exceptionally strong interest.

3

Emily St. Aubert, the virtuous and sensitive heroine held prisoner by a relentless male, has often been called a Clarissa in Gothic setting. The parallel is striking in a general way, but the differences in detail are more than a matter of sensational effect. In the first place, though various of Montoni's cohorts have amorous designs on Emily and though she is regularly menaced by abduction or rape, Montoni himself appears even less interested in her as a mistress than as a murder victim. If anything, Montoni serves as a restraint on the passions of his associates.

He agrees to keep Emily secure and in relative comfort so long as she promises not to be a nuisance to him, and twice he saves her from abduction by dissident members of his own band. Thus, imprisoned in a castle full of assassins, rapists, and thieves, the provocatively beautiful Emily, lodged in a bedroom with a door that cannot be locked from within, is spared a fate worse than death. In fact, the preservation of her chastity is not the central issue of the novel simply because the reader is never for a moment allowed to believe that Emily could be raped.

Sexual possession is hardly more of a moral problem in *The Mysteries of Udolpho* than it is in *Moll Flanders*. Both heroines are, in a sense, unravishable. Indeed, if Emily is Clarissa Harlowe's sentimental sister, she is also Moll Flanders' indestructible cousin. Mrs. Radcliffe often calls our attention to the practical means by which Emily gets through each day despite her excited emotional state. On the superficial narrative level, the mystery of *The Mysteries of Udolpho* is not whether Emily will or will not be raped, murdered, or morally destroyed, but whether she will manage to extricate herself from uncomfortable situations of an increasingly bizarre and complicated nature. What we wonder about is not her virginity but her ingenuity under stress. There is undeniable gratification in knowing how she finds her way around the darkest recesses of the castle in the middle of the night; how she heats up her damp room, barricades the unlockable door, gains the sympathy of the servants, eavesdrops on secret conversations, and dines on figs and wine after having gone hungry during two days of slaughter among Montoni's men.

But though she has traits of both the practical and sentimental eighteenth-century heroine, Emily St. Aubert differs from them in one important way: both the moral and material aspects of her ordeal are subordinated to the struggle which takes place within her mind. Neither Montoni and his surrogates who threaten her virtue nor the "world" and its possessions have as much substance to her or to the reader as her own fears. Montoni differs from Lovelace because Emily hardly exists for him but also because he exists only in a distant and dreamlike way for her. Barricaded in her chamber with her books, drawing instruments, and lute, sending servants on errands, venturing into the corridors at night to catch glimpses of horrible sights and snatches of mysterious conversation, Emily half-creates her own Udolpho. Every strange footstep and shrouded figure is imagined as a two-headed creature — one of Montoni's men coming to harm her or Valancourt coming to save her — which awakens such contradictory emotions as to unsettle her mind for days. As in the case of the moaning heard outside her window, attempts at logical explanation are fruitless until Mrs. Radcliffe is ready to provide them: "Inquiry only perplexed her. Who, or what it could be that haunted this lonely hour . . . she had no means of ascertaining; and imagination again assumed her empire." Having little knowledge of or control over what is happening in the castle, Emily is left to compose her unquiet mind and aroused feelings. This at least is what she tries to do as the dutiful daughter of her late father. But St. Aubert's philosophy of "self-command" proves even more difficult for the daughter to follow than it had been for the parent. He had "instructed her to resist first impressions, and to acquire that steady dignity of mind that can alone counterbalance the passions, and bear us, as far as is compatible with our nature, above the reach of circumstances." Such a philosophy assumes a clear understanding of what the circumstances are in order that they may be transcended. To St. Aubert the necessary counterbalance to a hasty and therefore unjust reaction is a lucid perception of things as they are. Thus, he views one untrustworthy character as having "neither humanity to feel nor discernment to perceive," whereas he insists that despite an impetuous nature, Valancourt's "perceptions were clear and his feelings just."

But, as the first view of Udolpho Castle in the fading twilight suggests, clear perception is precisely what Emily is deprived of in her imprisonment. Once inside the castle, things become even darker: "She entered an extensive Gothic hall, obscured by the gloom of evening, which a light glimmering at a distance through a long perspective of arches only rendered more striking." Both literally and metaphorically, Emily is unable to see exactly where she is or what is going on around her. Friendly servants are mistaken for villainous captors because all are "figures seen at a distance imperfectly through the dusk." During the long period of her heroine's confinement in Udolpho, Mrs. Radcliffe's imprecise prose becomes increasingly less specific and denotative. Everything seen through Emily's eyes is envisioned through a dim blur; walls are "massy," ceilings "lofty," faces "menacing," and the corners of rooms invariably "remote." One recalls Maria Edgeworth's remark on being introduced into an unusually large and dark hotel room in Bruges: "I am sure Mrs. Radcliffe might have kept her heroine wandering about this room for six good pages." [9] Emily herself may wander, but most other inhabitants of the castle "flit," "glide," or "float" from one "chamber" to another; doors are rarely opened but often "unclosed"; staircases are "ascended" and "descended." Montoni does not curse in any common or specific way; he utters "inhuman expressions." Curiously enough, these euphemistic fragments serve as accurate indications of the state of Emily's mind as well as of the limitations of her descriptive powers.

Though she gradually pieces together small bits of information, Emily is for a long time as ignorant of the intentions and motives of Montoni as she is of the ground plan of the castle. "Oh, could I know . . . what passes in that mind; could I know the thoughts that are known there, I should no longer be condemned to this torturing suspense." Unlike the landscapes through which she passed with Valancourt and her father, where sublime mountains and beautiful valleys were juxtaposed but distinguishable, the character of Montoni and some of his associates is disturbingly mixed and murky to Emily. The little she does see both repels and attracts her: she is suspended between contradictory emotions in a mental state which makes rational perception, already impeded by circumstance, almost impossible. "We feel," as Woolf says, "the force which the Romantic acquires by obliterating facts. With the sinking of the lights, the solidity of the foreground disappears, other shapes become apparent and other senses aroused." [10]

4

The ghosts and horrors of Emily's imprisonment in the male world of Udolpho, however "logically" explained by Mrs. Radcliffe at the end, are the projections of hysteria. Emily wants and does not want to know exactly what is going on in the castle; she wants and does not want Montoni to take more notice of her; and she wants and does not want one of his swarthy surrogates to come in the night and possess her. Mrs. Radcliffe justifies Emily's continuously putting herself in harm's way by defining the "faint degree of terror" she feels as one which "occupies and expands the mind, and elevates it to high expectation, is purely sublime, and leads us, by a kind of fascination, to seek even the object from which we appear to shrink." Not only does Emily tend to open unlocked doors and follow mysterious passageways, but she repeatedly reminds Montoni of her presence by sending her servant with messages to him, visiting him herself, and, on one occasion, throwing her arms around his knees to implore mercy.

Mrs. Radcliffe tells us more than once that Emily found Montoni and one or two of his friends "uncommonly handsome" despite their dark complexions and cruel expressions. One day, watching from a window, Emily observes a party of Montoni's men assembling in the courtyard.

As they mounted their horses, Emily was struck with the exulting joy expressed on the visage of Verezzi, while Cavigni was gay, yet with a shade of thought in his countenance; and as he managed his horse with dexterity, his graceful and commanding figure, which exhibited the majesty of a hero, had never appeared to more advantage. Emily, as she observed him, thought he somewhat resembled Valancourt in the spirit and dignity of his person . . . As she was hoping, she scarcely knew why, that Montoni would accompany the party, he appeared at the hall door.

There is no need to press the point further, although Mrs. Radcliffe does so for several hundred pages. Nothing drastic happens to Emily, either physically or morally. She does not die a martyr's death nor become the whore of outlaws. Imprisoned midway between the two extremes, she suffers the fate of the prototypical romantic character: deprived of a cathartic experience, incapable of tragedy, she is periodically immobilized by the imperatives of an imagination which transforms the limitations of present reality into a limitless future. As Coleridge remarked in an early review of the novel, "Curiosity is raised oftener than it is gratified; or rather, it is raised so high that no adequate gratification can be given it." [11]

Emily's constant quests and narrow escapes seem merely outlandish unless we judge the narrative not in an historical but in a psychological context in which everything is possible and nothing is achieved. As Mrs. Radcliffe points out several times, Emily's life in the castle "appeared like the dream of a distempered imagination." As long as the dream persists, everything must remain possible, that is, without fulfillment —

and the heroine's pursuers must be frozen in permanent chase. Though the minds which produced them differed vastly, Emily St. Aubert and the "still unravished bride" of Keats's Grecian urn have one thing in common: both are heroines to whom something is forever about to happen.

Even Emily's occasional periods of activity do not dispel the general atmosphere of hysterical paralysis. True, in her moments of self-composure, the Moll Flanders in her emerges, and she goes cannily about the business of self-preservation; but for every such hour there are days of weeping, fainting, and incapacity to act, and there are nights of sleeplessness and visions of ghostly presences. The hysterical heroine was not an invention of Ann Radcliffe's, nor does hysterical behavior have a particular importance for Romanticism except insofar as it exemplifies the power of the mind over external reality. The achievement of *The Mysteries of Udolpho* is not, then, the mere introduction of Gothic effects into an otherwise conventional sentimental narrative, but the projection of a nonrational mentality into a total environment.

One by one, Emily St. Aubert loses those anchors to objective reality which her father recommends as the only steadying influences on a highly "susceptible" mind. Like all romantic heroes and heroines, she is gradually separated from the world and imprisoned within her own consciousness. First her parents die; then she is taken from France and her beloved Valancourt by her aunt; then to an Apennine castle where her aunt dies. Bereft of relatives and friends, she turns for consolation to nature:

She rose and, to relieve her mind from the busy ideas that tormented it, compelled herself to notice external objects. From her casement she looked out upon the wild grandeur of the scene, closed nearly on all sides by Alpine steeps.

But though the view refreshes Emily at first, it is, after all, circumscribed by the window of her room. The interior darkness and spaciousness of the castle cause the landscape outside to shrink and fade. Emily never gives up her ideal love of nature, but as an effective influence in her life, as a counterbalance to self-absorption, it nearly ceases to exist during her confinement in Udolpho. Yet Emily's resources are not totally exhausted. Without human or natural support, she turns to music and literature for consolation and order, but even art eventually fails her:

> She endeavoured to withdraw her thoughts from the anxiety that prayed upon them, but they refused control; she could neither read nor draw, and the tones of her lute were so utterly discordant with the present state of her feelings, that she could not endure them for a moment.

Emily, then, has almost nothing and no one to lean on, except one or two faithful servants. She is a romantic heroine largely by default. Having removed the rationalistic and objective supports so carefully enumerated in the early chapters of the novel, Mrs. Radcliffe leaves her heroine to the devices of her own mind which, admittedly, turns out to be a fairly dark and empty place, save for the presence of a few lascivious-looking but impotent spectres. There is nothing salutary, creative, or formative about Emily's interior experience. She does not emerge from her captivity in Udolpho with a fuller comprehension of the complexities of human nature or sympathy for its weaknesses: she is willing to dismiss Valancourt from her life at the first hint that he had gambled and caroused during his stay in Paris and, in fact, becomes so hysterical at the thought, that the poor fellow can never attempt to explain himself without causing her to become faint. Her idea of nature does not change either: she does not find a deeper rapport or a greater incongruity between herself and her natural surroundings, but resumes in the last pages of the book her never-ending walks in search of melancholy vistas and moral edification.

5

It must be understood that for the Radcliffean heroine, the romantic experience is not a desired initiation into a new reality but a temporary deprivation. She is not pictured beholding herself and the world with a new and powerful vision, but as one blindfolded and sent into momentary panic. The phantoms conjured up out of the darkness may be more or less entertaining, but when the blindfold is removed, there is the same orderly universe, bright and clear as it had been before — mountains distinct from valleys, virtue undaunted by vice. Mrs. Radcliffe's explicit moral, despite her penchant for romantic atmosphere, is antiromantic. What her heroines must do during their ordeals is not simply preserve their lives and their virginity — that they would do so is taken so much for granted it is hardly at issue — but they must "hold fast" in every way, keep every old idea and emotion intact, prohibit the darkness from informing their view of the day. All the weeping and fainting and fantasying, then, are supposedly the signs of an endurance test which proves that a well-instructed young lady can sacrifice her nerves without losing her principles.

Although Jane Austen was not in the least convinced by such reasoning, Sir Walter Scott and others thought this an excellent moral justification for the exaggerations of romantic fiction. Even some modern critics excuse Mrs. Radcliffe her Gothic "intrusions" because of the serious moral intention of her work. One cannot, of course, deny Mrs. Radcliffe her moral intentions, but it would be as difficult to claim for her a major role in the literature of prudential prose as to argue that her influence on Lewis, DeQuincey, Maturin, and scores of other romantic writers was primarily of a didactic nature.

If Mrs. Radcliffe taught anything to later writers, it was that a region other than that presupposed by rationality and a middle-class moral code might be accessible to novelists without their having to resort to the irrelevancies of courtly romance. Today her ruined abbeys and menacing foreigners may seem nearly as absurd as the artifices of seventeenth-century romance, but in their own time they were exaggerations of a relatively new kind for the novel and, even more important, they were placed in juxtaposition to subject matter and character types which could be found in the realistic fiction of the day. In an introductory commentary to the 1826 edition of *Gaston De Blondeville*, T. N. Talfourd notes the success with which she interweaves "the miraculous with the probable," infuses "the wondrous in the credible," and imparts "human interest to the progress of romantic fiction." He reflects a common, if not universal, contemporary judgment when he concludes that Mrs. Radcliffe "occupied that middle region between the mighty dreams of the heroic ages and the realities of our own." [12]

Like Walpole, Mrs. Radcliffe meant to combine the excitement of earlier narrative and dramatic literature with the authenticity of the realistic novel. Oddly enough, the excessive conscientiousness with which she constructs the reasonable world outside Udolpho serves to weaken one's confidence in the reliability of that world. The more elaborately "logical" her explanations of mysterious apparitions, the more we find ourselves becoming skeptical, not so much of the ghosts as of the explanations. She has shown all too well that there are crucial moments when neither reason nor faith in cosmic order is the central factor in the experience of an individual.

In *The Mysteries of Udolpho* she dismantles her heroine's rationally ordered universe with breathtaking thoroughness. The stability of human relationships is challenged; the harmonizing power of nature is challenged; the efficacy of art is challenged; and, most significant of all, the clarity of routine sensory perception is challenged. Despite other doubts, the reader is perfectly willing to believe that Emily St. Aubert is bereft and frantic. To the degree that Mrs. Radcliffe convinces us of that and constructs a physical setting which corresponds to an aroused emotional state, she has succeeded in doing something new for the novel.

The ghostly sounds and, even more, the elaborate explanations which set everything right at the end may not in themselves be wholly convincing. But then the preliminaries of total irrational disruption have been so vigorously begun that one can hardly expect things to be creditably reconstructed at once. The more profound and creative works of romantic fiction were to come later, but Mrs. Radcliffe had done more for the form than Gothic needlework. In her dark forests, ruined convents, and haunted castles, she had prepared whole regions bereft of reasonable certainties — "silent, lonely, and sublime" — where later heroes and heroines, more complex than Emily St. Aubert, would encounter shadows more interesting and consequential than those cast by the ambiguous Montoni.

IV

CALEB WILLIAMS

William Godwin

1794

The greatest fault of Godwin's philosophy, according to Hazlitt, was "too much ambition." "He raised the standard of morality above the reach of humanity, and by directing virtue to the most airy and romantic heights, made her path dangerous, solitary, and impracticable." [1] One is tempted to add that the greatest fault in Godwin's fiction is his philosophy, and that what Hazlitt found above the reach of humanity was not capable of producing believable fictitious characters or situations. But to leap to such a conclusion is really no better than to assume that Ann Radcliffe would have been a greater novelist if only she could have resisted Gothic machinery. Like all artists, Radcliffe and Godwin required some organizing factor, some pattern through which their creative energy could be ordered. That each chose constructs which are cumbersome, eccentric, and often at odds with what to a modern reader seem the best elements in their fiction can hardly be denied. But it should also be remembered that in both cases the "machinery," far from being an idle choice, represented a deliberate departure from a literary norm, and answered a need peculiarly deep in each author.

Walpole and Beckford were antiquarians and collectors whose fiction repeatedly bears witness to their interest in useless old things. Godwin was best known in his own lifetime for his preoccupation with ideas. His acknowledged ambition as a novelist was to write fiction which would be both romantic and philosophical. Depending on their prejudices, readers have tended to choose one side of Godwin to defend. They have either preferred the radical idealist (and shrugged off the fiction as imperfect popularizations of his thought) or they have admired the innovative psychological novelist (and dismissed the philosophy as eccentric abstractions).

Godwin himself is partly to blame for this factionalism. In the preface to *Caleb Williams* which was originally suppressed for being politically inflammatory, he does indeed sound like an apologist for whom the novel is merely a convenient means by which to instruct a large audience:

> It was proposed in the following work, to comprehend, as far as the progressive nature of a single story would allow, a general review of the modes of domestic and unrecorded despotism, by which man becomes the destroyer of man. If the author shall have taught a valuable lesson . . . he will have reason to congratulate himself upon the vehicle he has chosen.[2]

Yet fiction was more than a "vehicle" to Godwin. The art of narrative had had an intrinsic appeal to him long before he established his reputation as a philosopher. Among his earliest works are two intellectually slight but fanciful and technically elaborate narratives. *Italian Letters or The History of the Count de St. Julian* (1783) is permeated by Rousseauian sentiment and the narrative devices of Richardson and Walpole. *Imogen: A Pastoral Romance* (1784) is a utopian story, yet Godwin's preface calls attention to it as a work of peculiar literary ingenuity rather than as a philosophical treatise. Pretending it is a translation from the Old Welsh, he takes advantage of and half-parodies the Ossianic poet and, at the same time, points out the parallels between his work and *Comus*.[3]

From his earliest years as a writer, Godwin was fascinated by the techniques and imaginative claims of nonrealistic narrative. Despite his reformist tendencies, however, he was a man rooted in the eighteenth century, and he saw the reasoning intellect and the imagination as two distinct faculties. What is rarely acknowledged is the energy and the persistence with which he tried in his own life and writing to bring the two together.

The opening sentence of his historical novel *St. Leon* (1799) is characteristic: "There is nothing that human imagination can figure brilliant and enviable, that human genius and skill do not aspire to realize." [4] Such an all-encompassing statement would seem to be a perfect target for Austenian irony, yet the chapter — in fact, the entire book — is conspicuously lacking in comic detachment. The statement may be taken as pure Godwin. Unfortunately, the formality of phrasing in this and similar pronouncements has led readers to assume that Godwin's ideas on the conjunction of imagination and rational "genius" are perfunctory and not really central to his intellectual growth. And yet it was the habit of most of his mature life to examine his theories — however extreme his early formulations of them were — in the light of felt experience. In a moving tribute to Mary Wollstonecraft at the end of *Memoirs of the Author of a Vindication of the Rights of Woman*, he praises her, above all, as an intellectual companion who continually provided "spontaneity," "taste," "sensibility," and "intuition" to his own mind, which he regarded as too skeptical and systematic.[5]

The point is that Godwin's writings, especially his philosophical and fictional work taken together, reflect what Camus calls, in speaking of his own philosophical fiction, an "intellectual drama." Godwin could praise Rousseau and Burke, he could advise an American student to read both Bacon and Burton,[6] he could write a romance of the sixteenth century filled with "incredible situations," [7] and, six years later, produce a novel whose merit depends on "the reality it gives to the scenes it portrays." [8]

When Godwin modified a previously held position, as he did his early stand against marriage, he was criticized for being contradictory or hypocritical. When he maintained a position despite social and political pressure, as he did his approval of the republican aims of the French Revolution, he was called a crank and a fanatic. His courageous and very romantic mistake was to insist on playing out his personal "intellectual drama" in public. And since his taste in drama and rhetoric tended toward the heroic, even his admissions of self-doubt have a regal resonance. "One of the leading passions of my mind has been an anxious desire not to be deceived," he wrote in 1798. "Endless disquisition however is not always the parent of certainty." [9]

The balance and generality of such sentences — even when the subject is anxiety and uncertainty — seem to chase the ghosts away. Godwin had to keep reminding those of his contemporaries who took his treatise on political justice as a statement of dogma that the full title of the work was *An Enquiry concerning Political Justice, and its influence on General Virtue and Happiness*. He meant it to be only an "enquiry." And as *Caleb Williams* and much of the later philosophical writing demonstrate, Godwin's mind spawned nonpolitical ghosts as quickly as it did political hypotheses. He was well able to anticipate objections to his arguments; what he was unable to foresee was the virulence with which his character would be attacked once the French Revolution had ceased to be a rallying point for English liberals. By the turn of the century, when France posed more and more of a threat to England, Godwin was attacked as a traitor and *Political Justice* denounced as an incitement to civil disorder, the tenets of which were "accompanied with a long and portentous train of evils." [10]

In 1801, Godwin spoke out in self-defense:

I wrote my *Enquiry concerning Political Justice* in the innocence of my heart. I sought no overt effects; I abhorred all tumult; I entered my protest against revolutions. Every impartial person who knows me, or has attentively considered my writings, will acknowledge that it is the fault of my character, rather to be too skeptical, than to incline too much to play the dogmatist. I was by no means assured of the truth of my own system. [11]

The argument is that of a speculative intellectual, not that of a doctrinal apologist or political activist.

2

An Enquiry concerning Political Justice was published in 1793, a year before *Caleb Williams*, and it is upon this work, more than his fiction, that Godwin's reputation was chiefly established. "No work in our time gave such a blow to the philosophical mind of the country," wrote Hazlitt. "Tom Paine was considered for the time as Tom Fool to him; Paley an old woman; Edmund Burke a flashy sophist." [12] Today, *Political Justice* seems a curious document, a peculiar combination of political theory, moral philosophy, practical psychology, and pure fantasy, but in its time it exerted considerable influence on liberal and radical thinkers. Herbert Read was only slightly exaggerating when he said that "no philosophy was ever so completely taken over and transmuted into the finer grain of poetry than Godwin's by Shelley." [13] The idea of Coleridge and Southey to found a "pantisocracy" in

America was largely inspired by Godwinian ideals. According to Hazlitt, even Wordsworth advised a young student to "throw aside [his] books of chemistry and read Godwin on necessity." [14] It is hardly surprising that poets, more readily than lawmakers, were attracted to Godwinian theory, for his was a dream — not really a plan — of a world of Houyhnhnms, where law and government would be unnecessary. [15]

Man, according to Godwin, is a perfectible being whose reason is his greatest strength but whose moral character is largely the result of accumulated associations. Since government, in all its principles and minutest ramifications, has a greater effect on human perception than do other external stimuli, it follows that man's imperfect state is largely the fault of government and that he can develop rationally only when released from the artificial constraints of laws and contracts. Man should not think of himself as having "rights" within the framework of a legalistic government, but rather as having moral "duties" — dictated by his own reason — to perform whatever acts would benefit society and to refrain from whatever would injure it.

Government, it should be pointed out, did not mean to Godwin only the direction of the state, but the ordering of all human affairs by means of contractual power. No man could benefit from placing himself at the disposal of another and no man had the "right" to act as owner or protector of another. Thus, all ideas of property which assigned to anyone more than he needed for self-sustenance were unnecessary and unjust. Public education fostered uniformity of mind and impeded the intellectual growth of each according to his own gifts and inclinations. And marriage was a contract, like any other, which "binds man to insincerity" because it is based on the false assumption that "the inclinations and wishes of two human beings should coincide through any long period of time." [16]

Sincerity was one of Godwin's key words and one of the great goals of his ideal society. All forms of convention, tradition, or custom, whether legally defined or not, hindered man from expressing his true self. And as Godwin's image of that self was so exalted, it seemed certain that once the bonds were loosed, reason and virtue could not help but prevail. In fact, so great was Godwin's confidence in man that, though a radical, he was opposed to violent revolution simply because he assumed it to be unnecessary. The promulgation of the word, by virtue of the very clarity and truth of the message, would, he predicted, convert even the rich and the wicked.

Godwin was aware that there were large numbers of people "whom books of philosophy and science are never likely to reach." For these he tried to combine his theories with exciting fictitious episodes and, more specifically, in the case of *Caleb Williams*, to demonstrate the need for reform by showing how bad things had become. The subtitle, *Things As They Are*, gives notice that the novel will be no utopian romance, but an exposé of contemporary reality — that is, of the pervasive influence of despotism in "every rank of society." *Caleb Williams* was intended to show, in fictional terms, a world which made the reforms proposed in *Political Justice* necessary and, by implication, a world in which they are possible.

On the surface of it, Godwin's plot would seem to suit his purpose. Two landowners of entirely different temperaments and education reveal through their behavior how power and wealth can corrupt human nature regardless of apparent differences in individual makeup. Ferdinando Falkland is the perfectly cultivated and cosmopolitan gentleman, educated in Italy, devoted to literature and the fine arts, graceful and courteous in manner, moderate in all things but his devotion to the honor of his good name. His just and generous nature are in sharp contrast to that of his neighbor Barnabas Tyrrel, equally rich and well-born, but coarse, arrogant, and overbearing, a muscular brute whose education was left to the gamekeeper and stablemaster. Fiercely jealous of Falkland's popularity in the community — and especially with his own niece — Tyrrel hounds the girl to her death. He insults Falkland publicly and is shortly after found murdered in the street. Though Falkland is suspected at first, the blame is finally placed on a tenant farmer and his son, whom Tyrrel had also persecuted. The two are hanged, and Falkland retires to his estate a subdued and changed man.

Enter Caleb Williams, the personification of Godwin's ideal of human nature in its full potential — young, unspoiled, limber of mind and body, unpossessed of property or wealth in any form. He combines the innocence of Joseph Andrews with the ingenuity of Robinson Crusoe. As Falkland's new secretary, he is ready to be formed by his learned master, but finds him strange and reticent in his retirement. Ultimately, Williams discovers that Falkland was Tyrrel's murderer, begs to be released from service, escapes, is captured and imprisoned, escapes again, and is pursued throughout the kingdom by Falkland's agents. Falsely accused of robbery and disloyalty, Williams decides after ten years of suffering to proclaim his master's secret before a judge and, thereby to release himself from further persecution. When, at the hearing, he sees Falkland a physically broken and ruined man, he praises his virtues as a gentleman and begs his forgiveness for having exposed his crime. The skeletal Falkland throws himself into the arms of the still sturdy Williams, begs *his* forgiveness, and dies three days later.[17]

Obviously, many of Godwin's criticisms of society are implicit in this narrative. None of the characters, including Tyrrel, is depicted as inherently bad, but rather they have been corrupted by the power which has been given them over other men. For Godwin, the moral struggle takes place between unregulated passion and reason. Each character has a "ruling passion" which circumstances — pervaded by what Godwin calls the "spirit of government" — allow him to indulge. The primary source of Falkland's unreasonable behavior is his obsessive pride in maintaining the honor of his name at any cost. Tyrrel's passion is an insane jealousy, especially directed at anyone who could engage his niece's affection more than he himself did. Even good Caleb is overcome from time to time by an irrational urge, an intense curiosity which leads him to spy on his master and to uncover the secret which leads to all his later misery. But phrases like "ruling passion" and "spirit of government" do not really convey the effect of Godwin's narrative. Once he begins to apply his mind to specific cases, the old-fashioned abstractions give way to perceptions of human nature which have little to do with political systems or dreams of utopian republics.

3

Though there are episodes of political and economic oppression, brief accounts of mistreated tenant farmers and unjustly sentenced prisoners, the novel's two major cases of oppression are curiously independent of the general rule they are apparently meant to exemplify. True enough, Tyrrel's persecution of his niece and Falkland's persecution of Caleb are reinforced by the political system which grants wealth and power to such men, but the true motive for the persecution, indeed its very nature, seems beyond the power of system to cause or rectify. The deeper God-

WILLIAM GODWIN

win probes into the subject of human possessiveness and oppression, the more personal, irrational, and complicated the problem becomes.

At first, Tyrrel's harshness toward his orphaned niece, Emily, seems a typical instance of family authoritarianism accentuated by the girl's total material dependence on her uncle. But as Tyrrel's jealousy of Falkland grows into an insane obsession, his treatment of Emily takes on the character of a cruel fantasy. Everything becomes distorted, oddly simplified, including Godwin's language, which is usually elaborately formal. Believing Emily to be under some "fatal enchantment" wrought by the artful and sophisticated Falkland, Tyrrel assumes that she holds him, "the rude and genuine offspring of nature, in mortal antipathy." Thus, he chooses as her punishment a "boorish and uncouth" farmer, Grimes, "the diametrical reverse of Mr. Falkland," whom he insists that she marry. It is not difficult to see that this "half-civilized animal," whose "features were coarse" and complexion "scarcely human," is a crude replica of Tyrrel himself, a rough surrogate who will carry out his master's unacknowledged desire to possess his niece sexually, as he already possesses her legally, and thereby make her unattainable to Falkland. Godwin refers to Grimes as Tyrrel's "instrument," his "engine" (two common eighteenth-century epithets for penis) and explains carefully that though "nearness of kindred and Emily's want of personal beauty prevented him from ever looking on her with the eyes of desire . . . habit had rendered her in a manner necessary to him."

With the inevitability and simple logic of a fairy tale, the story of Emily's oppression proceeds. Her conversations with Tyrrel are those of a disobedient princess and a wrathful king. When she refuses to marry Grimes and compares him to a "rough water-dog" taking up residence on a silk pillow in her dressing room, Tyrrel denounces her as a "whore," "a common trull" who would "rot upon a dunghill" if he did not save her from "destruction." He even speaks with a furious honesty in justifying his wish to marry Emily to Grimes:

"I am not your enemy . . . but if I were . . . I could not be a worse torment to you than you are to me. Are not you continually singing the praises of Falkland? Are not you in love with Falkland? That man is a legion of devils to me! I might as well have been a beggar! I might as well have been a dwarf or a monster!"

88

And so he becomes what he "might as well have been." He prompts Grimes to take Emily into the forest and rape her. But when he fails and she escapes, Tyrrel drives her to debtor's prison where she dies feverishly dreaming of Grimes and her uncle, their hands dripping with blood, and Falkland, a pale victim "deformed with wounds," beyond the reach of her love or help.

Tyrrel has brought his nightmarish fantasies of himself as a monster and his niece "rotting on a dunghill" into reality. He has made the dream true. And it is, of course, Godwin's point that Tyrrel's social and financial ascendancy gave him the power to do so. Yet the narrative raises questions which Godwin's philosophy does not fully answer. Though it may be true that Tyrrel's social position gave him the means to pursue his frantic design, it is by no means clear that his mixed feelings about his niece are the result of "governmental" influence on his character. We are given no reason to believe that possessive, jealous, and destructive "love" would flourish less easily in a republic than in a monarchy. Except for his method of persecuting her once she has escaped from Grimes, Tyrrel's relationship with his niece has few political overtones and, in fact, is so riddled with ambiguity that corrective social measures, however radical, appear more limited and clearcut than the problem.

By reducing the narrative to its emotional and melodramatic essentials, Godwin recreates the atmosphere of dream as well as the style of the fairy tale. External considerations of every sort fade beside the intensely imagined and narrow world of private event. The "landscape" of Godwin's novel — natural, political, sociological — is never fully sketched in, and at crucial moments vanishes altogether. The questions that remain are not strictly political or sociological because they are not posed in terms of groups or institutions. They are questions about individuals. Where, in a particular human relationship, does possessiveness begin and end? Who is really the possessor and who the possessed? Perhaps in all the obvious ways, Emily is "owned" and controlled by her uncle, but Tyrrel speaks an important truth when he says to her, "I could not be a worse torment to you than you are to me." Though not deliberately or consciously, Emily nevertheless exerts such a powerful emotional hold on Tyrrel that her admiration for Falkland does indeed become for him an insupportable torture. Tyrrel is a possessive tyrant, but he is just as surely a man possessed. Godwin goes beyond his own doctrine and shows human nature in precisely that subtly shifting light which makes all abstract theories so difficult to apply to specific cases.

4

The history of Caleb's persecution by Falkland goes even further than that of Emily and Tyrrel in defining the nature of human relationships and of individual identity in terms which either undermine those of *Political Justice* or make them seem irrelevant. Reason, sincerity, optimism, and the independence of the individual are the bywords of Godwin's philosophy, but passion, ambiguity, pessimism, and the dependence of human beings on one another are the realities which emerge from the adventures of Caleb Williams. To be sure, the subtitle of the novel is *Things As They Are*, but Godwin presents those "things" — insofar as they pertain to the mentalities of his characters — with such penetration that it is difficult to find in them the seeds of hopeful change.

Caleb's curiosity, though it leads him to a love of learning, is more like a physical hunger than a quality of rational intellect. When he begins to suspect Falkland of murder and decides to spy on him in an effort to learn his secret, Caleb feels a "strange sort of pleasure in it." His master's stern insistence upon privacy increases Caleb's sense of danger, but it also gives him "a kind of tingling sensation, not altogether unallied to enjoyment." The further Caleb penetrates into his master's private life, the less rational and more physical his pleasure becomes. Upon discovering a particularly incriminating piece of evidence, Caleb rushes into the garden and experiences a climax of a curiously sensual sort:

I felt as if my animal system had undergone a total revolution. My blood boiled within me. I was conscious to a kind of rapture for which I could not account. I was solemn, yet full of rapid emotion, burning with indignation and energy. In the very tempest and hurricane of the emotions, I seemed to enjoy the most soul-ravishing calm . . . I was never so perfectly alive as at that moment.

Caleb continues his search in a state which he himself refers to as an "infatuation," a temporary "insanity," a "passing alienation of mind." Unreason may not continually operate upon human behavior, but in this novel, when it does, it bursts forth with irresistible power. And though it may only govern the act of a moment — like Falkland's murder of Tyrrel or Caleb's invasion of Falkland's privacy — it has the capacity to change the course of a whole life.

But if reason is shown by Godwin to be fragile in a crisis, sincerity suffers an even worse fate — it appears as an ideal incapable of realization under any circumstances. Caleb is introduced as a frank and open youth, but from the beginning his attitude toward Falkland is ambivalent and their conversations a network of ambiguity. According to Godwinian doctrine, men should always say exactly what they think to one another. But since Caleb happens to think his master is a murderer, he is faced with an initial difficulty which he tries to overcome by putting his apparent innocence and frankness to work for him. He blurts out, with deliberate ingenuousness, stories of unpunished crimes in order to observe his master's reactions to them. Conscious use of his own apparent naïveté is already an act of insincerity, though Caleb might be justified even in Godwinian terms if his goal were simply to uncover the truth, to break down Falkland's more serious form of insincerity.

But Caleb is honest enough in his confessional narrative to admit that truth was not his only aim, that he took pleasure in the game itself and especially in creating a temporary reversal of roles between master and servant. As in the case of Emily and Tyrrel, Caleb is outwardly under Falkland's control, but psychologically there are moments when he is master and, unlike Emily, he senses and takes advantage of them. But rather than leaving us with this fairly simple view of Caleb as the outwardly innocent, inwardly sadistic servant who enjoys taking advantage of his master during unguarded moments, Godwin creates one more ambiguity. Throughout all of his apparently nasty and devious behavior, Caleb loves and admires Falkland. Among all the other motives for his spying is the genuinely innocent one of wanting to establish intimacy with Falkland, to break through his "distant and solemn" manner, to know what he knows. In this aim, Caleb is perfectly successful; a "magnetical sympathy" is established, master and servant become irrevocably linked in mind and soul.

What Caleb discovers is not simply his master's secret crime — which he has suspected for some time — but the consciousness of guilt. At the very moment when he knows the truth as a certainty from Falkland's own lips, he himself experiences extreme pangs of guilt for having forced his master into confessing it. In a sense, Caleb has achieved exactly what he wanted; he has possessed Falkland's mind and in doing so is forced to share the burden of its knowledge. That there was a kind of innocence at the bottom of Caleb's deliberate prying is suggested by his pathetic wish to cast off that knowledge by quitting his master's service. He longs for his former ignorance and, in begging Falkland for release, he writes him a letter asking: "Why should you subject me to an eternal penance? Why should you consign my youthful hopes to suffering and despair?" The release which Caleb is really asking for — a release from consciousness of guilt — is, of course, beyond Falkland's power to grant. His persecution of Caleb from this point on is merely the literal extension of a psychological event which cannot be undone. Terms like "mastery" and "service" suddenly take on a symbolic connotation much wider than that implied by the societal context. Caleb has succeeded in placing himself psychologically on equal terms with his master and he no longer can claim humble irresponsibility or the servant's right to "quit" service.

When Caleb runs away, Falkland accuses him of "having robbed [him] of a considerable amount," and, although it is literally a lie, symbolically it is perfectly true. Caleb has taken something which he cannot give back and engaged himself in a union which he cannot undo. Throughout the rest of the novel, he is imprisoned, pursued, and hounded because of Falkland, yet Falkland himself recedes into the background and is hardly seen again except at the end. The persecution of one human being by another ceases to be the central concern of the narrative. And the psychological torment of an attempted flight from conscience takes precedence as the real adventure.

Caleb finds himself suddenly alone with his hard-earned knowledge, and it is with his own newly informed, expanded, sorrier self — more than with any external enemy — which he must contend. Upon being thrust into prison because of Falkland's false accusations, Caleb tries to comfort himself by thinking that he and Falkland are opposites, since Falkland appears innocent to the world while he, though legally innocent, languishes in prison as a condemned thief. Caleb's solution is to retreat from the unreal and unjust realm of appearances to that of interior "reality." His description of his adjustment to prison life is a perfect account of psychological withdrawal:

To an ordinary eye I might seem destitute and miserable, but in reality I wanted for nothing. My fare was coarse; but I was in health. My dungeon

92

was noisome; but I felt no inconvenience . . . I had no power of withdrawing my person from a disgustful society . . . but I soon brought to perfection the art of withdrawing my thoughts, and saw and heard the people about me for just as short a time, and as seldom, as I pleased.

Whether thought of as the symptoms of psychological withdrawal or sturdy self-reliance, Caleb's behavior in prison signals the beginning of his shift to a world which is largely subjective. Misunderstood and mistreated by the world, he plunges into his own mind, content for a time to feed on the "stores" of his own knowledge and the contemplation of his innocence. But this "blessed state of innocence and self-approbation" does not last forever. Caleb meets a fellow prisoner who befriends him and believes in his innocence because he too has been unjustly condemned. When this companion dies, Caleb determines to escape back into the world in the hope of finding others like his dead friend who will "do [him] justice and sympathize with [his] calamity."

In the death of Brightwell, whose name suggests the qualities which Caleb lost when he penetrated Falkland's mystery, we have a repetition of the death of Caleb's innocence. His escape from prison, then, represents an attempt to seek a more substantial and durable reaffirmation of his essential goodness than prison or his own psyche can provide. But Caleb's brief experience of innocent friendship proves to be an illusion which he cannot recapture outside of prison. His life as a fugitive is even worse than his life as a convict because the world continually confronts him with images of his own guilt which make him feel more and more isolated from the rest of mankind. Once again Godwin's treatment of the individual psychological problem overshadows the social issues. Technically, Caleb is the victim of an unjust legal system which allows one class to oppress another. But what makes his suffering so moving is that he is the epitome of the misunderstood man forced into leading a dual existence because of the world's inability to see him as he sees himself.

5

Though Godwin may have begun by treating Caleb's misadventures as a case of appearance and reality, he tends, as the novel progresses, to treat it more and more as a split between different kinds of reality, subjective and objective, which can never be reconciled. The unjustly condemned fugitive from society is one of the types of the romantic hero who continually suffers from the disparity between his subjective vision and what the world calls objective truth. As long as society can provide him with no channels through which to express his true nature, he is condemned to live in perennial rebellion against that society — a criminal, a madman, a fugitive — or to try to play one of the available roles, in which case he becomes a hypocrite and a poser. As the novel progresses, society is seen less as a community of men organized in a particular way, and more as any assemblage of men whose collective judgments are inevitably different from and perhaps even opposed to those of the individual.

Caleb cannot find a home for his "true nature" with any group, whatever its composition. After escaping from prison and crossing another bleak, uninhabited terrain, he makes several attempts at re-establishing himself in the world, but each time he is discovered as a fraud pretending to be what he is not. He joins a band of outlaws in the forest, later masquerades as an Irish beggar, a farmer, a Jewish writer, and a hunchbacked watchmaker, but he is always found out — sometimes literally stripped naked of his disguise — and sent running to look for another mask. When he seeks obscurity in a Welsh village, assists the schoolmaster, and becomes more-or-less adopted by a local family, he believes himself finally to have obtained safety in a role relatively congenial to his temperament. But here too he is exposed as an imposter when a handbill is circulated giving "the most wonderful and surprising history and miraculous adventures of Caleb Williams," describing him as one of England's most notorious thieves, jailbreakers, swindlers, and imposters. Though the details are exaggerated, the handbill is at least partly accurate in its picture of Caleb, but since it causes him to lose his position in Wales, he decides, once and for all, to return home and make a formal declaration before a magistrate that Falkland is the confessed murderer of Tyrrel.

Caleb believes that by doing this he will not only clear his own name, but that he will finally be able to reassert his true character without having to assume any more false roles. But when he faces Falkland and finds him a withered and helpless invalid, he can derive no satisfaction from his revenge and, indeed, only suffers from a renewed sense of remorse and self-alienation. Even in this apparent act of justice and plain speaking, he has been unable to be true to the full complexity of his nature. In keeping his master's secret, he offends justice and destroys his own reputation; in choosing to reveal the secret, he breaks his oath, offends loyalty and self-respect. In the ambivalence of his nature, he can find no rest, no morality, no sanity, and finally no identity. Who is Caleb Williams when all the accusations have been withdrawn and all the disguises removed? He answers the question himself in the last paragraph of the narration, "I began these memoirs with the idea of vindicating my character. I have now no character that I wish to vindicate."

Finally released from the grip of his master and therefore relieved of the necessity of further pretense, Caleb Williams loses all distinctness of identity and strength of character. The struggle against a clearly defined antithesis had kept alive in him a firm concept of a "real" self. Once that antithesis is destroyed, this sense of the self dissolves into a nondescript assortment of mixed feelings and contradictory impulses. Caleb released from persecution is much worse off than he was in the darkest cell of the prison. And here, in a book filled with reversals and ambiguity, seems to lie the largest deception of all.

Ironically, Godwin's failure to sustain the theoretical framework of *Political Justice* in *Caleb Williams* is held against him even by critics like Leslie Stephen who think his political philosophy doctrinaire and silly.[18] Could it not be in this case — as is so often true of Lawrence and Yeats — that Godwin's imagination showed itself superior to his power of abstract conceptualization? David McCracken is quite right to argue that there is an important relationship between Godwin the novelist and Godwin the philosopher, and that it is false to say that the one "betrayed or simply ignored" the other.[19] It is the interplay of the two which produced *Caleb Williams,* and the fact that the artist prevails over the philosopher hardly seems a fair basis on which to condemn the novel.

The history of Caleb Williams may be an object lesson in the corrigible faults of government, but it is also something more than that — a tragedy of the incorrigible division in the human mind. When reminded, at one point in the book, of Falkland's "flawless" reputation, Caleb asks, "And can you imagine that the most upright conduct is always superior to the danger of ambiguity?" The question is meant to refer specifically to Falkland's duplicity, but it applies as well to every major character in the novel — to Emily and Caleb as well as to Tyrrel and Falkland. It is an early form of the deeply disturbing dilemma faced by Camus' "judge-penitent" in *The Fall*. Despite the apparent optimism of his philosophy, Godwin's fictionalized view of human nature is deeply pessimistic. He shows passion and reason yoked together in all individuals, creating division in the human personality which makes consistency, integrity, and therefore sincerity, impossible. Guilt, which is the fate of all mature beings, is not necessarily associated with sin as traditionally defined, but with the individual's constant sense of his inability to bring into being what he really is. Since the self is a composition of opposites, every act, every word, every gesture, is in some degree a self-betrayal.

Assuming polarization to be a permanent condition of human nature, Godwin's primary stay against despair became the internal dialogue, the pursuit of truth and of identity through dialectics. The injustice done to him in his own lifetime — and one which has been too often repeated — was to treat a single work, particularly *Political Justice* or *Caleb Williams*, as a final statement. If the one was intended, in part, to explain the other, it was also intended to question, modify, and even challenge it. This seems to have been taken so for granted by the philosophical Godwin that he was first surprised and ultimately stunned to see *Political Justice*, which was written early in his career, taken as an exposition of an absolute and fixed position.

In a passage which Coleridge thought reflected "great honour on Godwin's Head and Heart," [20] Godwin says of *Political Justice* what might be said of his writing generally: "I did not cease to revise, to reconsider, or to enquire." [21] Not all of Godwin's early admirers shared Coleridge's respect for open-mindedness. Many saw the "intellectual drama" as mere vacillation or as the substitution of one rigid position for another. Most simply remembered *Political Justice*, or some particularly exasperating passage from it, and used it as a weapon against Godwin throughout his later life without regard for the changes which occurred in his thinking as he matured.

In 1805, rejected by many of his earliest friends and disciples, Godwin adapted ancient and modern fables for children and published them under a pseudonym. One which has a poignant relevance to his own career as well as to that of Caleb Williams is the story of "The Dying Eagle." Seeing herself wounded by a hunter, the eagle looks down at the arrow which has penetrated her side:

It was the feathery end of the arrow that the eagle looked at, and she saw that it was winged with plumage from one of her own quills, which a few weeks before had dropped from her when she moulted. This is double cruelty! said the eagle: I am killed; and they have furnished themselves from my own person with the means of my destruction.[22]

V

THE MONK

Matthew Gregory Lewis
1796

It was Godwin's fate to have been, if only briefly, at the center of the intellectual life of his time, to have tasted early fame, sudden notoriety, and then long years of relative obscurity. Despite the furor created by the publication of *The Monk* in 1796, Matthew Gregory Lewis was socially and literarily, perhaps even temperamentally, a man of the periphery. One has the impression from his letters that wherever he was and whatever he was doing, he felt an outsider and would have preferred to be somewhere else, doing something different. Though he was relatively "satisfied" with a brief residence in Weimar, he wrote to his mother that he would "not like to be shut up in Germany" for very long.[1] Sent by his father to a post with the British embassy in Holland, he complained that he had "nothing in the world to do," and, in any case, had not "found a single soul whom I ever wish to see again."[2] In Lombardy, he thought of Holland because the two places were comparably ugly and flat; in Florence he thought of London, where, it seemed to him, one could hear better opera. As a member of Parliament, holding the seat vacated by Beckford, he demonstrated little interest in politics. And it was during his ennui-filled diplomatic service at the Hague that he completed *The Monk*.

But Lewis was not an outsider merely because his prosperous and respectable father urged him against his nature to be a man of affairs.

He was not truly at home in literary circles either. He knew Byron and Scott, but though they liked him, both found him eccentric and tedious. "Lewis was a good man, a clever man, but a bore, a damned bore," [3] wrote Byron. And Scott concurred: "Matt, though a clever fellow, was a bore of the first description." [4] Part of the problem seems to have been that when he was with literary acquaintances, Lewis put on aristocratic airs. According to Scott, he "had always ladies and duchesses in his mouth, and was pathetically fond of anyone that had a title." [5] He appears to have been a man so little at ease with himself that he was unable to be at home with anyone else.

In a different era and under somewhat different circumstances, Lewis would almost certainly have found his social and intellectual center in the theater. As it was, he wrote or translated eighteen plays, and exerted, especially through *The Castle Spectre*, a considerable influence on the growing taste for the sensational in English drama. He was fond of rich costumes, spectacular sets and pageantry, and he loved the special effects of the newly installed gaslights at Drury Lane and Covent Garden. But there were obstacles to a full participation in the theatrical life. He bitterly disliked Sheridan; he was repelled by the vulgarity of actors and actresses; and there were moments when, as the son of his father, the whole thing seemed to him a frivolous waste of time.

It has been said that Lewis led the invasion of German romantic drama and fiction into England, but it might be more appropriate to say that he opened the right gate at the right moment and let the invaders through. Superficially he had much in common with Beckford — the unwanted seat in Parliament, the inherited land holdings in Jamaica, the long periods of absence from England. But his relationship to his foreign literary sources was different from Beckford's. However exotic and authentic Beckford's oriental sources may have been, they were made into transparent adornments for a created image of the self. His journals and fiction are early works of romantic autobiography. He was called the Caliph of Fonthill because his enormous wealth, his extravagance, and his sexual notoriety earned him that title almost as much as the authorship of *Vathek* did. When people referred to M. G. Lewis as "Monk" Lewis, however, they usually meant it, as Byron did in *English Bards and Scotch Reviewers*, as a joke:

MATTHEW GREGORY LEWIS

Oh! wonder-working Lewis! Monk, or Bard,
Who fain would make Parnassus a churchyard!
Lo! wreaths of yew, not laurel bind thy brow,
Thy Muse a Sprite, Apollo's sexton thou.

It seemed incongruous to Byron that the talkative and boring little man should have written such a dark, Germanic book.

But if Lewis did not dominate his sources as Beckford did his, there were more than temperamental reasons for it. In the first place Lewis knew German very well — certainly better than Beckford knew Arabic. He did poetic and dramatic adaptations of Schiller, Kotzebue, and Goethe, and even translated parts of *Faust* aloud to Byron. Soon after his arrival in Weimar, he became immersed in German literature. His admission in the preface to *The Monk* that the book is probably filled with unconscious "plagiarisms" is undoubtedly a reflection of the extent to which his mind was occupied, to the point of clutter, with German works.

He was, as Louis Peck has pointed out, a "purveyor of German materials to the English Romantic movement." [6] But in this respect, too, he differs from Beckford, whose orientalism is as idiosyncratic in its historical timing as it is in its literary application. *Vathek* was published too early or too late to be regarded as part of any marked trend toward orientalism in English literature. *The Monk*, on the other hand, was just in time to add great stimulus to a movement which it epitomized but did not initiate. Veit Weber's *Die Teufelbeschwörung*, which Lewis knew in the original, was translated into English by Robert Huish and published in 1795. The following year — the year of *The Monk* — there were five English translations of Bürger's *Lenore*, including one by Scott and one illustrated by Blake. Also in 1796 there appeared two translations of Karl Grosse's *Der Genius*, one of which, *Horrid Mysteries*, is referred to by both Austen and Peacock as part of the popular literary fare of the period.[7]

In addition to particular turns of event and character types, German romantic narrative generally brought more explicit eroticism and violence to the realm of the English Gothic. Lewis liked *The Mysteries of Udolpho* and *Caleb Williams* (although he was sorry that Godwin was "half a Democrate"), but his major work, however tame it may seem in the era of Genet and Burroughs, treated sexual license and brutality

100

in a manner unprecedented in popular English fiction. When Scott said that *The Monk* was a "romance in the German taste." [8] he was not referring merely to its Gothic scenery. Uncontrolled appetite and physical pain and the emotional states which they produce are emphasized and particularized to such a degree in *The Monk* that the reader encounters them, not in permanent suspension as unrealized fantasies, but as nightmares come to life.

2

The effective representation of any human feeling may be partial justification for a work of art, but the meticulous and deliberate dissection of mental torment and physical abuse which forms the substance of the tale of terror raises aesthetic and moral problems of a complicated sort. Toward what end does such literature aim, if not the merely sensational? And in what way is it linked with the major concerns of the romantic aesthetic?

Like most fiction of the period, the novel of terror nearly always made claims, especially on final pages, of high moral intention. Man's inhumanity to man, the dangers of excess, the fate of pride, were all paraded for inspection in the last chapter so that any reader of bad conscience and little discrimination could close the volume content that he had been given a stern lesson. What makes the didactic protestations in *The Monk* ring slightly hollow is the tone rather than the narrative context of the whole book. There is no reason to assume that Lewis set out to write an immoral novel or that his didactic intrusions are mere cynical compromises with public taste. The fact is that his novel does show the dangers of excess and the fate of pride, but the power and originality with which he treats the physical, emotional, and psychological elements of the story tend to obscure the moral assertions even when they do not contradict them. Lewis's vocabulary of violent emotions was part imitation and part artistic creation, but his moral terminology was an inherited rhetoric which lacked the energy of belief or discovery.

The monk Ambrosio is a Faustian protagonist who sells himself to the devil for the sake of temporary pleasure, but there is little space given to rational analysis, theological dispute, or metaphysical speculation. Plot and the conventional implications of chronology and causal relationships are relegated to a position of unobtrusive significance. The author concentrates not on how things come about but on how they look and feel. The main narrative is repeatedly interrupted by the details of a subplot and, at one point, by a long digressive tale. Nevertheless, *The Monk* does have a unique structure which derives from an accumulation of strikingly realized scenes rather than from a logical knitting together of events. More than any fiction which preceded it, the novel of terror is picturesque. It appeals first to the eye and only secondarily to reason and conscience.

Lewis sought to reproduce an intensely private vision of a character in extreme circumstances, an institutional man suddenly at war with every kind of convention. Given the novel's roots in social convention and common speech, it would seem that he was attempting the impossible. (It is no coincidence that, like Walpole and Maturin, he turned from fiction to poetry and drama.)

For most serious romantic writers, the composition of a novel was an endurance test as well as an experiment. Long, loose, and prosaic, the novel obviously did not have the formal restrictions of a sonnet or even of verse drama, but its thematic and stylistic traditions were pedestrian. Seeking out the novel for its apparent capaciousness, Lewis nonetheless found himself struggling against inherited formulas of situation and expression, and using the genre as a medium for debate between strict form and freedom in life as well as in art. The nuns of Wordsworth's sonnet may not fret at their convent's narrow room, but those of Lewis's novel most definitely do.

The limits of the prison and "the weight of too much liberty" are the major themes of *The Monk*. The mood is one of constant and agonizing struggle between two equally undesirable alternatives, both of which seem to tempt and betray the author along with his characters. There are, on one hand, the victims, innocent and noble, whose beauty shines all the brighter for being shut up in a cell, cloaked in a monk's habit or stretched upon the rack. On the other hand, there are the free spirits who have escaped the bonds of convention, but who, in doing so, have escaped distinct identity as well and have disappeared into a timeless, spaceless limbo where all distinctions are prison walls seen from the outside.

The author may identify himself partly with both character types, but the artist in terror novels is most often depicted as the destroyer, the executioner, the gatekeeper, whose victims are confined in the name of order and tradition by the imposition of one will upon another. The artistic process is seen not as an imitation of the divine creation, but as devil's work, taking away life in order to make dumb idols. It confines, restricts, torments into shape, even at moments when that is what is least intended. In a world of subjective extremes, the ultimate in aesthetic license for the individual artist lies in his uninhibited use of other people and things for his own pleasure. Thus understood, the artist's freedom necessitates the subject's constraint. Hence, the convent cell and the torture chamber may be seen not as mere backdrops but as the symbolic conditions of "captured" beauty.

3

It is not surprising that the Marquis de Sade put *The Monk* at the top of his list of favorite contemporary novels.[9] Its brutal episodes seemed to him to reflect the mood of an age of bloodshed and rebellion and to be the only means by which a writer could hope to move readers accustomed to calamity. This new kind of novel was, according to Sade, the result of

those shocks of revolution which were felt by all of Europe. For those who knew the miseries which the wicked could cause men, the ordinary novel became as difficult to write as it was monotonous to read . . . It became necessary to call on hell for help in order to compose works of interest and to find in the realm of monstrosities those things which one knew were currently being unfolded in the history of man in this age of iron.[10]

Sade's argument is an important one, and it should not be shrugged off as the self-justification of an isolated mind. Much of the "madness" of the *roman noir* imitates and caters to the madness of an unstable society. Despite the theatricality and superficial contrivance of a book like *The Monk*, there is a sense in which it may be called realistic. Moreover, Sade's stress on the need to "move" readers is a common romantic preoccupation and one which poses a particular problem for the artist living in a period when human sensibilities are repeatedly overstimulated. Though his purpose was to lament rather than to justify the popularity of the novel of terror, Coleridge reasoned in his review of *The Monk* much as Sade did in *Idée sur les Romans*:

The horrible and the preternatural have usually seized on the popular taste, at the rise and the decline of literature. Most powerful stimulants, they can never be required except by the torpor of an unawakened, or the languor of an exhausted appetite.[11]

In attempting to explain the growing taste for sex and violence in the contemporary theater, twentieth-century critics also have used the theory proposed by Sade. The argument has become familiar: "Because of all the shocks that are being given by the real world these days, there is need for real shock in the theater." [12]

Such statements are not only observations about historical reality but, as Sade makes explicit, about inherited artistic conventions. Many artists, particularly in the last hundred and fifty years, have felt an increasing need for originality and a corresponding difficulty in attaining it. Sade, like Lewis and Beckford and the aging Walpole, thought that he lived in an age when, literarily, "everything seemed to have been done." [13] Many of his own experiments, like those of his English counterparts, appear to be aesthetic as well as moral outrages. And that, in part, is exactly what they were intended to be.

More positively, Sade argued that the subject of fiction should not be social man acting for the benefit and approval of others, but rather the inner man as he truly feels and thinks. Once again, the general point is both familiar and romantic. But it is Sade's peculiar application of the theory rather than the theory itself for which he is remembered.

If Wordsworth's sonnet reveals a romantic spirit accommodating itself to the discipline of external form, Sade's fiction reveals a mind pressing well beyond the usual limits of Romanticism in an effort to accommodate itself to a universe of absolute license. "There is neither God, nor virtue, nor justice in the world; there is nothing good, useful or necessary but our passions," according to Sade. Man therefore should adopt as his rule of conduct "whatever suits his taste without worrying whether it is or is not in keeping with custom." [14] Though Sade insisted that all men are basically cruel, he admitted that nature produces such diversity in human character that it is impossible to establish moral, psychological, or aesthetic norms. For him, the good, the sane, and the beautiful must be defined separately by every man. He looked for no ideal society which would permit the free exercise of individual whim, since he was enough of a realist to recognize that compromise, regulation, and consistency of any sort pose a threat to the total liberty of the self. As Maurice Nadeau has pointed out, Sade's conception of freedom "obliges the individual to be in a perpetual state of insurrection; no society, real or utopian, could accommodate it." [15]

Among the victims of the *roman noir* were the sentimental heroine, the noble hero, the respectable parent, the devout cleric, and, in fact, nearly all ideal character types associated with the structured society of prerevolutionary eighteenth century. Sade's motives were hardly democratic, yet he did literally and symbolically strip his characters of the roles to which society had assigned them in order that they could see themselves and be seen as they "really" were. We need not accept his vision of reality to see how deeply he had thrust a wedge between the external social criteria of characterization and the representation of a strange, private, and, in some respects, genuine self. It is through the interplay between these two aspects of the self — public and private — that the best romantic novelists were able to fashion remarkable psychological portraits even out of the crude materials of melodrama.

In his characterization of the monk Ambrosio, Lewis goes well beyond the simplistic psychology of Sade in exploring the dual nature of man. Despite his theoretical allowance for great diversity in human nature, Sade's fiction is populated by characters whose "true" selves are invariably the clear reverse of what they seem to be in public. Thus, the chaste virgin is a whore at heart, the pious hermit a debaucher, the brave soldier a coward, the kindly matron a murderess, and so on through an almost infinite monotony of predictable opposites. Lewis begins his novel in much the same vein, showing a contrast between appearance and reality with an ease which even he must laugh at. For the first hundred pages, the novel wavers between melodrama and burlesque; and when the pious young monk Rosario throws himself before Ambrosio, confessing, "Father, I am a woman," burlesque seems to have gained the day. Lewis is too taken by the absurdity of the situation to insist upon reaching for a tragic note. After Rosario/Matilda, threatening to stab herself, exposes the "dazzling whiteness" of her bosom, the grave superior muses, "I have never seen her face; yet certainly that face must be lovely, and her person beautiful, to judge by her — by what I have seen." [16]

If *The Monk* had continued in this vein it would have been a psychologically slight and ultimately silly book. But even from the beginning, in the midst of the formulaic contrasts and "shocking" reversals, there are signs that the familiar Gothic devices are being manipulated by an artist who never fully trusts the "unconventional" conventions which he has adopted. The dagger against the bared breast cannot be taken seriously because the author himself sees it as a bit of theatrics, even as, later on, the rape in the charnel house, though externally more detailed and grotesque, seems a stage pantomime in comparison to the successfully realized horror of the rape of Clarissa. Unlike Sade, Lewis recognized the frustration of meeting one cliché with another opposite one. To substitute a knife for a fan, a lie for a promise, a murder for a marriage, can become, despite its initial shock value, another routine, another formula, another language without sufficient range to suggest the complexity of life.

4

Lewis's "adjustment" to the Gothic mode is altogether different from Wordsworth's avowed acceptance of the sonnet as a consoling discipline. Lewis, in fact, appears to have adopted a literary form not altogether worthy of his imagination. *The Monk* derives much of its interest from the curious division between a narrative voice which seems wittier, subtler, and more human than the narrative framework to which it has committed itself. One often has the feeling in reading *The Monk* that it is about to become a much funnier or sadder book than it is. A new Rabelais or Marlowe seems always about to be revealed, but then the stock devices — the Gothic properties and the melodramatic reversals — intrude and bring us back to a world of artifice and infuriating limitation. Of particular importance is the fact that Lewis, as revealed in his tendency to burlesque or treat with perfunctory interest certain episodes in the narrative, felt this disparity himself.

In 1801 he admitted in a postscript to *Adelmorn* that he might better have spent his early career "reading sense than in writing nonsense." [17] And though Scott and others praised the poetry which appeared in *The Monk*, Lewis parodied his own ballad of "Alonzo and Imogine" in the fourth and fifth editions of the novel. Yet the fact remains that, despite misgivings, Lewis returned again and again to devices which he knew to be cheaply theatrical. If *The Monk* is a morbid and disturbing book, it is also one which seems to flaunt its own artificiality. Byron said that it was composed of the "philtered ideas of a jaded voluptuary." [18] And Trollope complained that everything in it was "pretended, made up, and cold." [19]

Neither of these opinions would have been news to Lewis. For him, the artist, no less than the priest or the member of Parliament, was a role player who affected a costume, a voice, even a kind of behavior, which could never fully represent the changeable and complex being of the total man. Unlike Sade, he does not try to show human character stripped down to its supposed animal essence because, for him, to play the brute was still to act out only a part of the self. The proper metaphor for personality was not, therefore, one of depth, but of surfaces. The closest the artist or any man could come to a realization of his "whole" self was to take into account the variety of roles he could imagine himself playing.

In the context of Freudian psychology, this sounds naïve and superficial. But then, despite patterns which correspond to Freudian theory, *The Monk* is not interesting primarily as a precursor of early twentieth-century psychology. It is not sufficiently optimistic, mechanistic, or deep. Too many modern critics have tried to rescue it from the rubbish heap by claiming profundity for it, but this is doing no favor to Lewis, who knew rubbish when he saw it. No one could have been more conscious than he of the trivial and charade-like quality of his art, and few, except in our own post-Freudian age, could have better understood the appeal of such obvious imposture. Genet's prison fantasies in *Our Lady of the Flowers* are repeated imaginary escapes from one self, the convict, into a multitude of selves masquerading as virgins, whores, princes, and vagabonds.

Our Lady, in his pale-blue faille dress, edged with white Valenciennes lace, was more than himself. He was himself and his complement. I'm mad about fancy dress. The imaginary lovers of my prison nights are sometimes a prince . . . and sometimes a hoodlum to whom I lend royal robes . . . I love imposture." [20]

It is out of a similar sense of life as confinement without release except through the imagination that Lewis might also have said that he loved imposture. If he cannot really change anything, man can at least impose his mind temporarily on the intractable stuff around him. One reason that such impositions are so tawdry is that they are, by definition, admissions of failure — either of the earth's failure to provide coherent form or the artist's failure to find it. *The Monk* is not an early account of an identity crisis, but an exploration of imposture and the chaos which it so imperfectly conceals.

Ambrosio is not simply the holy man who eventually yields to temptation; he is the hero too large for any of the roles which society or nature provides for him. Until the age of thirty, given to study, prayer, and the mortification of the flesh, he is a model priest at the expense of the passionate side of his nature. But when he finally succumbs to the charms of Matilda, the young monk who is not a monk, he is not released into a state of full self-realization, but only harnessed by a different and even more limiting role. Lewis's concern was not with the psychological damage caused by a conventual life — hardly a problem in the England of 1796 — but with the dilemma of an ego unwilling to accept a life of moderation and unable to find fulfillment in extremes. Ambrosio's tragedy is not so much that he "falls" from a state of pious chastity into an obsessive lust, but that, in either case, he is forced to be something less than his true self. Neither sexual abandon nor ascetic mortification answers the real longings of Ambrosio's heart. Both force him into a kind of servitude, both close out other areas of experience, both turn into mechanical rituals, and both are finally false and temporary diversions from the infinite possibility which he seeks.

Like the artist superior to his art, Ambrosio is the priest superior to his religion and the male superior to his gender. His ego is a vast universe of which society and nature can give only imperfect representations. That the scenes of sexual possession in *The Monk* are as elaborately and artificially staged as the liturgical ceremonies is perfectly appropriate since they bear the same peculiarly detached relationship to Ambrosio's potential life. All choice of mind or body, insofar as it limits and subdues the self with relation to an external object, is a sign of defeat or dishonesty. Man's professions of faith, whether to a god or a mistress, are, at best, fragments of a temporary reality and, at worst, outright lies. The world of *The Monk* is theatrical, a world of performers and spectators, because every word and act is a work of art, and every work of art a pretense.

We first see Ambrosio preaching in a great cathedral in Madrid, casting a spell over his congregation, many of whom are said to be nonbelievers. Lewis does not give the exact words of the sermon and, in fact, makes it clear that Ambrosio's hold over his audience is not one of rational persuasion but primarily a result of his "style" of speaking, his "distinct and deep" voice from which "the thunder seemed to roll," or which could swell into a "melody," transporting those who heard it "to those happy regions which he painted to their imaginations in colours so brilliant and glowing." Ambrosio is, in other words, an artist who spellbinds his listeners with oratory. The truth of what he says is not important, and though his subject is supposedly the Scriptures, the attention of believer and nonbeliever, of male and female, is drawn to the speaker himself rather than to the lesson. Even the innocent and pious Antonia finds her thoughts drawn more to Ambrosio than to Christ: "His voice inspired me with such interest, such esteem, I might almost say such affection for him, that I am myself astonished."

From the beginning, then, art, even when identified with religion, is a form of self-projection which makes its appeal to the feelings rather than to reason. It is not an imitation of nature or a reordering of truth, but an enhancing disguise by means of which one attracts and temporarily holds sway over others. The artist himself may be deluded both by his own craft and by that of other artists. Hence, we find that Ambrosio, who has half of Madrid under his spell, is himself the captive of a painting of a voluptuous Madonna which hangs in his cell. When it is revealed that the model for the painting had been the wanton Matilda who had dressed in monk's clothing in order to be near Ambrosio, we see that the portrait is merely another disguise. Whatever Matilda really is — a witch of Satan, a figment of Ambrosio's imagination, a woman possessed by lust — art can only hint at and we can only guess. What is real about her is her effect on Ambrosio's mind. She changes his allegiance from a god of chastity to a god of sexual abandon, but both deities require self-denial of one sort or another.

When Ambrosio tires of Matilda and begins to lust after the beautiful Antonia, the cooperative Matilda promises to aid him by means of the "devil's art." The black magic ceremony performed in a charnel house is for Lewis what Daedalus fashioning wings was for Joyce, the type of the artistic imagination. Working with dead materials, cast-off bits of rag and bone, Matilda draws a small circle around Ambrosio and herself and calls forth "a figure more beautiful than fancy's pencil ever drew." It is the devil, though he appears as a naked youth "scarce eighteen, the perfection of whose form and face was unrivalled." Matilda's — or the devil's — art is like Ambrosio's oratory and Lewis's idea of his own craft as novelist and playwright. Gaudy, theatrical, narcissistic, such art gilds the ego and diverts it briefly — very briefly — from the darkness and ruin which encompass it.

In a sense, each stage of the novel's plot repeats the peculiar creative act of the author and shows it to be a form of self-indulgence. Lewis conjures up Ambrosio, who conjures up Matilda, who conjures up the devil, who conjures up Antonia. Lewis's artist is creator, audience, and critic. He fashions, enjoys, and, ultimately, distrusts his own pleasures. What force his art has derives from the individual will, not from a correspondence to external reality. Writing at the end of the eighteenth century, Lewis could not expect to convince many of his readers that Matilda had raised the devil. He could expect to convince them that Ambrosio wanted his way enough to believe, temporarily, whatever appeared to give it to him.

Art, as conceived by Lewis, is the lie which makes human longing, whether for an ideal or material goal, appear capable of fulfillment. Ambrosio's descent from his monastery cell to the magic circle drawn by Matilda is a movement from one deception to another rather than a conventional fall from grace. Like all Gothic novelists, Lewis uses Roman Catholicism primarily for the show of it — and for his Protestant readers, the obviously empty show of it. Imperfectly concealed by the orderly processions, the chants, and the purple reflections from stainglass windows are wretched, ambitious, and doubt-ridden souls. The convent of St. Claire is built above a particularly gruesome sepulcher, and the famous statue of the patron saint conceals a black pit where insubordinate nuns are put to meditate on their sins among the bones of their predecessors. The arts of sex are no more substantial or genuine than the arts of religion: Matilda's portrait, her harp-playing, and her incantations in the charnel house produce temporary illusions, but they do not long keep Ambrosio from experiencing satiety and disgust. Hardly a week has passed before he tires of Matilda and her harp.

5

The moral, it would seem, is obvious — so much so that it hardly carries any force at all when Lewis states it. Ambrosio's sin is pride which eventually leads him to the excesses of lust and wrath. A moral (and sensible) man would be humbler, avoid extremes in all things, and distrust the snares of art. Yet, *The Monk* is not finally a drama of moral alternatives. Indeed, like a great many later romantic heroes, Ambrosio is a being for whom reform and salvation are unthinkable. He has most of the attributes of a conventional hero — beauty, strength, intelligence — but they are inhibited by the circumstances of his life, by the monastery cell, the forbidden bedchamber, the magic circle. What assumes central importance in the novel is the spectacle of energy imprisoned, given hope of escape, and then disappointed. In Ambrosio's case, moral culpability is admitted, but the fact that nearly all the characters in the novel — innocent and guilty alike — suffer the same fate casts some doubt on its relevance.

All who reach out for a life beyond their own — even by means of unselfish love — are greeted by a nightmare and thrust into confinement, darker and more isolated than the prison they had originally sought to escape. Thus, in the subplot of Raymond and Agnes, though the young lovers are guilty of no crime other than their desire to be together, they encounter supernatural as well as mundane obstacles of the most gruesome sort. When Raymond arranges to meet his mistress at midnight, he finds himself embracing a vision of death: "I beheld before me an animated corse. Her countenance was long and haggard; her cheeks and lips were bloodless; the paleness of death was spread over her features . . . My blood was frozen in my veins . . . My nerves were bound up in impotence, and I remained in the same attitude inanimate as a statue." An elaborate explanation about the origins of this ghost is given, but it adds almost nothing to the psychological pattern of the narrative. What is more to the point is that the beautiful Agnes is very nearly turned into a living corpse because of her attempt to run off with her lover. Her family consigns her to a covent where, when it is discovered that she is pregnant, she is locked in the vault under the statue of St. Clare. There her baby dies and there she is eventually found by her brother, "a creature stretched upon a bed of straw, so wretched, so emaciated, so pale, that he doubted to think her a woman." Lewis permits Agnes to recover and marry Raymond in the end, but not without repeating in a minor key the basic theme found in the narrative of Ambrosio.

Whereas Raymond and Agnes are primarily victims of circumstance, Ambrosio is both victim and victimizer. He embraces a body which becomes a corpse on his first visit to the lovely Antonia's bedchamber, though this is no spectre but Elvira, the girl's mother, whom he murders when she discovers him about to rape her daughter. Ambrosio arrives in the room imagining Antonia's youthful beauty and suddenly, as in a nightmare, finds himself wrestling with an aged demon: "He dragged her towards the bed . . . and pressing his knees upon her stomach . . . witnessed without mercy the convulsive trembling of her limbs beneath him . . . Her face was covered with a frightful blackness . . . her hands were stiff and frozen." Ambrosio's reaction is much like Raymond's. He is not sufficiently sadistic to be stimulated by his crime, but, on the contrary, suffers from it almost as though he had been his own victim: "He staggered to a chair, and sank into it almost as lifeless as the unfortunate who lay extended at his feet . . . He had no desire to profit by the execution of his crime. Antonia now appeared to him as an object of disgust."

Two patterns are woven through the different accounts of these strange embraces. One is the reversal of the medieval tale of the "loathly lady" in which the courage and fidelity of a young knight married to an old hag are rewarded when the bride turns into a beautiful damsel. True beauty is seen not only as the prize of virtue but as a durable quality which may be veiled but not defeated by ugliness. The union of the real and the ideal is possible. In *The Monk*, beauty, physical and spiritual, is a deception, an apparition as unattainable and incredible as a stock Gothic ghost. The only reality outside the self is seen in the second pattern, in which the sexual drive ends in an act of murder. Sex, no more than religion, can provide the self with a route to transcendence. The reality beyond the sex act, like that beneath the church floor, is a tomb.

All of the encounters with female corpses are, in addition to their intrinsic unpleasantness, stylistically striking. Lewis's touch is nearly always lighter and surer than Mrs. Radcliffe's, but for the most part he

112

THE MONK

shows a similar reliance on Latinate abstractions, circumlocutions, euphemism, and a connotative rather than a denotative vocabulary. Nearly every page contains such sentences as, "Her distress was beyond the power of description" or "Excessive was the universal grief at hearing this decision." Yet in the scenes where a desirable sexual partner is replaced by a dead body, irony and euphemism vanish, and a sudden specificity of language brings the scene into shocking focus. The blackened face of Antonia's mother has a substantiality lacking in the "ivory" arms, the "coral" lips, the "inexpressibly sweet" smiles of the living heroines, and in the "bloodless cheeks" of ghosts.

It is Ambrosio and his surrogate Raymond in the subplot who give credence to what they see. The reaction to the vision of death is a trance in which the human witness becomes like the thing he sees. But Lewis takes his protagonist beyond the ephemeral confusion of Walpole's heroes or the hysterical paralysis of Mrs. Radcliffe's heroines. True, Ambrosio is a confused hero, subject to contradictory impulses, desirous of obtaining incompatible goals, but his solution to complexity is violence. Strangely enough, despite his reputed intelligence and emotional strength, Ambrosio is a character who seems to have almost no capacity to assimilate change. Every new and unexpected idea or event makes him flutter and reel. It is perhaps natural enough that his original discovery that his attentive novice is a beautiful woman should bring on the confusion of "a thousand opposing sentiments," but this is by no means the last of Ambrosio's nervous palpitations. At Matilda's first advances, he is "confused, embarrassed, and fascinated"; at first sight of Antonia, "a thousand new emotions" sprang into his bosom "and he trembled to examine into the cause which gave them birth"; when unable to seduce Antonia in the conventional ways, he is filled with shame and "the most horrible confusion"; when Matilda promises to help him by means of black magic, "his hand trembles as she leads him toward the vaults"; and, finally, when apprehended by Elvira by the side of her daughter's bed, he is struck by "terror, confusion, and disappointment."

Still, despite certain resemblances in sensibility, Ambrosio is no Emily St. Aubert, nor is he merely the buffoon seducer caught without his trousers (except for a brief moment when he stands "pale and confused, the baffled culprit" trembling before his victim's mother.) Fearing humiliation and scandal, Ambrosio breaks out of both roles, adopts "a

113

resolution equally desperate and savage," and "turning around suddenly, he grasp(s) Elvira's throat." Lewis's language as well as Ambrosio's behavior is suddenly simplified. The author cannot release his protagonist from all convention; murder, under such circumstances, is not unprecedented in history and literature. But he can release him from impotence, confusion, and triviality. He can keep him from being altogether ridiculous by making him momentarily and believably monstrous. The impostor monk makes life conform to his will by destroying it.

In a Gothic distortion of the tomb scene in *Romeo and Juliet*, the drugged Antonia is presumed dead and brought to rest near the remains of her murdered mother in the vaults under the convent of St. Clare. There Ambrosio pursues her, wakens, rapes and kills her in an insane frenzy which repeats not only the violence of his previous murder but of another which is occurring simultaneously in the streets of Madrid. Stopped while leading a religious procession, the abbess of St. Clare is accused of murdering Agnes and is torn to pieces by a furious mob. Lewis, who often finds more commonplace events "indescribable," once again chooses his words with apparent ease:

They tore her one from another, and each new tormentor was more savage than the former. They stifled with howls and execrations her shrill cries for mercy, and dragged her through the streets, spurning her, trampling her, and treating her with every species of cruelty which hate or vindictive fury could invent. At length a flint, aimed by some well-directing hand, struck her full upon the temple. She sank upon the ground bathed in blood, and in a few minutes terminated her miserable existence. Yet though she no longer felt their insults, the rioters still exercised their impotent rage upon her lifeless body. They beat it, trod upon it, and ill used it, till it became no more than a mass of flesh, unsightly, shapeless, and disgusting.

In a novel in which so much is theatrical and ornamentally grotesque, these scenes of violence possess an energy and realism for which the reader is not fully prepared. The abbess is without question presented as a wicked woman, but, like Elvira in the role of interfering parent, she is an uninteresting caricature *except* at the moment of her terrifying death when she becomes for a brief time the vivid image of a tormented human being. It is almost as though Lewis had played an unfair trick on the reader by endowing his Gothic stereotypes with life at unexpected and fatal moments.

When we speak of "realism" or truth to life in a novel like *The*

Monk, it is not a Defoe-like accumulation of detail that is meant, but a contrast between static and stylistically formal scenes and short episodes of concrete action, presented in relatively straightforward language. The murder of Elvira follows the long, elaborate, and ritualistic conjuring scene in the sepulcher; the mutilation of the abbess interrupts a slow, stately procession described with almost Spenserian solemnity. Lewis displays a detachment and control over his mode, first, by means of the amusing ironical aside and, increasingly and more effectively, by means of the pathetic aside, the quick glimpse at pain as inflicted and felt. From one point of view, conventional Gothic cruelty is too preposterously exaggerated, and therefore laughable. From the other, it does not go nearly far enough; it is only a weak charade when compared with human brutality and suffering as they really are.

6

What seems to have held Lewis's imagination more than institutional despotism was the more intimate and essentially psychological subjugation of one individual by another. Unlike Walpole's caricatures, his characters do relate to one another, but primarily as slaves to masters or victims to tormentors. The conventional pairs of lovers, Raymond and Agnes, Lorenzo and Antonia, are kept apart during most of the narrative, whereas emphasis is given to Ambrosio's contact with Matilda, Elvira, and Antonia, all of whom he presumes to overpower while, in another sense, he is himself being overpowered.

It is precisely this question of power — the conditions under which it increases and those under which it is transferred from one individual to another — which seems to have fascinated Lewis and led him to the rigidities and excesses of Gothic fiction. He appears to have recognized that the one could not exist without the other; that excess of any kind could not tolerate contradiction or complexity, and that excess of individual freedom thrives on the potential subjugation of everything but the self. The combination of the extreme gesture of release from convention, on one hand, and the imposition of an absurdly rigid reductionism, on the other, defines a human predicament as well as a peculiar stage in the history of the novel.

It is often said that in Gothic fiction there are either no believable characters at all or else there is one so monstrously absorbent as to make the form seem a kind of obscene exhibitionism. There is nothing between the cipher and the creature of gargantuan potency in an empty world. If this is not true of *The Monk* from the beginning, it becomes true in time. As Ambrosio casts off old roles, he deserts simplicity, bypasses complexity, and finds contradiction and confusion the corollaries of uninhibited power. The history of his personality is not one of growth, but one of painful constriction alternating with disastrous expansion.

Turning for the last time to the scene in the monastery garden where the young novice reveals he is a woman, we can learn something of Lewis's attitude toward personality. When Walpole engineers an unmasking, the onlookers gape and bless themselves and that is the end of it. But Lewis's Gothic disguises tend to have consequences. The sudden external change of sex signals the beginning not only of a breakdown in the conventional distinction between the strong and aggressive male and the weak and submissive female but a generalized blurring of gender and temperament. If Rosario begins as the too delicate and graceful novice, the transformation into Matilda does not bring about a more stable gender:

But a few days had passed, since she appeared the mildest and softest of her sex, devoted to [Ambrosio's] will, and looking up to him as a superior being. Now she assumed a sort of courage and manliness in her manners and discourse . . . She spoke no longer to insinuate, but command.

Simultaneously, Ambrosio, for a while, loses his masculine assertiveness along with his chastity and self-command. What is important is not that this is some sort of transvestite game, but that it shows human personality as essentially unstable, inconsistent, capable of so much that it is often productive of nothing. Lewis does not treat Ambrosio as Sade might have done — as a simple lecher in monkish habit. In attempting to escape one confining role, Ambrosio discovers his "true" self is some combination of lecher-virgin-saint-murderer-man-woman-rapist-victim — with no stress and no stability in any one part.

The nightmare of this novel is the spectacle of a creature whose nature dilutes and immobilizes itself. Where is a hero, a man in control of his own power, in a world of mannish women, effeminate men, servile masters, commanding slaves, where the dead often seem more animated than the impotent, rigid, terrified living? How does one wake up from the double nightmare of a realm of excessive and inhibiting classification which gives way to one of vanishing distinctions? Though Lewis's symbolism is largely sexual and sepulchral, the questions have obvious political, social, philosophical, and aesthetic applicability.

And so too do the outbursts of physical violence. For Ambrosio, having at last had enough of half-measures, can, when everything else fails, summon up the power to destroy. His murder of Elvira, if not the explicit cause of all the other destruction in the novel, is nonetheless quickly followed by the mutilation of the abbess, the burning of the convent, the rape and murder of Antonia, and finally his own death, which seems to put the order of Genesis itself into reverse. Having been seized by the devil and thrown from a "dreadful height," he "rolled from precipice to precipice, till, bruised and mangled, he rested on the river's banks . . .

Six miserable days did the villain languish. On the seventh a violent storm arose: the winds in fury rent up rocks and forests: the sky was now black with clouds, now sheeted with fire: the rain fell in torrents; it swelled the stream; the waves overflowed their banks; they reached the spot where Ambrosio lay, and, when they abated, carried with them into the river the corse of the despairing monk.

In no other scene is Lewis's language so charged, his rhythm so insistent, his feelings so obviously engaged, as in this last, where he smashes his own creation. Righteous anger against the sinning monk? Perhaps, in some measure, but, more fundamentally, he seems to be taking over the work of his own protagonist by revealing his greatest strength in a brutal revolt against the limits of human nature and the myth of an orderly universe. Lewis's final vision is of a chaos which neither man nor art has the capacity to control or avoid. Indeed, uncontrollable energy would seem to be the only energy there is in the world of *The Monk*. The artist, like the monk who seeks liberation from lifeless conventions, is apt to find himself unexpectedly on the side of the flood.

VI

NORTHANGER ABBEY

Jane Austen
1803

In 1802, the year before Jane Austen completed *Northanger Abbey*, a reviewer in the *Scots Magazine* wrote: "All the faults and immoralities ascribed to novels will be found realized in *The Monk*: murders, incest, and all the horrible and aggravated crimes which it is possible to conceive, appear in every chapter." [1] Earlier, a literary biographer recorded it as a circumstance "remarkable in the history of our times" that such a "flagrant . . . outrage against decency and propriety," should come from a Member of Parliament.[2] The most furious and prolonged attack was launched by T. J. Mathias, who accused Lewis of publishing "the arts of lewd and systematic seduction" and of thrusting "upon the nation the most unqualified blasphemy against the very code and volume of our religion." [3]

It was to be expected, as with all departures from convention, that romantic fiction would come under attack. It was perhaps also to be expected that the attacks would grow increasingly bitter as the experiments became more radical and more influential. What is surprising is the virulence with which "literary" critics assaulted the characters of authors, imputing to them imbecility, insanity, perversion, and diabolically inspired malice. Often at a loss for words which would convey a coherent reaction to disturbing and irregular works of art, critics turned in bewildered irritation to the minds and morals of those who produced them.

Mrs. Radcliffe, Lewis, and Godwin were all accused of madness and immorality, but it is worth remembering that the critical violence brought on by the works of these novelists was only a foretaste of that engendered by the romantic phenomenon in its full flowering. Shelley, in recognition of "the stupid trash" which he named poetry, was called a candidate for "a cell, clean straw, bread and water, a strait waistcoat, and phlebotomy";[4] Byron was denounced as "the greatest enemy of his species" whose poetry "flows on in one continued, unvarying stream of pollution";[5] Wordsworth, as the author of "moral and devotional ravings," was said to exhibit himself through his poetry either in a state of delirium or "of low and maudlin imbecility";[6] and Keats was described less than a year after his death as a "radically presumptuous profligate . . . a foolish young man, who, after writing some volumes of very weak, and, in greater part, of very indecent poetry, died some time since of consumption: the breaking down of an infirm constitution having, in all probability, been accelerated by the discarding his neckcloth, a practice of cockney poets, who look upon it as essential to genius." [7]

The primary "fault" of all romantic literature — what made it threatening in any form — was that it was antisocial. Hostile critics saw its effects not from the point of view of the individual seeking to free his spirit from artificial restraint, but from the point of view of communal stability. Depending upon the orientation of the particular reviewer, that stability might be associated most closely with the Church, the body politic, the profession, or the family, and the bitterest outrage reserved for the atheism, anarchism, amateurism, or sexual license of the artist and his works. In all cases, it was the group which was being undermined and which needed guarding. Even the consternation over the atheism of Byron and Shelley stemmed not so much from a horror of blasphemy — the Deity, it was presumed, could deal with that — but from a fear of the damage which might be done to the continuity of the Christian community. As one Methodist minister put it: "Society may flourish without genius; and may be refined without poetry, but it cannot exist without virtue; and when genius arms itself against the body politic, and wages war with the whole human family — I am determined, for one, to make common cause with my country; — with my species." [8]

It is not surprising that Godwin's literary "offenses" were treated as sins against society. His "kind affections" were said to have been "writhed around the unsocial" (which seems to be a way of calling him a good-natured enemy of the people). He was called a sage "rapt in beatific visions," given to "wily insinuations" and "declamatory harangues, to the discredit of gratitude or patriotism." [9] According to Mathias, in his satirical *Pursuits of Literature, The Monk* too was a crime against the State committed by one whom the State should have punished:

> Another Cleland see in Lewis rise.
> Why sleep the ministers of truth and law?
> Has the State no control, no decent awe,
> While each with each in madd'ning orgies vie,
> Pandars to lust and licens'd blasphemy? [10]

In cases where it was difficult to bring specific charges of political or religious unorthodoxy, general and often quite vague suspicions were aroused by the solitary — and therefore presumably unproductive and queer — habits of writers who sought inspiration in the seclusion of the countryside. One reviewer frankly admitted that lakes and mountains seemed to him "paltry idols" upon which Wordsworth and his imitators wasted talents which might have been better employed: "Solitary musings, amidst such scenes, might no doubt be expected to nurse up the mind to the majesty of poetical conception, — (though it is remarkable, that all the greater poets lived, or had lived, in the full current of society)." [11]

The spokesmen for social continuity and stability had legitimate reasons to be aroused by the potential dangers of Romanticism. However, the tendency on the part of so many to respond irrationally, even hysterically and with personal vindictiveness, produced a mirror image of the worst faults of the phenomenon they were opposing. More to the point was criticism in which the values of tradition were brought into clearer focus precisely because of the challenges posed by romantic writers. What was needed was not an echo or a collision — though a certain number of both could hardly be avoided — but an intelligent exchange. On the highest level of literary criticism, this was provided by Coleridge and Hazlitt, both of whom conducted a continuous inquiry into the ways in which romantic values related to the traditions of English literature and, especially in the case of Coleridge, to the larger developments of Western philosophy.

Less sympathetic to Romanticism than Coleridge and Hazlitt and less righteous than the reviewers, Jane Austen brought the techniques of intelligent dialogue to bear on the excesses of romantic fiction. She satirized the Gothic novel, but, more importantly, she based her narrative on that enemy of solitude and cornerstone of society: conversation. She seemed convinced that the antidote to "delirious ravings," "pathetic confessions," and "solitary musings" was not raving of another sort, but talk — polite conversation in which questions were asked in anticipation of answers, and in which mutual comprehension, however modest, was presumed to be the object. Jane Austen's critical method is to introduce one "romantic" character into the non-romantic world of marriage and money. Talk is difficult, but necessary. The romantic figure is not permitted the luxury of addressing a mute and spellbound stranger who "cannot choose but hear." In the world of Jane Austen, nearly everyone talks back, even to heroes and heroines. And having said his piece, a speaker cannot count on vanishing mysteriously or sinking into the grave, but must expect to meet his auditors again the next day, strolling in the pump room, opening doors, offering chairs, or sitting across the table and asking for the cream and sugar.

That every romantic hero or heroine worthy of the name would, at some time, be confronted by a situation which words could not describe or overcome with a feeling which language could not convey, was taken for granted by most romantic novelists. But where characters are speechless, authors cannot afford to be. The poet could interrupt his line with a dash or exclamatory "Ah!" but the romantic novelist, feeling the need of a longer pause, often spent a great many words to impress his reader with the inadequacy of language. The inaccessibility of the sublime, the unreachable depths of human feelings, the persistent elusiveness of the mysteries which lay behind the veil, within the forest, around the corner of the next corridor, were among the favorite topics of romantic novelists. For some, words seemed to serve best when declaring their own uselessness and novels to be most serious only when novelists confessed their inadequacy.

2

Jane Austen thought the capabilities of language, correctly used, considerable, and early in *Northanger Abbey* she opens her gentle assault on romantic fiction with a defense of the novel:

I will not adopt that ungenerous and impolitic custom so common with novel writers, of degrading by their contemptuous censure the very performances, to the number of which they are themselves adding — joining with their greatest enemies in bestowing the harshest epithets on such works, and scarcely ever permitting them to be read by their own heroine, who, if she accidentally take up a novel, is sure to turn over its insipid pages with disgust. [A novel at its best can be a] work in which the greatest powers of the mind are displayed, in which the most thorough knowledge of human nature, the happiest delineation of its varieties, the liveliest effusions of wit and humor are conveyed to the world in the best chosen language.[12]

That is what a novel *might* be. But it is clear from the start that Catherine Morland, the heroine of *Northanger Abbey*, while an enthusiastic reader of novels, admires that class of fiction in which human nature, wit, and choice language are secondary considerations. Catherine Morland is an admirer of Ann Radcliffe. She reads, not to be instructed or entertained, but to be frightened.

Northanger Abbey embraces two worlds — the world of Catherine's subjective fancy and that of social convention as it is interpreted primarily by Henry Tilney. As nearly all critics of the novel have recognized, the book is, because of this juxtaposition of worlds, part parody romance and part realistic novel.[13] But what may appear as a division of purpose — an early and therefore forgivable lapse on Austen's part — is really a precise comic analogue to a genre which was itself divided. By contrasting Bath to the Abbey, Austen is not doing anything that Radcliffe, Godwin, and Lewis had not done before her in placing rational, social, daylight worlds against dark, subjective prisons. If Catherine's "prison" is of her own making, so, to a large extent, were those of Emily St. Aubert, Caleb Williams, and Ambrosio.

There *is* parody in *Northanger Abbey*, and though it is broader in the romance sections, it pervades both worlds, romantic and realistic, without totally rejecting either. The book is entertaining, and it was obviously Austen's purpose to ridicule the excesses of an untutored imagination. But though she shows us that Catherine's Gothic dreams are derived from false suspicions and inadequate information, Austen does not pretend that the collision of a susceptible mind with the world of hard reality is a false situation or even a wholly ludicrous one. *Northanger Abbey* is split in a way familiar to a close reader of romantic novels and it shows, despite its surface frivolity, that Austen understood the source and nature of that division very well.

Young, impressionable, good-hearted and a little simple-minded, Catherine imagines herself a romantic heroine in a world fraught with Gothic possibilities. Unlike Ann Radcliffe, however, Jane Austen does not allow her heroine's emotions to dominate the vision of reality presented to the reader. On the contrary, through the speeches of other characters and through the steady narrative voice of the author, the reader is constantly shown a world which corresponds in almost no way to the apprehensions of the heroine. Having set down her copy of *The Mysteries of Udolpho* to attend a ball during her visit to Bath, Catherine finds sufficient cause for romantic musings when momentarily "abandoned" by her dancing partner:

To be disgraced in the eye of the world, to wear the appearance of infamy while her heart is all purity, her actions all innocence, and the misconduct of another the true source of her debasement, is one of those circumstances which peculiarly belong to the heroine's life.

That the language is far in excess of what the situation justifies is obvious, but Jane Austen also shows that it is not even an apt indication of the girl's own feelings. For within ten minutes she is roused out of her "humiliation" by the approach of another and preferable partner. The episode is trivial and amusing, but through it Jane Austen demonstrates how language can exceed as well as fall short of human experience. There are words to describe balls at Bath and the disappointment of young ladies who have not been asked to dance, but Catherine's reading habits have not helped her to find them.

But if Catherine's misuse of language is the innocent result of inexperience and undiscriminating susceptibility to romantic fiction, there are other examples of exaggerated language which are of less innocent origin. The first acquaintance Catherine makes at Bath is Isabella

Thorpe, an attractive and comparatively sophisticated girl, who over-whelms her new friend with repeated professions of undying devotion and sisterly affection. It soon becomes clear to the reader, if not to Catherine, that Isabella overestimates the Morlands' wealth and hopes to marry Catherine's brother James. The more convinced she becomes of the family's wealth, the more extravagant become her praises of the beauty and brilliance of the relatively plain and intellectually unexceptional Catherine. At first, Catherine takes her friend's exaggerations as signs of her romantic nature and high spirits. For Isabella, the most ordinary things, when associated in any way with the Morland family, become "inconceivable, incredible, impossible"; to be separated from her friend for an afternoon seems "ages"; to wish to question her about her brother is to have "thousands of things to say to her"; to take leave of her until the next morning is to part in "utter despondency."

Even Catherine eventually becomes aware that Isabella's language, far from being the spontaneous overflow of a brimming heart, is a consciously manipulated instrument with which she attempts to satisfy herself while seeming to think of others. One day when Isabella has her mind set on taking a ride with Catherine and her brother, she is irritated to learn that Catherine has already promised to spend the day with other friends. She urges her to do what "would be so easy," that is, tell them that she had "just been reminded of a prior engagement." "No, it would not be easy," answers Catherine. "I could not do it. There has been no prior engagement." Carelessness about the correspondence between words and events can be, as Catherine realizes, a form of dishonesty. Truth, as understood by Jane Austen, is not determined merely by the urges of the ego, but by the discernible events of a world outside the self. If some of those events are beyond mortal powers of articulation, others are perfectly capable of being named. One danger of romantic scorn for the reliability of words is that it introduces confusion where there is none, creates a muddle for the innocent and a camouflage for the disingenuous.

Two other examples of the mismanagement of words — without benefit of Radcliffean aura — are provided by Catherine's companion and hostess at Bath, Mrs. Allen, and Isabella's braggart brother John. Both are vain and dull-witted characters who demonstrate the folly, selfishness, and tedium of using words as adornments of the self rather than as means of communication. Mrs. Allen has one subject, fashion, and nearly all of her talk, wherever it begins, comes around eventually to the tilt of her bonnet or the state of her muslin. While she is a relatively harmless and comic character, she is also incapable of doing good. She cannot comfort Catherine nor serve as a moral guide, because she cannot think of her except as the wearer of so many yards of material. When Catherine asks her opinion about the correctness of riding in an open carriage with a man to whom one is not engaged, Mrs. Allen displays the limit of her understanding and sympathy: "Open carriages are nasty things. A clean gown is not five minutes wear in them. You are splashed getting in and getting out; and the wind takes your hair and your bonnet in every direction. I hate an open carriage myself."

John Thorpe is a vulgarized, stupider version of his sister. Also thinking the Morlands are wealthy, he continually attempts to impress and flatter Catherine. He boasts about his horses, his carriage, his drinking parties at Oxford, repeats and contradicts himself, and punctuates every other sentence with an oath. Words fail him only when he tries to enumerate Catherine's qualities:

"You have more good-nature and all that, than anybody living I believe. A monstrous deal of good-nature, and it is not only good-nature, but you have so much, so much of everything; and then you have such — upon my soul I do not know any body like you."

The humor of the scene stems from the fact that the missing word for which Thorpe seems to be groping is all too plain. It is not language which fails the man, but the man who fails language, and in doing so reveals his want of honesty, affection, and wit along with his want of words. Catherine, too, at this relatively early point in the novel may be said to fail language — she does not use words precisely and does not easily see through the muddled jargon of the Thorpes. But her failure is not of a moral sort. She is merely ignorant. By learning the ways of words, she will gradually come to know more of the world and of herself.[14]

Her teachers are Eleanor Tilney and, more particularly, Eleanor's brother Henry, two conventional, yet sincere, charming, and even noble persons. Through them — and especially through the way they speak — Jane Austen makes an impressive defense of social convention and

125

shows the egotism and futility of ignoring or scorning it. When Catherine and Eleanor first meet, they exchange the usual pleasantries, but after the absurd exclamations of Isabella Thorpe, polite commonplaces seem almost rich with meaning. At least, they convey the idea that two young ladies are happy to have met and are content in one another's company, though neither may find the other, after five minutes, dearer than her own life, the sweetest creature she ever saw, "amazingly" clever, ravishing, clairvoyant, in short, a combination of virtues altogether "inconceivable, incredible, impossible." In the company of Eleanor Tilney, Catherine does not reach for superlatives nor is she showered with them. Jane Austen merely tells us that they met with "civility" and "good will":

And though in all probability not an observation was made, nor an expression used by either which had not been made and used some thousands of times before, under that roof, in every Bath season, yet the merit of their being spoken with simplicity and truth, and without personal conceit, might be something uncommon

3

Catherine's most instructive teacher is Eleanor's brother Henry, the hero of the novel. He is, in nearly all respects, the reverse of the male protagonist of a romantic novel. He is at home in society, a minister and country gentleman, cheerful-natured, an obedient son and courteous brother, well-educated, slightly pedantic, presentable but not striking, intelligent but not a genius. His courtship of Catherine takes the form of a series of lessons in semantics, through which he reveals his own affection for her and teaches her to judge and discriminate among words as an aid in judging and discriminating among people and circumstances.

Henry's first lesson stresses the importance of language as a conventional approximation of reality, an artificial convenience which can express much so long as it is not confused with the reailty itself. He draws a comparison between a dance and a marriage which demonstrates the metaphorical nature of language while defining the necessarily conventional basis of all social intercourse:

"We have entered into a contract of mutual agreeableness for the space of an evening, and all our agreeableness belongs solely to each other for

that time. Nobody can fasten themselves on the notice of one, without in-
juring the rights of the other. I consider a country-dance as an emblem of
marriage. Fidelity and complaisance are the principal duties of both; and
those men who do not choose to dance or marry themselves, have no
business with the partners or wives of their neighbors."

"But they are such very different things! — "

"That you think they cannot be compared together."

"To be sure not. People that marry can never part, but must go and
keep house together. People that dance, only stand opposite each other in
a long room for half an hour."

For the moment, Catherine has missed the point of the lesson as well
as the bantering tone of the teacher. But Jane Austen's hero, thinking it
unnecessary to speak up for order, speaks up instead for the importance
of recognizing its essential components. For Catherine, marriage is marriage and dancing is dancing. Like most other things in her mind, they
have no connection. Different names for different things with no
apparent basis for comparison. Yet Tilney has begun to show that the
most trivial as well as some of the most important social actions involve, in one way or another, making contracts which involve rights,
duties, and, most un-Godwinian of all, voluntary mutual conformity.
The characters in *Northanger Abbey*, as in all of Jane Austen's novels,
are constantly "engaging" themselves to others, to walk, to dine, to
visit, to marry. And the worst thing a person can do is to enter into an
engagement dishonestly — like Isabella with James Morland — or to
break it without sufficient cause — again like Isabella, or like General
Tilney when he expels Catherine from his house after having invited
her to stay as long as she pleased.

In the next lesson, Henry attempts to show that language too is a
kind of "contract of mutual agreeableness" with principles and rules
which ought to govern those who "engage" to use it in the presence of
others. Though he is a minister, it is not the meditational but the con-
versational precision of Catherine which he seeks to improve. Like
Isabella, though without her ulterior motives, Catherine tends to use
words like "amazing," "horrid," and "tremendous" to describe matters
of little consequence. One day, while walking with Henry and Eleanor
Tilney, she asks Henry if he does not think *The Mysteries of Udolpho*
"the nicest book in the world."

"The nicest; — by which I suppose you mean the neatest. That must depend upon the binding."

"Henry," said Miss Tilney, "you are very impertinent. Miss Morland, he is treating you exactly as he does his sister. He is forever finding fault with me, for some incorrectness of language, and now he is taking the same liberty with you. The word 'nicest,' as you used it, did not suit him; and you had better change it as soon as you can, or we shall be overpowered with Johnson and Blair all the rest of the way."

"I am sure," cried Catherine; "I did not mean to say anything wrong; but it *is* a nice book, and why should not I call it so?"

"Very true," said Henry, "and this is a very nice day, and we are taking a very nice walk, and you are two very nice young ladies. Oh! it is a very nice word indeed! It does for everything."

In a world of Catherine Morlands — to say nothing of Isabella and John Thorpes — Henry's schoolmarmish manner seems forgivable if not heroic. Having demonstrated something of the analogical nature of language in his first lesson, Tilney proceeds to argue that a verbal representation of reality — even if it cannot reproduce that reality to perfection — need not miss it by a mile. Human experience is rich and varied, but Jane Austen and her hero, both admirers of Dr. Johnson, could not agree that the English language was without resources to describe a considerable portion of it. One remedy for speechlessness or, what amounts to the same thing, the indiscriminate use of a few words, is a larger vocabulary — a mind in touch with other minds through the conventional but many-faceted medium of language.

Of course, a good heart is essential, for, without it, language, however precise, can become a fashion like any other, vain, inconsequential, and inert, a piece of mental apparel to be put on and off without feeling or taste. Right feelings we know Catherine possesses: Jane Austen explains that though she often "knew not what to say and her eloquence was only in her eyes . . . the eight parts of speech shone out most expressively, and [one] could combine them with ease." But taste, or the ability to see connections and to make distinctions, Catherine lacks from want of instruction and practice. When Isabella Thorpe decides, for example, to wear exactly the same dress as Catherine at a ball so that the men will take notice of them both, Catherine does not see it as a tasteless and unfeeling maneuver to flatter and outshine her at the same time. Isabella borrows styles in dresses, as in words, without regard to elegance or sensitivity to the feelings of others, but to gratify a momentary vanity. She lives from whim to whim and from day to day, changing her manners and moods as the wind blows, and following no governing principle beyond that of "improving her situation." She is without taste for the same reason that, on another level, she is without morality: she does not make coherent connections between herself and other people; between her words and her actions, or even among her own utterances, which Catherine eventually recognizes as a tissue of "inconsistencies" and "contradictions."

Unlike Isabella's, most of Catherine's mistakes originate from an excessively high opinion of nearly everyone. Still, there is a narrowness, a kind of selfishness, even in this, for it stems from judging the world only in terms of the self rather than in relation to a larger social context. Catherine always means what she says, even when her words are not well chosen, and she assumes therefore that everyone else is the same. Tilney's third lesson, then, is an attempt to urge Catherine to weigh words against the habits and actions of the speaker rather than simply against her own feelings. When she attributes Henry's brother's flirtatious interest in Isabella to his "good-nature," Henry tries to show her the basis of the error:

"With you, it is not: How is such a one likely to be influenced? What is the inducement most likely to act upon such a person's feelings, age, situation, and probable habits of life considered? — but how should I be influenced, what would be *my* inducement in acting so and so?"
"I do not understand you."
"Then we are on very unequal terms, for I understand you perfectly well."
"Me? — yes; I cannot speak well enough to be unintelligible."
"Bravo! — an excellent satire on modern language."

Catherine has unwittingly put her finger on one of the most important points that Henry has been trying to make: that language is worthless if not intelligible. But she has not yet seen that the "intelligibility" of words depends upon several things, including their emblematic relationship to external reality, their logical relationship to one another, their personal relationship to the speaker, and their circumstantial relationship to the one being addressed. Until she can see the importance of these relationships she will continue to misuse words and misjudge people.

4

Jane Austen realizes that, though Henry Tilney is an excellent teacher, his lessons are too abstract and subtle to have immediate effect on his pupil. Catherine needs a concrete confrontation with the errors of her ways and the applicability of his theories. Her opportunity comes when General Tilney, the widowed father of Eleanor and Henry, invites Catherine to visit their country house, Northanger Abbey. Already fond of the brother and sister, and intrigued by the thought of living in a reconstructed Gothic ruin, Catherine accepts. Actually, the house is bright, cheerful, and Gothic only in a few minor details, but Catherine is hardly in it before she begins imagining herself in the role of a Radcliffean heroine. She digs for ancient parchments in chests and cabinets, lies awake trembling on windy nights, and deduces, from the strict and domineering manner of the General, that he must have persecuted his wife and sealed her up in some hidden chamber of the house until she went mad or died.

Determined to get to the bottom of the "mystery" and expose the General to justice, Catherine resolves to visit the bedroom where Mrs. Tilney is said to have died of a fever nine years earlier. All the more suspicious because the General does not show her this room when giving a tour of the house, Catherine ventures to it alone one afternoon before tea, expecting she hardly knows what "gloomy objects," what "proofs" of the General's cruelty. She finds, instead, a "well-proportioned apartment, an handsome dimity bed, arranged as unoccupied with an housemaid's care, a bright Bath stove, mahogany wardrobes and neatly painted chairs on which the warm beams of a western sun gaily poured through two sash windows!" Disappointed and ashamed, she dashes out into the hall where she meets Henry and confesses her suspicion, which he greets with mild dismay and a rational explanation.

The point, of course, is that Mrs. Tilney's death is a subject about which Catherine really has nothing to say. It is both amusing and rather touching that she should crave so frantically to "explain" — even in absurd terms — the death of her friends' mother. It is the only subject in the novel which Jane Austen seems to admit is "beyond words." The image of death — one of the rare examples in all of Austen's works — is not a blood-stained dagger or a murky chamber, but an "unoccupied" bed in a perfectly neat, ordinary, though empty room. Mrs. Tilney dead is Mrs. Tilney "not present," a vacancy except in the memory of her family. Neither Catherine Morland nor the reader has cause or capacity to say anything more about her. And in the world of Jane Austen, the best thing to do when one has nothing to say — that is, nothing which can add to the instruction or comfort of others — is not to lament the impotence of words, but to turn to subjects where they can be of some use.

If, for example, Catherine had devoted the time spent wondering about the late Mrs. Tilney in speaking to and, above all, listening to General Tilney, she might have deduced, not that he was an English Montoni, but a prosperous parent with military fondness for order and obedience, and a tendency to petulance when his dinner was not served on time. She might further have deduced, from his comments about his house, his son, and her family (which he has never met), that he thinks her a good match for Henry and, for some reason, imagines her wealthier than she is. General Tilney is a quick-tempered snob, not a murderer, but Catherine learns that these unsensational vices are quite enough to cause her a kind of pain which has nothing to do with old parchments or phantom footsteps. When the General conveys through his daughter that Catherine must terminate her visit and return unaccompanied to her parents' home, she suffers genuine anguish for the first time in the novel. In comparing the distress of her first and last nights at North-anger Abbey, Catherine finally perceives distinctions of the sort Henry Tilney had tried to show her from the beginning:

That room, in which her disturbed imagination had tormented her on her first arrival, was again the scene of agitated spirits and unquiet slumbers. Yet how different now the source of her inquietude . . . Her anxiety had foundation in fact, her fears in probability; and with a mind so occupied in the contemplation of actual and natural evil, the solitude of her situation, the darkness of her chamber, the antiquity of the building were felt and considered without the smallest emotion.

Though Catherine is not altogether sure why the General is angry with her, she realizes that his rude termination of her visit is an "evil" more immediate than the sort evoked by Mrs. Radcliffe. His sudden breaking of a social engagement is both cause and symbol of serious ruptures in the life of Catherine, of her friendship with Eleanor and her love for Henry. Catherine learns from the General's treatment, that a human being need not be a murderer or rapist to do harm. Later, it turns out that John Thorpe, who had originally exaggerated Catherine's wealth to the General, had also informed him, upon seeing his own suit discouraged, that she was an opportunist from a family of scheming paupers. Henry finally clears away the confusion, apologizes to Catherine and her family, secures his father's grudging consent, and marries his well-instructed pupil.

5

It may be argued that, in dismissing physical violence and emotional extremes from her novels, Jane Austen too artificially limits, not only the size of her own canvas, but, by implication, the range of describable reality; that in a novel like *Northanger Abbey*, she seems to be saying, not simply, "I choose to write about 'this' because it is what I know," but "I do not choose to write about 'that' because it is silly, unimportant, or unreal."

Though by no means her richest or greatest work, *Northanger Abbey* is perhaps the most useful of her novels to consider in a discussion of this problem. It is more than a joke at the expense of Ann Radcliffe. Aside from the epistolary parody, *Love and Freindship*, it is the one sustained and explicit example we have of Jane Austen's reaction to the subject matter and technical devices common to much romantic fiction. As for subject matter, our insight into Jane Austen's attitude comes, as usual, from a speech of Henry Tilney's. When Catherine blurts out her suspicion that his father is a murderer, Henry reacts with characteristic logic:

"Dear Miss Morland, consider the dreadful nature of the suspicions you have entertained. What have you been judging from? Remember the country and the age in which we live. Remember that we are English, that we are Christians . . . Does our education prepare us for such atrocities? Do our laws connive at them? Could they be perpetrated without being known in a country like this, where social and literary intercourse is on such a footing?"

We know what William Godwin's answers to such questions were only eight years earlier. And we know that Jane Austen's answers would not be the same. But if we take Tilney's dismay at face value, we have neither followed the advice he gave Catherine to judge a person's words in relation to his "feelings, age, situation, and probable habits of life," nor have we understood the extent to which Austen's irony enlarges possibilities even at the expense of her own heroes and heroines. Tilney himself is not too perfect to fall into priggish overstatement which reveals the limitation of his otherwise "nice" perceptions.[15] That Catherine's particular suspicions are without substantial cause or probability is evident, but that a concealed murder is unthinkable in Christian England is by no means so.

If Catherine's behavior has often shown ignorance of the value of social and verbal convention, Henry — like his father, though with less rigidity — shows in this speech the absurdity of overreliance on conventional assumptions. True, Catherine is shown to be foolish to have mistaken the world for a Gothic romance, but then Jane Austen does not quite let her hero get away with endowing his countrymen and era with all the virtues of reason and self-control. In fact, she emphasizes the silliness of Henry's speech by making Catherine believe it wholeheartedly, just as she had believed what was contrary to it three minutes before. Later, in the privacy of her room, she meditates and elaborates upon her new-found wisdom: "Among the Alps and Pyrenees, perhaps, there were no mixed characters. There, such as were not as spotless as an angel, might have the dispositions of a fiend. But in England it was not so; among the English, she believed, in their hearts and habits, there was a general though unequal mixture of good and bad."

By viewing her hero's complacency ironically, Austen reveals that her own had its bounds. Her circumvention of the dark and "large" themes characteristic of romantic fiction, represents, not a failure to see all painful realities, but one way of acknowledging their force. Like her favorite, Dr. Johnson, her representations of rational order often derive their vigor from a vivid sense of the alternatives. True, those alternatives were not madness or violent death, but isolation, sterility, the sense of a life without security, affection, or use. Yet they were no less desperate for being unsensational.

What Johnson achieved through constant inquiry and argument, Jane Austen achieved in her own way through irony: elasticity within a convention. "Freedom" is not a word she uses very often, whereas "grace" is everywhere in her fiction. As she demonstrates in *Northanger Abbey* and all of her other novels, an ironical vision is cynical only when the conventional forms employed are thought to be without value and are manipulated for purposes contrary to mutual "convenience." As Henry Tilney sees, at least most of the time, where more than one person is involved, conventional forms are necessary stays against intellectual confusion and moral riot. They are, in the literal sense, guardians of sanity. He also sees that any convention — verbal or social — insofar as it is a sign of a "coming together," must involve compromise and never can, under any conceivable circumstance, suit all the peculiarities and complexities of a single human being. Austen's — and to some degree, Tilney's — recognition of the importance of the individual sensibility and its inevitably imperfect adjustment to established form is one source of the ironic tone of the novel.

Henry Tilney, when not lapsing into priggishness, speaks with a witty lightness which shows that he can appreciate a convention and express himself through it without letting it manipulate, rigidify, and annihilate his human nature. His realm is not a prison cell but a ballroom, and his wish is not to escape it but to master the rules and share their benefits with others. Convinced that some form is necessary and that no form suits all temperaments, he is not interested — as so many romantic heroes are — in changing the laws of society or nature. He maintains enough distance to show that he sees the inadequacy even of those conventions he finds necessary and pleasing. Though he is forever talking about precision, his primary lesson is one of balance. Just because people, like words, are imperfect, there is no reason for them, through carelessness, to permit themselves to be irrational and immoral as well.

Jane Austen's answer in the same period of challenge which produced so much radical and passionate literature, is reached not by rebellion and flight, but through education. When Catherine tells Henry that she has "learned" from Eleanor to love a hyacinth, he congratulates her, saying, in his briefest but perhaps most effective lesson, "It is well to have as many holds upon happiness as possible." Jane Austen nowhere denies the splendor of Mont Blanc; she merely speaks up for hyacinths. Northanger Abbey is a modest, even slight book, about one quarter the length of The Mysteries of Udolpho. But as a display of the disciplined mind and the well-chosen word it does more than all the hysterical criticism of the periodicals to deflate some of the poses and excesses of

Romanticism. When Catherine suggests to Henry that "to torment" is a good synonym for "to instruct," he agrees that discipline is often painful:

> "But . . . even you yourself, who do not seem altogether particularly friendly to very severe, very intense application, may perhaps be brought to acknowledge that it is very well worth while to be tormented for two or three years of one's life, for the sake of being able to read all the rest of it. Consider — if reading had not been taught, Mrs. Radcliffe would have written in vain — or perhaps might not have written at all."

Once again, Catherine has used a word imprecisely and Henry has corrected her. And once again his lesson appears to be after Jane Austen's own heart. Yet the impression lingers after reading this book that if one character makes too much of words like "torment," the other makes too little of them. A reasonable and socially conventional man can educate a young woman out of her unfounded fears, but he is not, therefore, St. George. There are dragons he cannot touch. Through a crack in the door of an empty bedroom and the petulance of a narrow-minded father, Austen gives a glimpse of the demons which prevent Henry Tilney from looming with perfect invulnerability over the fretful Catherine Morland. Austen's mode is ironic and her range modest, but she has explored the same division of mind which is at the core of romantic fiction.

VII

WAVERLEY

Sir Walter Scott
1814

Sir Walter Scott liked *Northanger Abbey* and *The Monk*. Indeed, he praised the writer of each book for precisely those traits which most irritated their critics: Austen for her detailed treatment of the unexceptional and Lewis for his bold excursions into the extraordinary. Such critical pliability has caused some readers to wonder whether Scott was large-minded or merely inconsistent. Probably the fairest reply is that he was both, that his particular kind of breadth consisted not in harmonized diversity but in unresolved contradictions.

It has already been noted that Scott admired Lewis for being among the first "to introduce something like the German taste into English fictitious, dramatic and poetical composition." Scott's notion of the special virtues of German literature is interesting. He speaks first of the language itself, which is "possessed of the same manly force of expression" as English.[1] But more important is his attitude toward the influence of German literature on the themes and structure of English narrative. For the first time since Shakespeare and Milton, he argues, there was "a race of poets who had the same lofty ambition to spurn the flaming boundaries of the universe, and investigate the realms of chaos and old night." Scott's terms may be inflated and vague, but the general point is clear. Goethe, Schiller, Kotzebue, and Bürger showed the way out of the tightening circle of contemporary manners and morals. What is more, by risking "occasional improbabilities" and "scenes of wildest contrast," the Germans disclaimed the "pedantry of the unities"

136

and demonstrated their "emancipation from the rules so seriously adhered to by the French school."

For Scott, *The Monk* was not mere artifice and bombast, but a brave and salutary experiment which "seemed to create an epoch in our literature." Though he disapproved of "the indelicacy of certain passages," he did not join the chorus of outraged critics in condemning the Gothic extravagance, the brutality or superstition of the book. On the contrary, he saw strength in these excesses and recognized in them an artist's effort to assert himself in the face of the domesticated trivia which was published in the name of prudence and the common good. Lewis, he said, "introduced supernatural machinery with a courageous consciousness of his own power to manage its ponderous strength." Far from being a source of embarrassment, this was, for Scott, precisely the ground upon which Lewis "commanded the respect of his reader."

Scott's review of *Northanger Abbey* and *Persuasion* was written in 1821, nine years before the *Essay on Imitations of the Ancient Ballad*, in which he discussed *The Monk*, but there is no evidence that he changed his mind about Austen or Lewis in that period. Various remarks in his journals, letters, and miscellaneous prose suggest that his admiration for both authors was constant. It is true that he is always careful to qualify his praise by reminding his reader that each writer excelled at a particular kind of narration. Despite allusions to Shakespeare and Milton, he makes no universal claims for Lewis or his imitators. If Austen was narrow in her way, those who wrote in the "German taste" were narrow in theirs.

What is curious is not that Scott recognized the limitations and virtues of two very different kinds of writers, but that he was able to treat their antithetical tendencies with such perceptive and sympathetic warmth. His famous and casual remark about being capable of the "big Bow-wow strain" [2] himself, without having Austen's skill in everyday matters, has too much of courtly condescension in it. But the studied analysis of Austen's fiction in the 1821 review reveals a genuine appreciation of precisely those traits which set her novels apart from Lewis's and, in many ways, from his own. Her novels "have all the compactness of plan and unity of action which is generally produced by a sacrifice of probability: yet they have little or nothing that is not probable." [3] There is no note of a needed emancipation from the unities, but only praise for the success with which she illustrates "the precepts of Aristotle." As for subject matter, Scott comes to Austen's defense against those who find her details tedious, her situations commonplace, and her fools too realistic for comfort. He refers to the precedent of Shakespeare's comedies and draws an analogy with the Dutch school of painters, much as George Eliot (who admired Scott *and* Austen) would do nearly forty years later in *Adam Bede*.

Scott himself was not unaware of the aesthetic contradictions implicit in a juxtaposition of the productions of Austen and Lewis or, to put it more generally, between those "fictitious biographies" whose purpose it was to instruct and amuse, and those romantic fictions whose purpose it was to arouse strong feelings. The Austen review is only one of many places where he attempts to come to terms with various kinds of truth in fiction, the "probable" and the "improbable," the "natural" and the "unnatural."

It was a major concern of his career to determine the "right" relationship between factual detail — especially of a social, historical or political nature — and a work of imaginative fiction. In a famous and much criticized apology at the beginning of *Waverley*, Scott explains that, for the sake of "probability," he must present certain political information which he admits is dull and slows down his story. He promises "to get as soon as possible into a more picturesque and romantic country, if my passengers incline to have some patience with me during my first stages." [4] Political data are not the only impediments to a swift-moving narrative, for once in "picturesque" country, the place itself and its inhabitants must be minutely described. Fergus MacIvor is examined brogue to bonnet before he is set in motion.

But narrative speed is only one question — and not the most important — raised by the introduction of extensive detail into literature in which adventure, emotional extremes, and fanciful characters play a central role. The larger question has to do with two kinds of perception, public and private. Or, perhaps, more accurately in the case of historical fiction, two kinds of memory, one of which is collective and rationalized, and the other of which is individual and intuitive. The problem, then, is not only one of the relationship between history and legend, but between analytical empiricism and creative synthesis. For many Romantics, the answer was clear. History was inferior to literature, and "cold facts" untransformed by the individual imagination were limitations, if not downright obstacles, to the truth. Wordsworth, in his Preface to the Second Edition of *Lyrical Ballads*, elaborates upon the Aristotelian position:

Aristotle, I have been told, has said, that Poetry is the most philosophic of all writing; it is so: its object is truth, not individual and local, but general and operative; not standing upon external testimony, but carried alive into the heart by passion . . . The obstacles which stand in the way of the fidelity of the Biographer and Historian, and of their consequent utility, are incalculably greater than those which are to be encountered by the Poet who . . . writes under one restriction only, namely, the necessity of giving immediate pleasure to a human Being possessed of that information which may be expected of him, not as a lawyer, a physician, a mariner, an astronomer, or a natural philosopher, but as a Man.[5]

In 1819 Shelley wrote, "Facts are not what we want to know in poetry. They are the mere divisions, the arbitrary points." [6] And in 1825, Hazlitt suggested that Scott's heavy reliance on factual detail was a sign of his creative weakness: "Sir Walter would make a bad hand of a description of the Millennium, unless he could lay the scene in Scotland five hundred years ago, and then he would want facts and worm-eaten parchments to support his drooping style. Our historical novelist firmly thinks that nothing is but what has been." [7] It is true that at the conclusion of his first novel, Scott pointed out that "the most romantic parts of this narrative are precisely those which have a foundation in fact." It is also true that his fondness for footnotes, genealogies, and what he called *vraisemblance* did not diminish as his career progressed.

2

One way out of the difficulty is to reject the "romantic" label which has so long been attached to his works and to claim for him a place among realistic novelists. Georg Lukács argued that Scott's ordinary and passive protagonists reveal his rejection of hero-worship and therefore express "a renunciation of Romanticism, a conquest of Romanticism." David Daiches has said that Scott's best fiction is anti-romantic and, more recently, Edgar Johnson has argued that *Waverley* is "not a romantic novel at all but an ironic novel of a young man's education." The reasoning in support of these claims cannot be dismissed and, in any case, we can certainly agree with Johnson that Scott was "no belated minstrel sentimentally eulogizing the past." Yet perhaps in an effort to correct a popular misconception of Scott, the case has been stated too strongly. In a balanced introduction to his study of Scott, Francis R. Hart suggests that it may be as misleading to call Scott "anti-Romantic as it is to call him Romantic . . . It is more useful to classify him . . . as an ironist for whom Romantic values are an essential part of a serious ironic vision." [8]

Certainly, in most of Scott's fiction the values of Romanticism — especially the validity of individual imaginative perception — and the demands of the external world come into conflict. Whether one argues that "fact" intrudes on the more interesting realm of imagination or that absurd fancies spoil engrossing probabilities depends more on the reader's taste than on Scott's practice. The point is that there are two distinct tendencies in most of his novels and that one of them, despite efforts to change Scott's image, is romantic.

Scott often spoke of art and his own role as an artist in romantic terms. Though most of his works are morally instructive, he wrote in his Journal that "all the Fine Arts have it for their highest and more legitimate end and purpose, to affect the human passions, or smooth and alleviate for a time the more unquiet feelings of the mind — to excite wonder, or terror, or pleasure, or emotion of some kind." [9] His intent was to appeal first to the feelings of his readers and only secondarily to their judgment and conscience. Despite his eagerness to achieve verisimilitude in his fiction, he saw his life, after ten years of publishing novels, as "a sort of dream, spent in 'chewing the cud of sweet and bitter fancy.' I have worn a wishing cap, the power of which has been to divert present griefs by a touch of the wand of imagination, and gild over the future prospect by prospects more fair than can ever be realized." [10]

In addition to his admiration for Lewis and the Germans, he was a lover of Oriental tales and exotic adventures of all sorts. He wrote an introduction to an Edinburgh edition of *The Castle of Otranto*, calling the "wild interest of the story" and its capacity to "excite the passions of pity and fear" praiseworthy and "remarkable." He even started a romance in imitation of Walpole's "with plenty of Border characters and supernatural incident" which he called *Thomas the Rhymer* and allowed to be published in its unfinished form in the 1829 edition of his works. He corresponded with Maturin, who sent him the manuscript of *Bertram*, and he projected an edition of that author's works until the bankruptcy of his publishers and his own financial losses made it impossible. He reviewed *Frankenstein*, finding it sufficiently impressive to think it the work of Shelley himself and, according to Ballantyne, preferred it to any of his own romances. In short, Scott did not devote all of his time to the study of "facts and worm-eaten parchments."

Of his Scottish novels, the three which hold up best as works of fiction without attaining an altogether satisfactory integration of history and legend are *Waverley*, *Rob Roy*, and *The Bride of Lammermoor*. Of the three, *Rob Roy* is the most conventionally heroic; *The Bride of Lammermoor*, with its ghostly apparition, its three churchyard crones, and its mad damsel, is the most nearly Gothic; *Waverley* (1814), the first of the great series, is not only one of the best, but it is also one of the narratives in which Scott tries most explicitly to define the romantic sensibility and its relation to the world of social and moral responsibility. In this novel Scott writes with detachment about the mind of a Romantic, as well as, from time to time, revealing its habits from the inside.

3

Edward Waverley, a dreamy young Englishman whose imagination is the "predominant faculty of his mind," spends his youth, as Scott did, reading Shakespeare, Milton, and Spenser "and other poets who have exercised themselves on romantic fiction," in addition to "picturesque and interesting passages from our old historical chronicles" and the "chivalrous and romantic lore" of France and Spain. Commissioned at an early age into the British Army, he joins his regiment in Dundee and, when summer comes, requests a leave of absence to visit a friend of his uncle's near the Highlands. Though still in Lowland country, Waverley's approach to the Highlands brings him to the edge of a world which hitherto he had only dreamt of or read about in books.

Upon his hero's arrival at the Bradwardine Manor House at Tully-Veolan, Scott applies the term "romantic" with judicious caution three times to Waverley's initial impressions. Upon first seeing the house itself, the young hero finds the "solitude and repose of the whole scene

. . . almost romantic," but what presumably prevents it from being more than that is an open gate which lets in the sunlight, "a long line of brilliancy . . . flung upon the aperture up the dark and gloomy avenue."

The first member of the household who greets Waverley is the simple-minded Davie Gellatley who is described as having a "prodigious memory stored with miscellaneous snatches and fragments of all tunes and songs." His is indeed a private nonhistorical memory since it was from a gifted and adored brother that he learned his songs and from the shock of that brother's early death that he lost his reason. His songs do not convey coherent ideas, but rather reflect moods of deep melancholy or sudden gaiety. Though charmed and fascinated by Gellatley, Waverley finds his story only "bordering on the romantic." His background is sad but not mysterious and he has preserved "just so much solidity as kept on the windy side of insanity." Gellatley is not quite crazy enough to satisfy the hunger of Waverley's imagination.

Finally, the young and beautiful lady of the house, Rose Bradwardine, does not at first stir Waverley's heart because, as Scott explains, "she had not precisely the sort of beauty or merit which captivates a romantic imagination in early youth. She was too frank, too confiding, too kind; amiable qualities, undoubtedly, but destructive of the marvellous." She gives Waverley no opportunity "to bow, to tremble, and to adore," and, therefore, cannot qualify in his mind as even "bordering" on the romantic. To him, she is a nice girl who would make a tolerable cousin or sister, but who could hardly be thought of as the mistress of his affections.

In all three cases, Scott is treating his hero's romanticism ironically as a kind of adolescent fever fed by exotic reading. He comes to Tully-Veolan craving, or imagining that he craves, darkness, solitude, mad passions, and a *femme fatale* at whose feet he can worship. He is a bit disappointed to find a cheerful house, a good-natured simpleton, and a healthy Lowland lass. In fact, up to this point in the novel, Waverley seems a masculine Catherine Morland about to be instructed in the ways of conventional modes of behavior and modest expectations in the civilized world. But at precisely this crucial moment, Scott's hero — and, in a way, Scott himself — takes leave of his sensible companions and, through a series of unlikely circumstances, finds himself irresistibly

142

led into a world which does indeed correspond to the yearnings of his imagination.

Waverley accepts an invitation to visit the Highland retreat of a robber chieftain and, later on, the manor of Fergus MacIvor, the head of a great Highland clan in rebellion against the House of Hanover. As the contour of the land and the nature of the characters encountered resemble more and more nearly the expectations of young Waverley, Scott's ironic tone diminishes and the personality of the hero — his way of seeing things — becomes a matter of less and less significance. Edward is quite literally swallowed up by his new environment. The discrepancy between the hero's perceptions and his surroundings no longer prevails because, temporarily, Scott has allowed the romantic vision to become the reality.

Waverley had wanted darkness and solitude and, as he follows his Highland guide who speaks almost no English, he finds himself as though alone, crossing at sunset into the Highlands, through a "path which was extremely steep and rugged," past an ancient burial ground, through a "thick, and, as it seemed, an endless wood of pines . . . [where] the path was altogether indiscernible in the murky darkness." Like Emily St. Aubert entering the Castle of Udolpho, Waverley is gradually deprived of his normal sensory perception as he is conducted further and further north. He cannot see well and, unacquainted with Gaelic, he can understand little that is said. Moreover, he does not know the way and must rely upon someone else to guide him.

On more than one occasion he is struck down and unable to move under his own power. Soon after his arrival at the house of MacIvor, he is nearly crushed by a herd of stags during a hunt and, as it is, sustains a badly sprained ankle when his host saves him by throwing him abruptly to the ground. Waiting for his injury to heal, Waverley is unable to return to his regiment on time and is assumed to be a traitor and deserter. When, finally, he tries to return he is placed under military arrest, is subsequently "rescued" against his will by his Highland friends, once again is thrown to the ground and injured, and once again finds himself "hurried along" through the night nearly "deprived of sensation." When his Highland attendants protectively wrap "our hero's body in one of their plaids," Waverley's symbolic initiation into their alluring but forbidden world is almost complete. His conscience and

143

reason subdued, he is conducted by the Highlanders as though they are the personified agents of his own imagination.

4

And where does Waverley's dark journey lead him? In the beginning, as he might have hoped, it takes him to the imperious, raven-haired lady of his dreams. The beautiful Flora MacIvor, the Highland chieftain's proud sister, instantly captures the young Englishman's heart. The description of his first important rendezvous with her, to which he is conducted by one of her ladies-in-waiting, sets the tone of their relationship:

It was up the course of this last stream that Waverley, like a knight of romance, was conducted by the fair Highland damsel. A small path . . . led him through scenery of a very different description from that which he had just quitted . . . This narrow glen seemed to open into the land of romance. The rocks assumed a thousand peculiar and varied forms.

Waverley notices a narrow footbridge made of two pine trees laid between the points of two high projecting rocks:

While gazing at this pass of peril, which crossed, like a single black line, the small portion of blue sky not intercepted by the projecting rocks on either side, it was with a sensation of horror that Waverley beheld Flora and her attendant appear, like inhabitants of another region.

In the preparation of this scene, Scott has done everything in his power to present Flora MacIvor to the reader as well as to his hero as though she were the inhabitant of "another region." It is Scott who likens his hero to a knight and who calls the place a "land of romance." And, of course, it is Scott's imagination, not Waverley's, which contrives to make the lady materialize against the sky like a celestial apparition. As usual, everything is, as it were, technically propped up, but Waverley, despite his susceptibility, cannot be altogether blamed for finding the sight unusual. Once well north of the Tweed, Scott is not so ready as Jane Austen to present his excitable hero with prosaic companions in conventionally furnished rooms.

Of course, it is as unthinkable for Waverley to marry Flora as it would be if she were a spirit instead of a woman. First, she does not love him; second, she is a Catholic; and third, her single ruling passion is to stand by her brother and the Jacobite cause. Across the perilous and dark pass is a mysteriously beautiful woman, but, behind her is the real object of Waverley's journey, her brother and masculine counterpart, the opposite of the young English gentleman, and yet the very image of his privately imagined self. Superficially, Fergus and Waverley seem to form contrasts in everything: Fergus is dark, physically robust, a man of action, strong will and quick temper; Waverley is pale and fair, unused to physical exertion, a dreamer more than a doer, and possessed of a mild, even passive, temperament. But Fergus represents a way of life which Waverley, though he has never considered the political or moral consequences, has spent his youth reading about and imaginatively living. Fergus MacIvor lives in the feudal past as the patriarch of an ancient clan, the chieftain of his own army, the lord of his own castle, surrounded by retainers and minstrels, and given to presiding over boisterous banquets, battle games, and lusty hunts. Fergus lives in a glorious madness, specifically because of his single-minded intention to risk all for the Stuart cause, but, more generally, because his whole way of life constitutes a rebellion against the present. This clinging to the past attracts Waverley, while the legal and moral implications of its concrete form remain dimly in the background.

It is some time before Waverley consciously realizes where MacIvor's ambitions and his own reveries are leading him. When Fergus speaks out against the "usurping House of Hanover" for the first time in Waverley's presence, telling him that his own grandfather would no more have served it "than he would have taken wages of red-hot gold from the great fiend of hell," the young Englishman coolly points out that "since the time of my grandfather, two generations of this dynasty have possessed the throne." But Waverley's practical English sense and his partial willingness to accommodate himself to present reality is no match for the glamor of his Highland friends and the inclination of his own imagination. He allows himself to be carried further and further along in the process of identification with MacIvor and therefore with his dream-self. Not only does he admire his host's life and make love to his sister, but soon after the Highland blanket is thrown over his shivering form, he finds himself sufficiently recovered to pay homage to Prince Charles and to don a uniform ordered for him by MacIvor:

"Get a plaid of MacIvor tartan, and sash . . . and a blue bonnet of the Prince's pattern . . . My short green coat, with silver lace and silver buttons, will fit him exactly . . . The Prince has given Mr. Waverley broadsword and pistols, I will furnish him with a dirk and purse; add but a pair of low-heeled shoes, and then, my dear Edward . . . you will be a complete son of Ivor."

MacIvor and Prince Charles have not only decked Waverley out in a fetching costume, they have equipped him for battle against his own army and nation. At the point where Waverley seems most literally to have assumed his new persona as another MacIvor, the claims of his English home to the south — law, order, and present circumstances — reassert themselves against those of his Highland retreat into the past. Vaguely disturbed by the rapidity and confusion of events, Waverley fully realizes the consequences of his behavior when he is faced with the concrete reality of being on the opposite side of the battlefield from his own countrymen:

They approached so near, that Waverley could plainly recognize the standard of the troop he had formerly commanded, and hear the trumpets and kettle-drums sound the signal of advance, which he had so often obeyed. He could hear too the well-known word given in the English dialect, by the equally well-distinguished voice of the commanding-officer, for whom he had once felt so much respect. It was at this instant that, looking around him, he saw the wild dress and appearance of his Highland associates, heard their whispers in an uncouth and unknown language, looked upon his own dress, so unlike that which he had worn from his infancy, and wished to awake from what seemed at the moment a dream, strange, horrible, and unnatural.

In an instant, Waverley's reason regains ascendancy over his imagination. He, of course, does not raise his hand against his countrymen nor does he injure or betray his Highland friends. Almost as suddenly and inexplicably as he had found himself in the Highlands, he finds himself on the way home, a sadder, wiser, and humbler man. "He acquired a more complete mastery of a spirit tamed by adversity than his former experience had given him . . . He felt himself entitled to say firmly, though perhaps with a sigh, that the romance of his life was ended, and that its real history had now commenced."

When his case is discussed by a clergyman and a military magistrate, the sympathetic parson attempts to excuse Waverley's Highland adventures:

"Surely youth, misled by the wild visions of chivalry and imaginary loyalty, may plead for pardon."
"If visionary chivalry and imaginary loyalty come within the predicament of high treason," replied the magistrate, "I know no court in Christendom . . . where they can sue out their Habeas Corpus."

In making his hero see his dangerous journey as somehow not real, as a dream or an adolescent phase to be outgrown, Scott, like the kindly parson, relieves him from responsibility. But, of course, by doing so, he also deprives him of greater interest as a character. After presenting a serious confrontation between the irrational urges of a romantic sensibility and the demands of an ordered society, he retreats from the most important issues of the conflict. If Scott could not take his Catholics and his Jacobites with sustained seriousness, one feels he might at least have had more faith in the psychological truth, if not the practical wisdom, of his hero's dream. But, like Beckford, he mistrusted his own visions and had unsettling doubts about the "holiness of the heart's affections." Ruskin's remark comes to mind: "The most startling fault of the age being its faithlessness, it is necessary that its greatest man should be faithless. Nothing is more notable or sorrowful in Scott's mind than its incapacity of steady belief in anything. He cannot even resolve hardily to believe in a ghost." [11] The title of the novel prepares us for a wavering hero; it does not prepare us for a wavering author.

5

But if Scott is to be blamed for failing to believe in his Highland "ghosts," it is partly because he has been so successful in creating them in the first place. His evocation of the "land of romance" in the central portion of the novel is too compelling and disturbing to be dismissed as an adolescent's idealization of a few crude outlaws. During many important chapters of the book, Scott, as well as Waverley, is under the spell. A reader can only balk at being told that those parts of the narrative which are most lively and, in one sense, most nearly true, cannot be thought of as part of the hero's "real history." [12] The moral lesson in prudence does not obliterate the experience for the reader, and it hardly seems possible that it could for Waverley. His dangerous and shocking encounter with an unconscious and forbidden aspect of himself would seem more likely to arouse than to subdue his mind. It is disappointing to find Scott stopping where Conrad would have begun.

It must be admitted, however, that some warning is given that Edward Waverley will be no Lord Jim to agonize over inconsistencies within himself. In her analysis of his character, Flora MacIvor paints Waverley's nature in a manner which resembles the placid hero of an Ann Radcliffe novel more than it does the tormented protagonists of later romantic literature:

"High and perilous enterprise is not Waverley's forte . . . He will be at home . . . and in his place — in the quiet circle of domestic happiness, lettered indolence, and elegant enjoyments, of Waverley-Honour. And he will refit the old library in the most exquisite Gothic taste, and garnish its shelves with the rarest and most valuable volumes; and he will draw plans and landscapes, and write verses and rear temples, and dig grottoes; and he will stand in a clear summer night in the colonnade before the hall, and gaze on the deer as they stray in the moonlight . . . He will repeat verses to his beautiful wife . . . and he will be a happy man."

The speech contains a good description of fashionable romantic melancholy and an even more sharply ironic view of Waverley than Scott presents as the narrator earlier in the novel. Scott's earlier inferences, like Jane Austen's concerning Catherine Morland, were that his hero's foibles were largely the consequence of youth, inexperience, and an inadequately supervised education. Flora, rather than excusing Waverly because of his past, projects an image of him in the future as a comfortable dilettante, a collector of rare volumes and exquisite moments, savoring melancholy vistas while inwardly feeling perfectly content with himself. For her, Waverley's "Romanticism" is not a deep discontent, a vision or way of life, but a taste, a mood, a mannerism, which may affect the way he decorates his house, but not the way he conducts his life.

Thus, we are served two views of Waverley, as a gullible adolescent or a hopeless aesthete, both of which excuse him from the consequences of a mature involvement in his departure from duty. In the beginning and again at the end of *Waverley*, Scott "explains" the dream by discrediting the dreamer. Just as he apologizes for his facts in the name of probability, he apologizes for the glamor of the Highland episodes by stressing the ephemeral nature of his hero's susceptibilities. Neither apology is worth much, and the latter makes us want to come to Waverley's defense. He may not be much of a hero, and there are times when his indecision is annoying, but there are signs of something more than a weakling and a dummy in him. Scott's ironic attitude, as has been pointed out, is not altogether consistent. In some of the best Highland scenes — the courting of Flora MacIvor, the banquets and ballad singing, the piping and preparation for battle, the secret meeting with the dashing young Chevalier — Scott unites with his hero in relishing the moment. After the vigor and pageantry of the Highland scenes, the attempt to resume the ironic note seems clumsy and unconvincing. If the hero has been a fool to be attracted by the Jacobites, then so has the author.

But if there is inconsistency in the tone Scott adopts toward Waverley, there are also inconsistencies in factual detail which, if we are receptive to the author's wish for authenticity, we cannot overlook. Waverley may have started his Highland adventure as a weak and inexperienced youth, but despite his various injuries and fevers, he does make progress. During the march south toward battle, we are told:

As Colonel MacIvor's regiment marched in the van of the clans, he and Waverley, who now equalled any Highlander in the endurance of fatigue, and was become somewhat acquainted with their language, were perpetually at its head.

Only a few pages earlier, Waverley refers to the "uncouth and unknown language" of his associates. But what is more important than the hero's sudden knowledge of Gaelic is the fact that he is not, at this point, being dragged along, but is stoutly leading the regiment with MacIvor. Furthermore, despite Flora's remarks about his not being fit for "high and perilous enterprize," he shows skill and courage on the battlefield when he saves the life of an English officer separated from his troops. Later on, in another skirmish, Waverley sees MacIvor and two others surrounded by English soldiers, but "the moon was again at that moment totally overclouded, and Edward, in the obscurity, could neither bring aid to his friends, nor discover which way lay his own road to rejoin the rear-guard." It must be noted that neither the obscurity nor the weakness is *in* Waverley. Scott draws the shade on his hero and leaves him fumbling about in the dark. Despite the narrator's patronizing ironies and Flora MacIvor's disparaging evaluation, one sometimes has the impression that Edward Waverley is a hero whose potentialities are externally suppressed rather than internally thwarted by his own frail character.

If Scott were really so detached from his hero as he appears to be in the ironic passages of the novel, he would probably have been less anxious about "saving" him from himself and absolving him from the responsibility of his rebellious interlude. But the author's peculiarly protective attitude toward his wayward hero suggests that he sympathizes with him to the point of being afraid *for* him. But afraid of what? The most obvious answer and the one provided openly in the text is, of course, treason. Scott himself was a Lowlander and, despite his admiration for Highland pluck and old clan traditions, he was a loyal British subject. He did not want his own glorification of the Scottish past to be misconstrued by English readers as disloyalty. Yet the specific shapes which his romantic dreams often took did tend to hover close to political ambiguity. By making Waverley, in part, an unconscious victim of adolescent imprudence, he avoids a crisis with which he is not ready to cope.

6

But perhaps of even more significance than the concrete question of political loyalty is the larger, more general one of allegiance to present realities rather than to past glories. It is once again the interaction between the historical "facts" which are responsible for the institutions, boundaries, and customs of the present and the legendary visions which endow men and events with ideal qualities. When Scott means most earnestly to have the past come alive, he usually loads his narrative with factual details which are intended to endow it with the substantiality of the present. If, however, the heavily weighted descriptions are not shaped by the enthusiasm of his imagination, the opposite effect occurs and the past remains remote and inert. In *Waverley*, the reader is introduced to two realms of experience, one of which is evidently *supposed* to seem more real than the other because it is more thoroughly presented and more closely linked with the world as it was in the year the novel was published. And it should be said that the Lowland scenes in *Waverley* are richly and convincingly rendered. Yet the color and emotional variety of the forbidden realm give it a life which possesses authenticity of another kind. At his best, Scott is capable of creating both Highlands and Lowlands, two versions of reality, one of which is ultimately repudiated in favor of the other. In the end, what seems most stimulating to his creative imagination is almost invariably that which is unacceptable to his reason.

By speeding his hero quickly home, Scott not only saves him from the course of treason, but he also saves him from death. Fergus MacIvor, whose role Waverley had attempted to imitate, is captured by the English, executed, and his head gruesomely displayed on the Scotch Gate of Carlisle Castle. Waverley is not permitted to attend the last moments of his friend, but nonetheless MacIvor's death represents the symbolic amputation necessary to save Waverley's rational self. He is not destined, like so many romantic heroes, to go on haunted by a dangerous dream because the personifications and symbols of the dream are made to vanish. The prognostication for Waverley who returns to marry Rose Bradwardine and to resume his manly duties with a new sense of responsibility and self-discipline is that, unlike Davie Gellatley, he will be too little rather than too much disturbed by private memories.

The failure of Waverley's romantic vision to carry over into his conscious life is one sign of the quality of Scott's own romantic perception. If there is a part of Scott which recoils from the seductive extremes of his imagination, it is because there is also a part of him which recognizes where they tend. As Romantics like Keats and Shelley both realized, the imaginative pursuit of the ideal, when carried to the extreme, can result in a gradual loosening of ties with common life and a yearning for the ultimate absolute which can be found only in death. Scott's romantic ideal is often misunderstood or underestimated because it takes the form of legendary adventure rather than, as in much great romantic poetry, a natural or aesthetic symbol. But just as Keats imaginatively "joins" his protagonist in *Endymion* or in *The Ode to a Nightingale*, Scott cannot seem to help uniting himself imaginatively with Waverley until forced to rear back suddenly, shocked by his brief encounter with eternity and "forlorn" at the thought of returning to a mortal existence. Since Scott is writing fiction rather than poetry, the abrupt shift in attitude creates certain problems of credibility in the manipulation of the plot. But symbolically, the sudden "waking" from the dream is perfectly fitting. Scott sees *for* his hero that the rebellion against present circumstance in favor of the past, as represented by Fergus MacIvor in his championing of the Jacobite cause, is not only political treason but a rejection of life and inevitably a voluntary embracing of death.

Scott saves his hero from the battlefield and the executioner's axe, and he also saves him from the continuation of an ideal journey which leads him from liberty to alluring liberty, and finally to a wasteland of violence, destruction, and chaos. As Waverley moves further and further north at the beginning of the novel, he temporarily sheds his old self. He leaves behind his family, his country, his regiment, and the sunny clarity with which moral and legal problems are viewed and solved in a country of civilized law and order. And he enters a rude and dark wilderness where he dwells in a kind of trance, sees new and comely apparitions, and follows them for no other reason than that he wants to. But, though Waverley's movements may seem random and unpremeditated on his part, they were not so on the part of the author. Robert Louis Stevenson was justified in calling *Waverley* one of the best plotted of Scott's novels. From the beginning, when Waverley follows his Highland guide through the night until a "small point of light was seen . . . and gradually increasing in size and lustre, seemed to flicker like a meteor on the verge of the horizon," the hero is headed, stage by stage, to the limit of that horizon. First, there is the robbers' cave which, in its natural simplicity, diverts his mind from the civilized comforts of Lowland and English manor houses. Then, having in a sense left his era as well as his country, he is ready for the castle of the Highland chieftain and the manners of a medieval court. The sight of the beautiful dark lady, Flora, draws him emotionally further, not toward sexual union with her, but toward kinship with her brother and consequently with her brother's cause. His path is studded alternately with exotic beauties and colorful heroes, but it leads toward treason and self-destruction. When, at last, Waverley finds himself on the battlefield, he behaves as bravely as he can until, by special arrangement with the heavens,

Scott plunges him into darkness. Light does eventually return, the morning after battle, but it is neither lustrous nor meteroic:

A brief gleam of December's sun shone sadly on the broad heath, which . . . exhibited dead bodies of men and horses, and the usual companions of war — a number of carrion-crows, hawks, and ravens.

Waverley walks slowly over the "field of death," searching among the wreckage and the corpses for the body of MacIvor, but not finding it there, leaves the scene and begins the journey southward toward reason and "real history."

As we are discovering to be the case in most romantic fiction, the ending of this book raises as many questions as it answers. What is real for Waverley? Has he improved or worsened in the course of his "education"? Is his return a pathetic compromise or a triumph of reason and virtue? David Daiches and Harry Levin see an aesthetic and even temperamental flaw in Scott's tendency to conform. Daiches suggests that "the tragic sense that romantic man must compromise with his heroic ideals . . . gives way as the book comes to a close to the less elevated sentiments of the realistic common man." [13] Levin sees Scott himself as a curious combination of quixotic idealism and shrewdness: "His conducted tours of the highlands, starting from the library and returning to the counting-house, compromised discreetly between Jacobite adventure and Hanoverian comfort. Romance became his business." [14]

In defense of Scott, and arguing, as Lukács does, that his subject "is the history of a society not the dramatic interaction of particular individuals," Karl Kroeber points out that readers have too often made inappropriate demands on Scott: "Where we pity the individual, Scott celebrates the race." [15] As a corrective, the suggestion is useful, but it does not solve the problem. The truth is that there are moments when Scott, as well as the reader, pities Waverley, the dreamy individualist. Even so ordinary and bland a hero has been made too interesting to sacrifice to historical necessity without a qualm.

Thus, the narrowness of Waverley's escape and the cleanhandedness with which he is permitted to walk away from his harrowing adventure are likely to appear unsatisfactory to some readers. But they go far in explaining Scott's belief in the deceptive power of the imagination, his mixed feelings about the consequences of pursuing visions, and his insistence upon clinging to the reassuring materiality of facts.

Walter Pater, who made a distinction between "the literature of fact" and "the literature of the imaginative sense of fact," argued that truth for the artist ought not to be a matter of reliance on externals but of "the finer accommodation of speech to that vision within." [16] It is the kind of statement Scott would have liked. But Samuel Butler expressed a view which comes closer to Scott's own attitude toward the accommodation of the individual imagination to the day-to-day business of living in the world:

All our lives long, every day and every hour, we are engaged in the process of accommodating our changed and unchanged selves to changed and unchanged surroundings; living, in fact, is nothing else than this process of accommodation; when we fail in it a little we are stupid, when we fail flagrantly we are mad, when we suspend it temporarily we sleep, when we give up the attempt altogether we die.[17]

Extreme Romanticism was, for Scott, a failure or refusal to "accommodate" oneself to changed and unchanged surroundings at the expense of the "vision within." Throughout his life, he was attracted by this refusal to cooperate. But his was no flagrant failure. And he preferred temporary suspension to giving up the practice altogether.

VIII

FRANKENSTEIN

Mary Wollstonecraft Shelley
1818

It is something of a miracle that *Frankenstein*, originally published in 1818, has survived its admirers and critics. Although Scott had admired the Germanic flavor of *The Monk*, he praised the author of *Frankenstein* for writing in "plain and forcible English, without exhibiting that mixture of hyperbolical Germanisms with which tales of wonder are usually told."[1] On the other hand, Beckford, who had little use for earnest horror, noted on the flyleaf of his first edition copy of *Frankenstein*: "This is, perhaps, the foulest Toadstool that has yet sprung up from the reeking dunghill of the present times."[2]

Opinion about *Frankenstein* was strong from the beginning, but no critical thinking on the subject was more elaborate and self-conscious than that of Mary Shelley herself. The genesis of this novel was — even for a work of romantic fiction — uncommonly bookish and artificial. It was supposedly begun as part of a literary contest among Shelley, Mary, Byron, and Polidori to write a ghost story in a vein popular in Germany and France.[3] During the first year of her marriage to Shelley, Mary had set herself a formidable and exotic reading assignment which included *Clarissa*, *The Sorrows of Young Werter*, *Lara*, *The Arabian Nights*, *Wieland*, *St. Leon*, *La Nouvelle Héloïse*, *Vathek*, *Waverley*, *The Mysteries of Udolpho*, *The Italian*, *The Monk*, and *Edgar Huntley*.[4] She repeatedly acknowledged the influence of Milton and Coleridge during this period of her life and, of course, Godwin and Shelley were major forces in shaping her mind.

Frankenstein seems a little book to have borne up under such a mixed and mighty company of sponsors, midwives, and ancestors. Mary Shelley did not set out, like her father, to write a philosophical novel, yet her most famous work, written at Shelley's suggestion and dedicated to Godwin, is, to a large extent, an expression of her reaction to the philosophy and character of these two men. In places the narrative seems chiefly to provide the occasion for Mary to write a tribute to her father's idealism and a love poem to her husband. The hero of her novel, the young Genevese student of natural science, is a magnetic character, described by one admiring friend as possessing attributes which seem almost divine:

Sometimes I have endeavoured to discover what quality it is which he possesses that elevates him so immeasurably above any other person I ever knew. I believe it to be an intuitive discernment; a quick but never-failing power of judgment; a penetration into the causes of things, unequalled for clearness and precision; add to this a facility of expression, and a voice whose varied intonations are soul-subduing music.[5]

Yet despite such expressions of love and veneration for the nobility of Frankenstein, Mary expresses through her characters certain reservations about him which have led some readers to interpret the novel as an unconscious repudiation of Shelley. As M. K. Joseph puts it, "With unassuming originality, [Mary's] 'modern Prometheus' challenges the whole myth of Romantic titanism, of Shelley's neo-Platonic apocalypse in *Prometheus Unbound,* and of the artist as Promethean creator."[6] Frankenstein is brilliant, passionate, sensitive, and capable of arousing feelings of profound sympathy in others, yet he is the creator of a monster which causes great suffering and finally destroys his maker. Signs of impatience and outright disgust with the obsessive ambitions of the hero are certainly present in the narrative.

Still, Frankenstein remains the hero throughout; he is the "divine wanderer," his face lighted up by "a beam of benevolence and sweetness," his spirit enlivened by a "supernatural enthusiasm." He is compared not with Faustus but with Prometheus in his desire to grasp "the secrets of heaven and earth." No one suffers more than he from his failure, and, indeed, there is a strong hint that the fault is more nature's than his that his godlike ambitions result in a monstrosity. For Mary, as for Shelley, nature's imperfect character only confirmed a belief in the superiority of mind over matter. After her husband's death, Mary referred to him as "a spirit caged, an elemental being, enshrined in a frail image," [7] and confessed her reverence for the artist who would rather destroy his health than accept the limitations imposed by the body, whose "delicately attuned [mind] shatters the material frame, and whose thoughts are strong enough to throw down and dilapidate the walls of sense and dikes of flesh that the unimaginative contrive to keep in such good repair." [8]

In her novel *The Last Man*, published eight years after *Frankenstein*, Mary's narrator takes it as a universal truth "that man's mind alone was the creator of all that was good or great to man, and that Nature herself was only his first minister." [9] And in that same novel there is a character named Adrian, even more obviously patterned after Shelley than is Frankenstein, whose "slight frame was overinformed by the soul that dwelt within." [10] The fact that he is "all mind" does eventually make him behave strangely, but the implication is that the fault is the world's or society's, not his.

Applying the same logic to Frankenstein's attempt to manufacture a man, one might argue that the structural faultiness, the grotesqueness of the result, is another example of nature's failure to live up to man's expectations. Even the fact that the monster becomes a murderer and brings about the destruction of his master does not necessarily detract from the grandeur of Frankenstein's dreams. If he has not been able to create human life, he has been able to create a sublime facsimile. To some, a destructive force was still better than no force at all and the creation of a new menace better than a copy of a worn-out consolation. The Shelleys, like their friends Byron and M. G. Lewis, were fascinated by the correspondence between the terrifying and the magnificent, the proximity of ruinous and constructive forces at the highest levels of experience. "Nothing should shake the truly great spirit which is not sufficiently mighty to destroy it," said Shelley in reference to the personal relationships of geniuses.[11] The risk of calamity becomes the measure of all endeavor, and a great catastrophe is preferable to a small success. Viewed in this way the catastrophic abomination represented by Frankenstein's creature is not proof of its creator's folly, but an inverse indication of his potential greatness.

Potentiality is a key concept in the delineation of Frankenstein's character because, like so many romantic heroes, much of his allure derives from what he might have been, what he almost was, rather than from what he is. "What a glorious creature must he have been in the days of his prosperity," says his friend Walton, "when he is thus noble and godlike in ruin! He seems to feel his own worth and the greatness of his fall." The days of Frankenstein's prosperity do not occupy much of the narrative, but it is nonetheless clear that Walton is not altogether right. Though a good and gifted person before his "ruin," it is really afterward, by means of the uniqueness and depth of his suffering, that Frankenstein achieves superiority over other men. Having made a botch of his experiment, he may fail to impress any but the most loyal advocates in the days of his prosperity. But where actual achievement falters, the guilty and disappointed spirit can sketch the dimensions of its unfulfilled intention by describing the magnitude of its torment. We are reminded of Macaulay's remark about Byron: "He continued to repeat that to be wretched is the destiny of all; that to be eminently wretched, is the destiny of the eminent." [12]

2

Superiority through suffering is a major theme of Mary Shelley's novel, a romantic half-tragedy in which the fall from greatness is nearly all fall or, more accurately, where greatness is defined in terms of the personal pain which results from the consciousness of loss which cannot be recalled or comprehended by other men. In unique regret, Frankenstein discovers his true distinction: "I was seized by remorse and the sense of guilt which hurried me away to a hell of intense tortures, such as no language can describe." The failure of language, as always in romantic fiction, is meant to be a sign not of vacuity or of an imaginative limitation of the character or author, but of the singular noncommunicable nature of great experience.

It is unfortunate (though psychologically fitting) that in the popular mind the monster has assumed the name of his creator, because Mary Shelley considered it of some importance that the creature remain unnamed. As Elizabeth Nitchie points out, it was the custom in dramatic performances of *Frankenstein* to represent the monster's part on the playbill with "_____." On first remarking this, Mary Shelley was pleased: "This nameless mode of naming the unnameable is rather good." [13] If the phenomenon itself cannot be named, neither can the feelings it evokes in its maker. No one can know what it is like to be the monster or its "parent."

What cannot be described cannot be imitated, and the pain it causes cannot be relieved. The following lines are Frankenstein's, but they might as easily have been spoken by the creature as by its creator:

"Not the tenderness of friendship, nor the beauty of earth, nor of heaven, could redeem my soul from woe: the very accents of love were ineffectual. I was encompassed by a cloud which no beneficial influence could penetrate. The wounded deer dragging its fainting limbs to some untrodden brake, there to gaze upon the arrow which had pierced it, and to die — was but a type of me."

"Gazing upon the arrow" can be a fairly protracted occupation even when no use is expected to come of it. Mary Shelley spends a great part of her narrative confronting her hero with images which evoke the sublimity of his mental state where ordinary words fail. Frankenstein journeys to Chamonix, where the mountain views elevate him from all "littleness of feeling" and "subdue and tranquilize" his grief though they cannot remove it. Mont Blanc provides him with a moment of "something like joy," but the Alps, though briefly impressive, are not in the end any more able than words to express or alleviate what Frankenstein feels. Trips up the Rhine, across the sea, even into the Arctic, hint at his unrest, but "imperial Nature," in all her "awful majesty," can no more provide truly adequate images of his misery than she can provide the fulfillment of his ambitious dreams.

At the end of the narrative, Frankenstein accuses himself of overreaching, but even in doing this, he immodestly compares himself with the prince of overreachers: "Like the archangel who aspired to omnipotence, I am chained in an eternal hell." Rather than looking back on his ambition with disgust, he remembers it with pleasure: "Even now I cannot recollect without passion my reveries while the work was incomplete. I trod heaven in my thoughts, now exulting in my powers, now burning with the idea of their effects." Despite the conventional speeches about the dangers of pride, it becomes more and more evident in the last pages of the novel that Frankenstein, though regretting the result of his extraordinary efforts, is not ashamed of having made the effort in the first place. He repeatedly warns Walton, who is engaged in an expedition into the Polar Sea, to content himself with modest ambitions and a quiet life, but when Walton's men threaten to turn the ship back, the dying Frankenstein rallies to urge them on:

"Did you not call this a glorious expedition? And wherefore was it glorious? Not because the way was smooth and placid as a southern sea, but because it was full of dangers and terror . . . You were hereafter to be hailed as the benefactors of your species; your names adored as belonging to brave men who encountered death for honor and the benefit of mankind."

In his last breath, he begins to warn Walton once more not to make the same mistake he did, but then changes his mind:

"Seek happiness in tranquility and avoid ambition, even if it be only the apparently innocent one of distinguishing yourself in science and discoveries. Yet why do I say this? I have myself been blasted in these hopes, but another may succeed."

That Frankenstein does not die absolutely repentant once again raises the possibility that the monstrous result of his experiment was not the inevitable issue of pride but an accident of circumstance, the result of insufficient knowledge, or an imperfection in nature itself. If one wishes to accept Walton's reverent appraisal of his new friend, it can be said that Frankenstein has the immunity of all scientific and artistic genius from conventional morality, that he is somehow apart from and superior to material circumstances even when he himself seems to have brought them about. Just as Mary saw Shelley "caged" in a "frail image" and surrounded by misfortunes from which his superiority of mind detached and elevated him, so Walton sees Frankenstein as a man with a "double existence." "He may suffer misery and be overwhelmed by disappointments; yet, when he has retired into himself, he will be like a celestial spirit that has a halo around him, within whose circle no grief or folly ventures."

3

Mary learned her lessons in idealism well, and there is in her narrative a level on which her hero is above reproach. But it must be admitted that there is a mundane side to this fantastic tale. If genius can escape or withdraw from the material universe, ordinary mortals cannot.

And however great their admiration for genius may be, they cannot fully separate it from the lesser objects of their perception.

Mary Shelley was a young and impetuous woman when she ran off with the poet; she was also an intelligent woman, but her journals and letters reveal that despite her efforts to form herself after her husband's image, common sense often intruded and made the task difficult. She was never intellectually disloyal to Shelley, yet she admitted that her mind could not follow his to the heights. Her novel, like almost every- thing else about her life, is an instance of genius observed and admired but not shared. In making her hero the creator of a monster, she does not necessarily mock idealistic ambition, but in making that monster a poor grotesque patchwork, a physical mess of seams and wrinkles, she introduces a consideration of the material universe which challenges and undermines the purity of idealism. In short, the sheer concreteness of the ugly thing which Frankenstein has created often makes his am- bitions and his character — however sympathetically described — seem ridiculous and even insane. The arguments on behalf of idealism and unworldly genius are seriously presented, but the controlling perspective is that of an earthbound woman.

In making her hero a scientist rather than a poet or philosopher, Mary could hardly have avoided treating the material consequences of his theoretical projects. But, in almost all important respects, Frankenstein's scientific ambitions are at the level where they coincide with the highest desires of artists and metaphysicians, to investigate the deepest mysteries of life, to determine causes and first principles. The early descriptions of Frankenstein's youthful dreams are filled, like more recent forms of "science fiction," with outlandish schemes which combine the highest fancies of the imagination with an elaborate application of technical ingenuity. Though Frankenstein himself scorns the notion, his "scien- tific" method has a large dose of hocus-pocus in it and comes a good deal closer to alchemy than it does to physiology. The professor whom he most admires disclaims the inflated schemes of ancient pseudo- scientists, but then proceeds to claim for modern scientists the godlike ambitions previously invoked by poets and prophets:

"Modern masters promise very little; they know that metals cannot be transmuted, and that the elixir of life is a chimera. But these philosophers, whose hands seem only to dabble in dirt, and their eyes to pore over the microscope or crucible, have indeed performed miracles. They penetrate into the recesses of nature, and show how she works in her hiding places. They ascend into the heavens . . . They have acquired new and almost unlimited powers; they can command the thunders of heaven, mimic the earthquake, and even mock the invisible world with its own shadows."

The passage sounds like an answer to the Lord's questions about knowledge and power in the Book of Job. The obvious echoes of Biblical language show, among other things, that science is making religion (or, more particularly, the fear of God) obsolete. But, beyond this, the speech might be passed over as a conventional piece of hyperbole if Mary did not undercut it sharply by proceeding to show her hero trying literally to put his professor's words into practice by penetrating the "recesses of nature." Frankenstein digging about in graveyards and charnel houses, matching eyeballs and sawing bones, is not an inspiring sight. Even less so is the bungled construct of muscles, arteries, and shriveled skin which he had intended as a perfectly proportioned and beautiful being. The gap between the ideal and the real, the ambition and the accomplishment, produces a result as gruesome and absurd as any pseudo-science of the Middle Ages. Still, Mary is not criticizing exalted ambition, but the misapplication of it, the consequences of what Frankenstein himself describes as "unrelaxed and breathless eagerness," a "frantic impulse," a trance-like pursuit of one idea. Through the mouth of her hero, she raises a question which in life she could probably never bring herself to ask her husband: "Is genius forever separate from the reasonable, the reflective, and the probable?"

The question is one which troubled a great many romantic artists and critics. Hazlitt, for one, did not accept such a division as inevitable, and he criticized Shelley in words which parallel almost exactly Frankenstein's own terms of self-criticism after the failure of his experiment:

Shelley's style is to poetry what astrology is to natural science — a passionate dream, a striving after impossibilities, a record of fond conjectures, a confused embodying of vague abstractions — a fever of the soul, thirsting and craving over what it cannot have, indulging its love of power and novelty at the expense of truth and nature, associating ideas by contraries, and wasting great powers by their application to unattainable objects.[14]

Hazlitt's impatience with Shelley, as expressed in the opening analogy, is based, to a large degree, on the poet's departure from the natural.

Shelley himself was deeply aware of the problem, and *Alastor, or the Spirit of Solitude,* was, in part, a criticism of the pursuit of truth under unnatural conditions of isolation. The poet's invocation to Mother Nature could have been spoken by Frankenstein during the research which led to the creation of the monster:

> . . . I have made my bed
> In charnels and on coffins, where black Death
> Keeps record of the trophies won from thee;
> Hoping to still these obstinate questionings
> Of thee and thine by forcing some lone ghost,
> Thy messenger to render up the tale
> Of what we are. In lone and silent hours,
> When night makes a weird sound of its own stillness,
> Like an inspired and desperate alchemist
> Staking his very life on some dark hope,
> Have I mixed awful talk and asking looks
> With my most innocent love; until strange tears,
> Uniting with those breathless kisses, made
> Such magic as compels the charmèd night
> To render up thy charge.

The passage describes a kind of necrophilia, an unnatural probing into the secrets of nature; and yet, despite his disapproving moral, the poet appears to luxuriate in the contemplation of the forbidden and fruitless act. It is, after all, the poet-narrator, not Alastor, who is speaking in this passage. As the image of the "inspired and desperate alchemist" suggests, the question remains as to whether a poet of sufficient genius can transform inert and unlikely objects into "gold"; or, to extend the sexual metaphor of the lines, whether the intercourse of mind with dead matter can produce new and vital images of nature. Shelley seems to be reasoning in the negative and rhyming in the affirmative. He argues in the preface to *Alastor,* that no truly great human effort can succeed if it is removed from the nourishing warmth of "human sympathy." Yet neither his poetry nor his life provides consoling solutions to the solitude genius so often creates for itself. Even an early and, for Shelley, relatively simple definition of love must have given Mary uneasy moments.

Love . . . is . . . the universal thirst for a communion not merely of the senses, but of our whole nature, intellectual, imaginative, and sensitive; and which, when individualized, becomes an imperious necessity . . . The

163

sexual impulse, which is only one, and often a small party of (its) claims, serves, from its obvious and external nature, as a kind of type or expression of the rest, a common basis, an acknowledged and visible link.[15]

It is not the kind of statement D. H. Lawrence would have admired, nor can its Platonism have been altogether comforting to a companion for whom the "visible link" of sex was the one claim not rivaled by Byron, Peacock, Hogg, Hunt, or Trelawny.

4

In describing the way in which Frankenstein's experiment seems most "unnatural," Mary Shelley implies a definition of the natural which is peculiarly feminine in bias. For her, Frankenstein's presumption is not in his attempt to usurp the power of the gods — she quite willingly grants him his "divine" attributes — but in his attempt to usurp the power of women. "A new species would bless me as its creator and source," says Frankenstein in the enthusiasm of his first experiments. "No father could claim the gratitude of his child so completely as I should deserve theirs." He seeks to combine the role of both parents in one, to eliminate the need for woman in the creative act, to make sex unnecessary. At least that would be the net result of his experiment if it were successful, despite the fact that he himself tends to see its consequences in grander and vaguer terms. Thus, while Mary grants her hero the nobility and even the innocence of his intentions, she cannot help but undercut them with her own womanly sense of how things are.

Stripped of rhetoric and ideological decoration, the situation presented is that of a handsome young scientist, engaged to a beautiful woman, who goes off to the mountains alone to create a new human life. When he confesses to Walton that he has "worked hard for nearly two years" to achieve his aim, we may wonder why he does not marry Elizabeth and, with her cooperation, finish the job more quickly and pleasurably. But one must be careful not to imply that Mary's irony is flippant or altogether conscious. Quite to the contrary, her reservations about her hero's presumptuous idealism are so deeply and seriously felt that they produce a symbolic nightmare far more disturbing and gruesome than the monster itself. As soon as the creature begins to show animation and Frankenstein realizes that he has made an abomination, the scientist races to his bedroom, paces feverishly about, and finally falls into a troubled sleep:

"I slept indeed, but I was disturbed by the wildest dreams. I thought I saw Elizabeth, in the bloom of health, walking in the streets of Ingolstadt. Delighted and surprised, I embraced her; but as I imprinted the first kiss on her lips, they became livid with the hue of death; her features appeared to change, and I thought that I beheld the corpse of my dead mother in my arms; a shroud enveloped her form, and I saw the graveworms crawling in the folds of the flannel. I started from my sleep with horror . . . (and) beheld the wretch — the miserable monster whom I had created."

In this extraordinary rendition of an Oedipal nightmare, Mary shows, without moral comment, the regressive depths of her hero's mind. Frankenstein's crime against nature is a crime against womanhood, an attempt — however unconscious — to circumvent mature sex. For Mary, this is the supreme symbol of egotism, the ultimate turning away from human society and into the self which must result in desolation. Having moved away from family, friends, and fiancée to perform his "creative" act in isolation, Frankenstein later beholds the monster, in a grotesquely exaggerated re-enactment of his own behavior, "eliminate" his younger brother, his dearest friend, and his beloved Elizabeth.

All the crimes are sins against life in the bloom of youth and beauty, but the murder of the woman is the most effectively presented and, in a way, the most carefully prepared. Frankenstein's fears on his wedding night are presumably due to the monster's threat to pursue him even to his marriage chamber. But the immediate situation and the ambiguity of the language contribute to the impression that the young groom's dread of the monster is mixed with his fear of sexual union as a physical struggle which poses a threat to his independence, integrity, and delicacy of character. Frankenstein describes the event in the following manner:

"I had been calm during the day: but so soon as night obscured the shapes of objects, a thousand fears arose in my mind. I was anxious and watchful, while my right hand grasped a pistol which was hidden in my bosom; every sound terrified me; but I resolved that I would sell my life dearly, and not shrink from the conflict, until my own life, or that of my adversary, was extinguished.
"Elizabeth observed my agitation for some time in timid and fearful silence; but there was something in my glance which communicated terror

to her, and trembling she asked, 'What is it that agitates you, my dear Victor? What is it you fear?'

" 'Oh! peace, peace, my love,' replied I; 'this night and all will be safe; but this night is dreadful, very dreadful.'

". . . I reflected how fearful the combat which I momentarily expected would be to my wife, and I earnestly entreated her to retire, resolving not to join her until I had obtained some knowledge as to the situation of my enemy."

Frankenstein leaves the room, and it is while he is away that his bride is murdered by the monster on her untried marriage bed. The passage is filled with the language of anxiety, phallic inference, and imagery of conflict, yet it is in Frankenstein's absence — not in an eager assertion of his physical presence — that harm comes to Elizabeth. If we take the monster to be one side of Frankenstein's nature, an alter-ego, then we see his physically potent self as brutish, ugly, and destructive, completely unintegrated with his gentle spirit. To depict a radical separation of mind from sexuality is one way to explore an unsatisfactory rapport between the imagination and the natural world. But what is important in the thematic terms of the novel is not the mere existence of the separation, but the fact that physical life is made ugly (indeed, is made to wither and die prematurely) because it is inadequately tended by the mind. The problem is not abuse but neglect.

The importance of the wedding night scene lies in its sexual connotation insofar as that provides the basic and concrete context in which, once again, to exemplify the hero's withdrawal from physical and emotional contact with living human beings. There are earlier instances of his separating himself from his family and from his friend Clerval, even while protesting, as he has with Elizabeth, that he continues to love them in spirit. The outrage dramatized in this novel is not restricted to a specifically sexual offense — nor is it directed against genius or ambition or idealism. The enemy is an egotism which, when carried to the extreme, annihilates all life around it and finally destroys itself.

5

While the main theme of the novel is the monstrous consequences of egotism, the counter-theme is the virtue of friendship. For, as Frankenstein's crime is seen as a sin against humankind more than

166

against the heavens, it is through human sympathy, rather than divine grace, that it might have been avoided or redeemed. In her treatment of friendship, Mary shows the Coleridgean side of herself. She sees a friend as a balancing and completing agent, one who is sufficiently alike to be able to sympathize and understand, yet sufficiently different to be able to correct, and refine. Above all, the friend, in giving ear to one's dreams and sufferings, provides not only a temporary release from them, but the immediate excuse to order them by putting them into words.

The entire narrative of *Frankenstein* is in the form of three confessions to individuals with whom the speaker has unusually close ties. First, the young explorer Robert Walton writes to his sister in England as he journeys into the Arctic. There he rescues Frankenstein from a shipwreck and listens to his tale, which, in turn, contains a long narrative spoken by the monster to its creator. There is not a great deal of difference in the styles of the three narratives, though the emphasis in each is determined to a large extent by the speaker's relation to the listener. Walton's sister is an affectionate English lady who needs to be reassured that her brother is not in too much danger. He is lonely and he writes to her in detail about everything, trying usually to maintain an air of competence and calm. Frankenstein is a genius on the verge of despair and death, brought to glow again by the admiration of his rescuer. He tells his story to dissuade Walton from ruining himself similarly through excessive ambition, spares no emotion or rhetoric, and condescends to him from the superiority of his suffering. The monster wants pity from his creator; his narrative is the most sentimental of the three and the most pathetically modest in its claims.

Each narrator speaks of the importance of friendship — Walton and the monster because they feel the lack of it, Frankenstein because he has had friends and lost them. In Walton's second letter to his sister, he reports that he has hired a ship and is ready to set sail on his dangerous journey. The one thing that troubles him is that, though he has a well-trained crew, he has no soul companion:

I have one want which I have never yet been able to satisfy . . . I have no friend . . . When I am glowing with the enthusiasm of success, there will be none to participate in my joy; if I am assailed by disappointment, no one will endeavour to sustain me in dejection . . . I desire the company

167

of a man who could sympathize with me; whose eyes would reply to mine. You may deem me romantic, my dear sister, but I bitterly feel the want of a friend. I have no one near me, gentle yet courageous, possessed of a cultivated as well as of a capacious mind, whose tastes are like my own, to approve or amend my plans. How would such a friend repair the faults of your poor brother!

When Walton's ship picks up the nearly frozen body of Franken- stein, the explorer hopes that at last he has found the ideal friend. He nurses, consoles, and entertains the survivor, but when he approaches the subject of friendship, Frankenstein, as always, agrees in theory, but finds a reason not to become involved in the situation at hand:

"I agree with you . . . we are unfashioned creatures, but half made up, if one wiser, better, dearer, than ourselves — such a friend ought to be — do not lend his aid to perfectionate our weak and faulty natures. I once had a friend, the most noble of human creatures, and, am entitled, there- fore, to judge respecting friendship."

Frankenstein condescends to poor Walton even on the subject of friendship. It is too late for him to take up any new ties in life, he explains, because no man could ever be more to him than Clerval was and no woman more than Elizabeth. Of course, as Walton and the reader soon discover, despite Frankenstein's avowals of mutual influence and attachment, neither Clerval nor Elizabeth had any effect on him at all after his childhood and early youth. In fact, it is precisely the qualities which each of them personifies which might have saved Frankenstein from proceeding in his mad experiment. Clerval, though refined and cultivated, is essentially the outgoing, energetic, and enter- prising friend who would counsel Frankenstein to climb the mountain rather than brood over it. Elizabeth was the "saintly soul," whose love softened and attracted, and who, whenever with Frankenstein, subdued him "to a semblance of her own gentleness."

Mary was sufficiently her mother's daughter to assume that a woman, as easily as another man, could be the soul companion, the ideal friend, of a man. She did not regard sexual love as an impediment to ideal friendship, nor, it would seem, as a "small party" of the claims of true love. Elizabeth and Frankenstein almost always address one another as "dear friend," and she and Clerval simply complement different sides of Frankenstein's nature. If it were to come to a choice of one or the other, the novel leaves little doubt that the feminine companion is the more valuable since she can provide both spiritual sympathy and physical affection. It is a great and painful loss for Frankenstein when Clerval is killed, but the death of Elizabeth is the end of everything for him. He dedicates himself to the pursuit and destruction of the monster, follows him to "the everlasting ices of the north" where, surrounded by blankness and waste, he confronts the sterility and uselessness of his life in a setting which anticipates that of the conclusions of Poe's *A. Gordon Pym* and Lawrence's *Women in Love*, and which was itself inspired by *The Ancient Mariner*.[16] Walton writes to his sister that he goes to "the land of mist and snow" partly because Coleridge's poem has instilled in him "a love for the marvelous." But in *Frankenstein*, unlike *The Ancient Mariner*, the icy region is not an early stage of a long and redemptive journey, but an end point, a cold blank, an image of sterility and failure.

An earlier scene of frozen desolation associated with isolation from human — especially feminine — companionship takes place between Frankenstein and the monster on a glacier at the base of Mont Blanc. The monster begs his maker to listen to him and proceeds to explain in detail how he has observed and imitated the ways of man, but is shunned because of his ugliness and is forced to wander over glaciers and hide in caves of ice because these are the only dwellings "man does not grudge." In other words, despite the bizarre details associated with his creation, the monster's lament is much the same as that of the physically presentable Caleb Williams: the world does not see him as he really is. His narrative is punctuated by outcries of loneliness:

"Everywhere I see bliss, from which I alone am irrevocably excluded."

"When I looked around, I saw and heard of none like me."

"I had never yet seen a being resembling me, or who claimed any intercourse with me. What was I?"

"I am an unfortunate and deserted creature . . . I have no relation or friend upon earth."

The repetition of this theme, with slight variations, continues throughout the monster's narrative. However ludicrous or grotesque it may seem in the concrete, it is nonetheless in keeping with one of

the central arguments of the novel that the monster should ask Frankenstein to make him a wife. This, in fact, is the object of his narration:

"If I have no ties and no affections, hatred and vice must be my portion;
the love of another will destroy the cause of my crimes . . . My vices are
the children of a forced solitude that I abhor; and my virtues will necessarily arise when I live in communion with an equal. I shall feel the affections of a sensitive being, and become linked to the chain of existence and
events, from which I am now excluded."

The irony of the situation, though heavy-handed, is effective. Having
removed himself from human companionship and the sexual means of
procreation, Frankenstein brings into being a creature who, though not
innately evil, is a torment to himself and to others precisely because
he is without companionship and a sexual counterpart. In this respect
the monster may well be taken as Frankenstein's alter-ego, his strange
and destructive self, which finds no adequate means of communication
with others, no true resemblances, no reciprocation, a repressed and
hidden beast for whom all acceptable forms of human commerce are
unavailable and therefore hateful. Frankenstein himself calls the unnameable creature "my own spirit let loose from the grave . . . forced
to destroy all that was dear to me."

6

Mary saw, as did her father, the duality in human nature which is
capable of bringing misery and ruin to the most gifted of beings. Her
novel is not so pessimistic as *Caleb Williams* nor are the solutions implied in it so optimistic as those outlined in *Political Justice*. Neither
her father's trust in system nor her husband's unworldliness seemed
satisfactory to her. On the contrary, judging from the events of her
novel, both alternatives were too likely to lead to that single-mindedness
which, when carried to the extreme, was a kind of insanity. It would
seem, in fact, that of all the romantic influences on her mind and
work, Shelleys' undoubtedly stimulated, but Coleridge's comforted;
Shelley's provided confusion and enchantment, Coleridge's provided
psychological and moral consolation. The ethereal reveries of her hero
are loyal attempts to imitate Shelley, but they are among the most
strained and unconvincing passages of the novel. Mary's natural in-

clination was toward synthesis, integration, a constant effort to find balance, relationship, correspondence, to root all ideals in natural process, and to find in nature the external signs of an ideal region. Her heart is with those, described by Coleridge, "who measuring and sounding the rivers of the vale at the feet of their furthest inaccessible falls have learned, that the sources must be far higher and far inward." [17] Despite his supposedly scientific approach to things, Frankenstein's error is to circumvent an elementary principle of nature in trying to achieve his rather vaguely conceived ambition.

In stressing friendship, and especially heterosexual love, as her "river of the vale," the natural symbol of a higher necessity, Mary presents her own concrete version of the theory of correspondence. We must give her more credit than to think that she supposed the problems of all men — including geniuses — would be solved by marriage to a good woman. What she does mean is that no being truly exists — except in an insane wilderness of its own creation — unless it finds and *accepts* a relationship of mutual dependence with another. The rapport with otherness is both the link with the objective world and the condition for self-delineation.

In his tenth essay from *The Friend*, Coleridge says, "In a self-conscious and thence reflecting being, no instinct can exist without engendering the belief of an object corresponding to it, either present or future, real or capable of being realized." [18] Mary Shelley's definition of a monster is precisely that being to which nothing corresponds, the product of a genius who tried to exercise its will without reference to other beings. Even Caleb Williams, at least until Falkland's death, is better off than the monster in that he can draw energy to shape some identity for himself from his strange bond with his master. Godwin wrote in his preface that he amused himself with the parallels between his story and that of Bluebeard: "Caleb Williams was the wife, who in spite of warning, persisted in his attempts to discover the forbidden secret; and, when he had succeeded, struggled as fruitlessly to escape the consequences, as the wife of Bluebeard in washing the key of the ensanguined chamber."

Frankenstein's first act after creating a new life is to disown it. The problem is not, as in *Caleb Williams*, an ambiguous fascination leading to abuse and immediate and obsessive pursuit. As soon as his dream is realized in concrete form, Frankenstein wants nothing to do with it. Despite his claims to scientific interest, he demonstrates no wish whatever to observe and analyze the imperfect results of his experiment. When he does finally pursue the monster, it is not in order to possess, dominate, or torment it, but to annihilate it. Though there is something ludicrous in the way the monster stumbles upon books and learns to read during his lonely wandering, the thematic consistency of the episode is unmistakable. The monster is most impressed by *Paradise Lost*; he compares himself with Adam before the creation of Eve, but, like a good Romantic, he finds Satan an even "fitter emblem" of his condition. Still, neither emblems, nor words can really help or define him any more than ordinary men can. He can find parallels but no connections and he concludes his encounter with books by envying Satan like all the others, for even he "had his companions."

The two dominant themes of *Frankenstein* never truly harmonize, nor does one succeed effectively in canceling out the other. Surely, the most explicit "moral" theme of the novel — expressed by the author with genuine conviction — is that man discovers and fulfills himself through others and destroys himself alone. Yet played against this, not so much as an argument but as an assumption, is the idea that the genius, even in his failures, is unique, noble, and isolated from other men by divine right.

Frankenstein is neither a pure hymn of praise to Godwin and Shelley nor a simple repudiation of them. Mary's uncertainties are not reflected in parody or burlesque, as Beckford's and Lewis's are in *Vathek* and *The Monk*. Her prose style is solemn, inflated, and imitative, an unhappy combination of Godwin's sentence structure and Shelley's abstract vocabulary. Whatever else she may have thought, Mary obviously did not regard her father or husband as silly. Her reservations about them were deep, complex, and mixed with genuine admiration.

After Shelley's death, Mary considered how best to educate her son, and a friend advised that she teach him to think for himself. Mary is said to have answered, "Oh my God, teach him to think like other people!" [19] If the young wife had been able to speak with the emphatic clarity of the widow, she probably would have had fewer nightmares and *Frankenstein* might never have been written. The book is a bad dream entwined with a moral essay. Like all romantic fiction, it resounds with the fascinating dissonance which usually results from intimate encounters between irrational symbols and reasonable statements.

IX

NIGHTMARE ABBEY

Thomas Love Peacock

1818

Shelley played a prominent role in another novel published the same year as *Frankenstein*. But if Mary Shelley's work is based on a troubled and qualified admiration, Peacock's appears on first reading to be founded on unqualified scorn. The fact, however, is not that simple. Peacock once said, with what might be taken as understated mockery, that "there was not much comedy in Shelley's life," [1] yet he was one of the few men who found Shelley amusing and at the same time liked and admired him. In his *Memoirs of Percy Bysshe Shelley*, Peacock presents an anecdotal and sympathetic picture of the poet's career, but though he describes the tragedies of Shelley's private life, he prefers to remember him as a charming eccentric rather than as a figure of pathos.

He recalls how Shelley "fancied that a fat old woman who sat opposite to him in a mail coach was afflicted with elephantiasis . . . and that he had caught it from her." The poet developed the habit of pinching his skin to check for symptoms and on occasion "he would seize the person next to him, and endeavour by a corresponding pressure to see if any corresponding deviation existed. He often startled young ladies in an evening party by this singular process." [2] Peacock also recalls how in the summer of 1816 Shelley announced one day that a strange man unseen by others in the house had visited him, walked with him to Egham, and warned him of "immediate personal perils." Peacock, believing that Shelley suffered from "semi-delusions," decided to cross-examine his friend:

I said, "What hat did you wear?" He said, "This, to be sure." I said, "I wish you would put it on." He put it on, and it went over his face. I said, "You could not have walked to Egham in that hat." [3]

And, finally, though he often speaks of Shelley's good humor and kind nature, Peacock likes to recall the poet's displeasure and alarm when his solitude was threatened. He describes him leaping over a hedge and throwing himself in a ditch to avoid a passerby in Bishopgate and, on another occasion, he remembers him jumping out of the window when the servant announced a caller he did not wish to see. [4]

Hypochondria, paranoid delusions, and a morbid fear of strangers are hardly comic in themselves, yet it is characteristic of Peacock to show that excesses of the mind may be diminished, if not entirely dispelled, by encounters with the commonplace. The process is not one whereby insanity is converted to sanity by patient reasoning, but rather one whereby an obsession is reduced by circumstances to a quirk.

Controlled irony and mild amusement were not Peacock's weapons against Romanticism. He knew too many Romantics too well to be able to preserve detachment in writing about them; he also delighted in theoretical dispute for its own sake, even if few of the theories in question conformed with his own notion of things. As a house guest of the Shelleys, he seems to have alternated between feeling himself a mediocrity among geniuses and a sane intruder in an asylum of madmen. A poet of no particular distinction himself, he was fascinated by the minds of poets. Though not really a philosopher, he followed the metaphysical and epistemological disputes of his period with perception and interest if not with approval. Though not professionally a critic, his *Four Ages of Poetry* provoked one of the great defenses of poetry in English and remains in itself a stimulating piece of criticism. In short, to say Peacock was not a Romantic is by no means to place him outside the circle.

In his fiction, as in his well-known essay on poetry, Peacock wields his common sense like a crotchet. He carries it too far, talks about it too much, tries to make it do too many things, and finally amuses himself with it as much as he does with the excesses which he appears to be criticizing. The introduction of reason is not for Peacock, as for Jane Austen, a way of restoring order to a world which had begun to lose its balance, but a way of exposing absurdity by joining it at its own level. There is no stabilizing, "saving" irony behind the crazy speeches in Peacock's novels. The voice of reason joins the general babble, and, if anything, is compromised by the gusto of participation. In the end, it is not the sanity of Peacock's humor which one admires, but its gaiety, its refusal to be serious in an age when frivolity was not the literary fashion.

The satirical method of *The Four Ages of Poetry,* though more limited in scope, is essentially the same as that of the novels. Peacock begins what appears to be a serious discussion in which his own case is presented in an orderly and sensible manner and that of the opposition as a tissue of illogical quirks and contradictions. As his own argument grows more and more insistent and elaborate, however, it too takes on the coloring of singularity, of a personal passion rather than an unprejudiced inquiry. He becomes a good-natured Swift, imitating the voice of the sober critic and then turning with amusement on the eccentricities of his own argument and, by implication, of any argument which is carried too far. There is no anger or bitterness in his method because he does not attempt finally to demolish either his own original position or the position of those being attacked. The point of his satire is the scuffle itself; each side is meant to come out dishevelled and perhaps slightly bruised, but certainly not ruined. Pomposity, affectation, and fanaticism were meant to be shaken all around, but there is little sense of moral outrage or despair. While critics of the period liked to see themselves as defenders of the faith and the "species," wielding swords against the offenders, and artists liked to imagine themselves as fugitives and outcasts, reincarnations of Prometheus tormented on a Caucasian crag, Peacock tried to change the metaphor to that of a schoolboy tussle with much name-calling and rolling in the mud, after which the participants brush themselves off and go home to have dinner together.

It may be said that Peacock's approach is even less appropriate a response to romantic art than the high-pitched battle cries of the hostile reviewers. Certainly his criticism is not completely serious. He oversimplifies and underestimates many problems, but in an era characterized by so much intellectual inflation, the opposite tendency comes as a refreshing antidote. In *The Four Ages of Poetry* the writer is able both to laugh at the romantic fondness for the remote and to parody the rhetoric of petulant utilitarian critics:

While the historian and the philosopher are advancing in, and accelerating, the progress of knowledge, the poet is wallowing in the rubbish of departed ignorance, and raking up the ashes of dead savages to find gewgaws and rattles for the grown babies of the age. Mr. Scott digs up the poachers and cattle-stealers of the ancient border. Lord Byron cruizes for thieves and pirates on the shores of the Morea and among the Greek Islands. Mr. Southey wades through ponderous volumes of travels and old chronicles, from which he carefully selects all that is false, useless, and absurd . . . and when he has a commonplace book full of monstrosities, strings them into an epic. Mr. Wordsworth picks up village legends from old women and sextons; and Mr. Coleridge . . . superadds the dreams of crazy theologians and the mysticisms of German metaphysics.[5]

Although Peacock relishes his own overstatement as much as he does making certain romantic practices appear foolish, he builds his elaborate verbiage around a grain of seriously intended criticism. His picturing of the Romantics as "raking," "wallowing," "digging," and "wading," is not merely a display of vivid language, but a characteristic attempt to bring poets and poetry "down to earth," even if it has to be done with a ridiculous thud. One of his persistent objections to romantic poetry was its unworldliness, by which he meant primarily its departure from the world of men living together in modern society. Shelley realized this when Peacock first sent him a copy of *Nightmare Abbey*: "I suppose the moral is contained in what Falstaff says, 'For God's sake, talk like a man of this world.' " [6] But although his main emphasis is social, Peacock also means the world of concrete matter where things are not negated by ideas. In a letter from Milan in 1818, Shelley wrote to Peacock about the way places and persons live on in the mind long after one is physically removed from them: "Time flows on, places are changed; friends who were with us are no longer with us; yet what has been seems yet to be, but barren and stripped of life." And then recognizing what Peacock thinks of visions "stripped of life," he adds, "See, I have sent you a study for *Nightmare Abbey*." [7]

Peacock's ridicule of the romantic interest in the past does not stem from a failure on his part to recognize the importance of history, but from a feeling that romantic literature too often failed to connect the past with the present. Furthermore, each antique invention seemed

177

unrelated to all the others. He saw romantic art as a phenomenon without internal or external coherence, "disjointed relics of tradition and fragments of second-hand observation . . . a modern-antique compound of frippery and barbarism . . . a heterogeneous congeries of unamalgamating manners." [8]

In his insistence upon taking the long view, in assessing many romantic writers at once rather than taking them separately, Peacock reveals his closeness to the eighteenth century. He prefers finding out how things fit together in a pattern to examining them one by one. For him, the Romantics had sacrificed the coherence of the whole for the sake of originality and intensity in the part. In his fiction, as in his essay on poetry, he would show them the folly of their ways — and enjoy a little vicarious foolishness himself — by lumping them all together to prove that they made as little sense to one another as they did to the uninitiated reader.

2

In Nightmare Abbey (1818), he assembles a party of romantic caricatures in a pseudo-romantic setting and gives them little to do but talk to one another. He forces each to strike his most individualistic pose, and to maintain it in the midst of such social conventions as dining in company or courting a wife. In making fun of the Romantics in this way, he demonstrates why there is no such thing as romantic comedy despite an abundance of what may be called romantic humor. Singularity is not comic except when measured against a norm or placed in juxtaposition to other kinds of singularity. Self-contemplation rarely provokes laughter, regardless of what is discovered, simply because it is impossible to preserve the necessary detachment. For most Romantics, detachment was precisely what was to be avoided in favor of imaginative sympathy, the capacity, discussed by Keats in his letter on "negative capability," to feel in and with the object of one's contemplation. Thus, even when Peacock allows them the sincerity of their ideas and the intensity of their feelings, he questions their ability to adapt them to the general welfare or to the simplest conventions of society or language.

Assembled in the "highly picturesque" and semidilapidated mansion of the melancholy Christopher Glowry and his son Scythrop is a company which includes Scythrop's fiancée, Marionetta, the mysterious

Stella, the obscure Mr. Flosky, the brooding Mr. Cypress, the devil-obsessed Mr. Toobad, and the Honourable (and lethargic) Mr. Listless. The parodic resemblance of most of the characters to well-known romantic figures is not particularly subtle and, occasionally, Peacock adds footnotes to make certain the connection is not missed. Scythrop is a caricature of Shelley caught between his love for the pretty but unexceptional Marionetta and the unconventionally intellectual Stella, as he was between Harriet and Mary. Flosky talks like a highly confused Coleridge, and Cypress quotes *Childe Harold* and strikes some of the more obvious Byronic poses. A few cheerful and sensible words are occasionally introduced by Glowry's brother-in-law, Mr. Hilary, who might be said to represent Peacock.

In a letter to Shelley, Peacock explained that his object in writing *Nightmare Abbey* was "to bring into philosophical focus a few of the morbidities of modern literature and to let in a little daylight on its atrabilious complexion." [9] His complaint is not simply that the Romantics occupy themselves too much with sorrow, but that they go about it in an idle, self-indulgent fashion, and invent imaginary miseries rather than coping with real ones. In one of the key dialogues of the book, Mr. Hilary upbraids Cypress for continually condemning nature, the world and mankind:

"To expect too much is a disease in the expectant, for which human nature is not responsible; and, in the common name of humanity, I protest against these false and mischievous ravings. To rail against humanity for not being abstract perfection, and against human love for not realizing all the splendid visions of the poets of chivalry, is to rail at the summer for not being all sunshine, and at the rose for not being always in bloom." [10]

It can hardly have escaped Peacock's notice that without the "disease" described by Hilary, a great deal of poetry, pre-romantic as well as romantic (and certainly including Shakespeare's sonnets), would never have been written. And yet he lets Hilary go on to accuse Cypress of talking like a man "who will love nothing but a sylph, who does not believe in the existence of a sylph, and who yet quarrels with the whole universe for not containing a sylph." Finally, Hilary offers a code, at least partly based on Peacock's rationalistic and humanistic views, outlining man's moral responsibilities: "To reconcile man as he is to the world as it is, to preserve and improve all that is good, and destroy or alleviate all that is evil, in physical and moral nature."

But, though a spokesman for reasonable compromise, Mr. Hilary does not dominate the narrative. He speaks his sensible piece from time to time, but his insistently cheerful practicality eventually appears as inflexible and almost as irrelevant as the melancholy fancies of the others. His approach to life is different from the others', but it is not necessarily broader or more vital. The only real advantage he has over the Glowry circle is that his philosophy and vocabulary are socially oriented while each of theirs is a form of private meditation. He is equipped for the salon and they are not. Furthermore, his primary objection is not to his friends' thoughts, but to what they say. When he protests "in the common name of humanity," it is against the "mischievous ravings" of Cypress more than against his beliefs or behavior. It is an assumption of Mr. Hilary, and it would appear of Peacock himself, that under the basic circumstances of life, men all think and behave in more or less the same way. When one is hungry, one eats; when tired, one sleeps; when lonely, one seeks company; when frightened, one runs; when in love, one mopes. In Peacock's world, the differences among characters are not so much revealed in what they do, but in the way they talk about what they do. "We live in a world of misnomers," declares Mr. Gryll during a discourse on the name of a soup in the first chapter of *Gryll Grange*. The main targets of Mr. Gryll's wrath are politicians and other holders of public office who deliberately misuse language to protect themselves. "I have found that a gang of swindling bankers is a respectable old firm . . . (and) that a man who successively betrays everybody that trusts him, and abandons every principle he ever professed, is a great statesman, and a Conservative, forsooth, a *nil conservando*." [11]

3

In the Peacockian view, Romantics are people who construct vocabularies and invent philosophical systems which obscure the common nature of man, not for political but for misguided poetical purposes. Hence, *Nightmare Abbey*, like most of Peacock's comic fiction, is a novel in which language is abstruse while the motivation of the characters is crystal-clear. It is the opposite of the Hemingway novel in which people speak with the simplicity of children even though they often do not know what they are doing or why they are doing it. Like Jane Austen, Peacock finds that despite their own laments and protestations, most Romantics were not at a loss for words. On the contrary, many of them had the tendency to say much more than a given situation warranted. It is important to see that the criterion for both Austen and Peacock *is* the situation, the event publicly unfolded rather than privately conceived. Peacock's satiric method is much closer to parody than Austen's, but he too forms tacit understandings with his reader by means of which his characters are viewed with reference to a standard different from that indicated by their own verbal formulations. An early conversation between Glowry and Scythrop is typical. The reader has already been presented with certain clear and simple facts: the speakers are father and son, the father has chosen a wife for his son, the son prefers another. The obvious question, asked by Glowry, is "What is to be done?" What follows is not a further examination of the problem, but a recitation of Godwinian philosophy, commenced by Scythrop:

"Indeed, sir, I cannot say. I claim, on this occasion, that liberty of action which is the co-natal prerogative of every rational being."
"Liberty of action, sir? There is no such thing as liberty of action. We are all slaves and puppets of a blind and unpathetic necessity."
"Very true, sir; but liberty of action, between individuals, consists in their being differently influenced, or modified, by the same universal necessity; so that the results are unconsentaneous, and their respective necessitated volitions clash and fly off in a tangent."

It is evident that the father is saying, "You must," and the son answering, "I won't," and that the elaborate Godwinian terminology is ludicrously out of place. It is the usual procedure in parody to employ a vocabulary or style out of its normal context, but Peacock's thrusts at various romantic styles have a double force because it is the particular object of romantic writers to create their own psychological contexts. Words cohere and make sense more in terms of the perceptions of a particular mind than in terms of an objectively presented world. But Peacock withholds the presence of one governing mind with which the reader can identify and through which he can ascertain the norms of the fictional world to which he has been introduced. Even

Mr. Hilary takes his place at table modestly among the others. What mocks inflated or foolish language is not, as in Jane Austen, better language, but life, daily events, which, even at the simplest, occur quickly and create new circumstantial contexts.

Peacock's "setting" for human experience is not a lonely chamber or a prison cell, but a full table or a crowded drawing room which people are constantly entering or leaving. In such a world, everyone is to some degree "out of context" simply because the context continually changes in accordance with movements and events largely beyond the control of any individual. Thus, even though the action may be relatively simple and consist only of entrances, exits, and a few minor frights and surprises, no one, including Mr. Hilary, possesses a vocabulary or a philosophical system which can keep him permanently free from "dislocation" of one sort or another. Life, in the novels of Peacock, is a series of episodes in which one is caught more or less off balance. The wise man is the one who recognizes that and busies himself restoring equilibrium before the next blow falls. The romantic "fool" is one who imagines his mind superior to circumstances and insists upon absorbing everything into his preoccupations.

Mr. Flosky, the character modeled after Coleridge, would seem to be a more thoroughgoing Romantic than Glowry or Scythrop. He repeatedly attempts to transcend circumstances with a vocabulary very much his own and to draw whatever fragmentary words and events he notices into the web of his own metaphysical and semantic meditations. When Scythrop's fiancée Marionetta goes to Flosky for information about her lover, she finds herself trapped in the involutions of his mind without learning anything about Scythrop. Flosky obstructs communication by taking up various of Marionetta's words as words rather than accepting them in their obvious context. Flustered by the strange dialogue, Marionetta tries to tell Flosky that she suspects Scythrop of being in love with someone else:

Marionetta. I think, Mr. Flosky — that is, I believe — that is, I fancy — that is, I imagine —
Mr. Flosky. The τουτεστί, the *id est*, the *cioé*, the *c'est à dire*, the *that is*, my dear Miss O'Carroll, is not applicable in this case . . . Think is not synonymous with believe — for belief, in many most important particulars, results from the total absence, the absolute negation of thought, and is

thereby the sane and orthodox condition of mind; and thought and belief are both essentially different from fancy, and fancy, again, is distinct from imagination. This distinction between fancy and imagination is one of the most abstruse and important points of metaphysics. I have written seven hundred pages of promise to elucidate it.

Flosky is presented as being either more eccentric, more withdrawn from reality, than even Glowry or Scythrop or as a greater fraud than either of them, since he uses his obscurantist talk on an innocent girl and they only on one another. Flosky is either too erratic to carry on a simple conversation or he is too proud to admit that he has no information about Scythrop.

There are moments, however, when Flosky shows himself capable of speaking and acting very much to the point. One such moment comes — and this may be said for most of the other characters as well — when he wishes to attack romantic practices which he has outgrown or romantic views which he has never shared. Flosky, like most of the Glowry circle, scorns making "connections," but can be surprisingly lucid in enunciating distinctions. He never describes anything so clearly as those literary schools from which he wishes to disassociate himself. Thus, one evening, he heaps fairly coherent scorn on "graveyard" poetry and Gothic fiction, even while admitting that in his younger days he had written a few ghostly poems himself:

That part of the *reading public* which shuns the solid food of reason for the light diet of fiction, requires a perpetual adhibition of *sauce piquante* to the palate of its depraved imagination. It lived upon ghosts, goblins, and skeletons . . . till even the devil himself . . . became too base, common, and popular, for its surfeited appetite . . . And now the delight of our spirits is to dwell on all the vices and blackest passions of our nature, tricked out in a masquerade dress of heroism and disappointed benevolence; the whole secret of which lies in forming combinations that contradict all our experience, and affixing the purple shred of some particular virtue to that precise character, in which we should be most certain not to find it in the living world.

Flosky's references to "experience" and the "living world" remind us that, despite his transcendentalism, he has not lost contact with earth altogether, especially when it comes to finding fault with his contemporaries. In fact, the empirical logic of his criticism as well as his scornful tone are hardly parodies of Coleridge at all, but faithful echoes of passages from the *Biographia Literaria* which had been published the year before *Nightmare Abbey*. Despite his own interest in the supernatural, Coleridge really did dislike Gothic sensationalism and he was morally offended by the increasing popularity of the "outlaw hero," treated sympathetically in the works of Schiller, Maturin, and Byron. He argued that some authors had found a formula for "originality," a sure way of surprising their audiences

by representing the qualities of liberality, refined feeling, and a nice sense of honor . . . in persons and classes where experience teaches us least to expect them; and by rewarding with all the sympathies which are the due of virtue, those criminals whom law, reason, and religion have excommunicated from our esteem.[12]

4

Hazlitt remarked in his essay on Coleridge: "The present is an age of talkers, and not of doers; and the reason is that the world is growing old." [13]

Though he saw the same symptoms as Hazlitt, Peacock's prescription was closer to that of Carlyle. He saw a remedy to melancholy and what he considered the incoherence of Romanticism in the establishment of a better balance between words and action. It is the major and least subtle irony of the novel that Scythrop, who is constantly analyzing and brooding over his feelings for Marionetta and Stella, never makes a decisive move and therefore wins neither of them in the end. When Stella first appears in Scythrop's study late one night muffled in a cloak, Peacock satirizes both Scythrop and the style of much romantic fiction by stopping the action to discuss the nuances of emotion which have been aroused. First, he compares the apparition to that of Geraldine in *Christabel*, "for, if it be terrible to one young lady to find another under a tree at midnight, it must, *a fortiori*, be much more terrible to a young gentleman to find a young lady in his study at that hour." He further refers to a treatise which Flosky intends to write on the "Categories of Relation, which comprehend Substance and Accident, Cause and Effect, Action and Reaction." And, finally, before allowing either character to do or say anything, Peacock considers the scene in a Burkean light:

Scythrop, therefore, either was or ought to have been frightened; at all events, he was astonished; and astonishment, though not in itself fear, is nevertheless a good stage towards it, and is, indeed, as it were, the halfway-house between respect and terror, according to Mr. Burke's graduated scale of the sublime.

The first and most obvious irony, like that of most of the book, is that a simple event is obscured with excessive and irrelevant language. Peacock, in mockery of his own characters, stops time and probes theories of the interior life at the very moment when external events cry out to be advanced. But there is a second irony which undercuts the first: Peacock takes a Shandean pleasure in precisely the kind of associationist verbal play of which he accuses his characters. Though he seems unable to take any one of them seriously, he is fascinated by romantic fashions and theories in clusters. Peacock bears a relationship to romantic morbidity not unlike that which Robert Burton bore to seventeenth-century melancholy. He is in and out of it, scornful of its follies, bewildered by its causes, but thoroughly captivated by its manifestations.

Even at the height of his apparently anti-romantic satire, Peacock comes to the aid of his romantic victims by showing other mentalities in an equally ridiculous light. Mr. Hilary's good-natured common sense paradoxically becomes a dampener of high spirits when he insists upon offering "medical" and "logical" explanations as all the rest sit about telling ghost stories. Peacock also introduces a "man of science" who speaks with apparent wisdom, but finally behaves as foolishly as any other character in the book. Mr. Asterias, the ichthyologist, joins the guests at Nightmare Abbey and lectures them sternly on the morbidities of modern literature and the usefulness of a scientific career in protecting one from the "inexhaustible varieties of ennui":

"A gloomy brow and a tragical voice seem to have been of late the characteristics of fashionable manners: and a morbid, withering, deadly, antisocial sirocco, loaded with moral and political despair, breathes through all the groves and valleys of the modern Parnassus; while science moves on in the calm dignity of its course."

Mr. Asterias speaks of keeping in touch with nature and working for the benefit of mankind, contrasting his own active existence as naturalist and explorer with the stagnant life at Nightmare Abbey. But when we hear that he and his son Aquarius have come to the region to hunt for mermaids and that they spend their nights and days combing the marshes with enormous nets, we realize that his wisdom is simply folly of another sort. Science, like poetry and philosophy, is subject to the temptations of reductionism, abstraction, and egocentricity. It too needs to be brought to earth, like the Science of Pantopragmatics in *Gryll Grange*, which is described as "a real art of talking about an imaginary art of teaching every man his own business." [14]

The relentless pursuit of a single object is what makes all the characters in *Nightmare Abbey* similar; yet, since no two are after exactly the same thing, it is also what makes them different. This is not romantic folly, but human folly. Peacock's Romantics are simply more melancholy and talkative than most other characters. And they are more determined than most to transform the world into an environment for their own moods.

5

Peacock makes a great deal of fun of those Romantics who seek picturesque settings where they can repose and contemplate their own misery. Nightmare Abbey is itself such a place, as is Scythrop's tower apartment, which is furnished in the most comfortable of lugubrious styles. Shelley himself suggested the epigraph for the novel, a passage from Jonson's *Every Man in His Humour* in which Stephen asks Matthew whether he can borrow a stool "to be melancholy upon." Shelley often described to his friend Peacock how he searched out "appropriate" settings for himself, a niche in the Milan Cathedral where he liked to read Dante by the rays of a stained-glass window, or a Ligurian pool by which he lay naked in the fine spray of a little waterfall reading Herodotus.[15] In *Crotchet Castle*, the hero and heroine meet by such a pool, both in search of "unsophisticated scenery," and the heroine gets into such a ludicrously contemplative position on the trunk of an overhanging tree that she nearly falls into the water.

What Peacock finds amusing is not natural beauty and not even an inclination for solitary musing, but the self-conscious combination of the two. His romantic caricatures talk so much about themselves because they are forever watching themselves and saying, in effect, "I am

186

in the depths of despair, how do I look?" Their particular folly is not that each rides his own peculiar hobbyhorse — for Peacock, all of human nature is one great assemblage of crotchets — but the Romantics, by making a cult of individualism have, in Peacock's eyes, created a religion devoted to the contemplation and worship of eccentricity. He saw them making a spectacle, a parade, out of the accidental differences in human nature rather than trying to understand and improve the bonds which hold men together.

Originality, as applied to human behavior, was not a new concept. There were "originals" to spare in the fiction of Smollett, Fielding, and Sterne. But the attitude toward originality was what had changed, according to Peacock, without sufficient justification. Whereas the "original" for Smollett was one who was amusing, often interesting, but limited by the extent of his peculiarity, the "original" in much romantic literature is an almost divine figure, presumed to be closer to the gods the farther away he is from ordinary men. Shelley once wrote to a friend: "As to real flesh and blood, you know that I do not deal in those articles; you might as well go to a ginshop for a leg of mutton, as expect anything human or earthly from me." [16]

Peacock could understand and even sympathize with the old kind of "originality," but he could not witness with reverence its apotheosis. His humor, unlike Austen's, was not so much aimed at moral correction and intellectual refinement, but at secularization. Like Aristophanes, from whom he learned much, he is a classically profane writer, at his best when confronting the "great" with their own pettiness, the ethereal with their own flesh, and the "unique" with their commonness.

One of the climactic scenes in *Nightmare Abbey* follows a discussion of ghosts in which each character calmly and airily describes his own "experience" with spirits and proposes some theory in explanation thereof. But when the mysterious Stella, not yet known except to Scythrop, makes an unexpected entrance in an outlandish costume, this mere hint of the supernatural makes the whole world kin:

Mr. Flosky, familiar as he was with ghosts, was not prepared for this apparition and made the best of his way out at the opposite door. Mrs. Hilary and Marionetta followed, screaming. The Honourable Mr. Listless, by two turns of his body, rolled first off the sofa and then under it. The Reverend Mr. Larynx leaped up and fled with so much precipitation, that he overturned the table on the foot of Mr. Glowry. Mr. Glowry roared with pain in the ear of Mr. Toobad. Mr. Toobad's alarm so bewildered his senses, that, missing the door, he threw up one of the windows, jumped out in his panic, and plunged over head and ears in the moat. Mr. Asterias and his son, who were on the watch for their mermaid, were attracted by the splashing, threw a net over him, and dragged him to land.

For once, Peacock's romantic "types" cannot savor their setting, dissect their emotional response, or insist upon their dissimilarity to the rest of mankind. The event, though a false and silly one, finally triumphs over poetical preoccupation and philosophical abstraction, forcing each character to show his "true" nature. The episode is, in fact, a representation in physical terms of the fundamental assumption which underlies the dialogue and dramatic action of the entire novel: every man for himself. In Peacock's view, it is the egocentricity of men which makes them all essentially alike. If he does not see it as cause for despair of the human race, neither does he see it as man's most noble or beautiful trait. Discipline, tolerance, good humor, may help, but the idea that it is the prerogative of poets and geniuses, a characteristic to be cultivated and idealized seems to him absurd. For Peacock, the analogy for a conversation among Romantics or, perhaps, an anthology of romantic literature, is the spectacle of various men diving out of different windows and describing it later as poetic flight.

Nightmare Abbey is not in itself an important work nor does it pretend to be. Yet it is worth considering in a study of romantic fiction because it shows so distinctly and to such an extreme the tendency of romantic novelists to discredit the moods and ideals which most fascinated them. Walpole, Beckford, Lewis, and Scott were all tempted to burlesque emotions and parody literary conventions to which they were attracted but which they feared were beyond their imaginative scope and half-suspected were morally and aesthetically beneath contempt. There is little ambivalence or tension in Peacock's fiction. If anything, his humor is too facile. Yet he exposes more graphically than any contemporary critic the most debilitating problem for the romantic novelist: the difficulty of rooting strong emotion in believable ground. Peacock was certain that he lived at a time in which it could not be done. Many of his more serious and gifted contemporaries were deeply troubled by the thought that he might be right.

X

MELMOTH THE WANDERER

Charles Robert Maturin
1820

Published more than two decades after *The Monk, Melmoth the Wanderer* is a late — some have said the last — Gothic novel. It was admired by Scott and Byron; Balzac wrote a sequel to it; and Baudelaire, dissatisfied with the French version of 1821, wanted to do his own translation. The book's thematic and stylistic links with Walpole, Radcliffe, and Lewis are not difficult to see, yet it is a wilder, more complicated, and, in many ways, a more daring work than most of its predecessors. In the first place, it is one of the rare works of Gothic fiction which dwells on the trappings of religion and is at the same time informed by a deep religious feeling. Living in southern Ireland as a Protestant minister, Charles Robert Maturin had a stronger and more lively emotional involvement with — if not a clearer understanding of — Roman Catholicism than did those English writers for whom "abbey" meant an ivy-covered ruin. Most of the properties of earlier Gothic fiction — the narrow cells, the dark cowls, the labyrinthine vaults — remain, but the attitude expressed toward them has little of antiquarian fondness or hesitant irony about it. On one level, *Melmoth the Wanderer* is a belated work of the Reformation, a roar of outrage against the bigotry, superstition, sadism, and hypocrisy which had infested the Roman Church.

Secondly, there is a good deal more authentic republican spirit in Maturin's novel than in those of many of his predecessors despite their conventional odes to liberty and denunciations of despotic rule. There

CHARLES ROBERT MATURIN

is a genuine distaste for authoritarian political systems, especially as they are linked with religious tyranny, and an insistence upon the right of the individual to determine his destiny on earth as well as to make his appeals to God without priestly interference:

"The inventive activity of the people of the world, in the multiplication of calamity, is inexhaustibly fertile in resources. Not satisfied with diseases and famine, with sterility of the earth, and tempests of the air, they must have laws and marriages, and kings and tax-gatherers, and wars and fetes, and every variety of artificial misery . . . These people . . . have made unto themselves kings, that is, beings whom they voluntarily invest with the privilege of draining, by taxation, whatever wealth their vices have left to the rich, and whatever means of subsistence their want has left to the poor, till their extortion is cursed from the castle to the cottage — and this to support a few pampered favorites, who are harnessed by silken reins to the car, which they drag over the prostrate bodies of the multitude . . . Another amusement of these people, so ingenious in multiplying the sufferings of their destiny, is what they call law . . . One of its most admirable triumphs is in that ingenuity by which it contrives to convert a difficulty into an impossibility, and punish a man for not doing what it has rendered impracticable for him to do." [1]

Though Maturin puts this diatribe against monarchy and oppressive laws in the mouth of the cynical Melmoth and appends to it a footnote assuring the reader that "the sentiments ascribed to the stranger are diametrically opposed to mine," the passage has a Swiftian lucidity and energy which are difficult to ignore. If Maturin did not intellectually embrace the political and social consequences of rebellious individualism, he at least felt sufficiently in sympathy with it to make the "agent of the enemy of mankind" speak with eloquence and vigor.

But however serious the religious and political levels of the book may be, *Melmoth the Wanderer* has as its main subject the dark side of the human mind. As Douglas Grant has said, "If it belongs to the Gothic novel of the past . . . it anticipates the psychological, metaphysical novel of the future. Dostoevsky and Kafka are low on the horizon." [2] In the dedication to *The Milesian Chief*, Maturin characterizes his talent as "that of darkening the gloomy, and of deepening the sad; of painting life in extremes, and representing those struggles of passion when the soul trembles on the verge of the unlawful and the unhallowed." [3] Like Lewis, he was fascinated by extremes of freedom and repression and the various kinds of anguish which they caused body and mind. But even more than was the case for Lewis or Beckford, painful subjects seemed to have stimulated his imagination into an extraordinary state of productivity. According to one of his own characters, "in situations of peril, the imagination is unhappily fertile." This seems to have been true of Maturin's imagination, which initiates "peril" and then divides and multiplies it like a Shakespearian pun. The structure of *Melmoth the Wanderer*, a series of narrations within narrations — often compared with a nest of Chinese boxes — defies conventional chronological sequence and replaces it with obsessive variations on the single theme of human misery. It is like a gruesome contest among the suffering to tell the worst tale of woe. Though the speakers are different, their narratives are given unity by a common pattern of torment and by the presence of the wraithlike Melmoth, who usually enters at a critical moment to tempt the sufferer into despair.

Though none of the main characters does yield to despair, almost all seem to enjoy lingering close to the edge and analyzing the various moods, emotions, and thoughts produced by enduring the nearly unendurable. While Maturin has his narrators discuss the effects of pain on the human personality, he implicitly suggests much about its uses as a subject for the artist. One of the points first and most often made is that extreme suffering reduces human nature to its essential character, undisguised by artifice and convention. A particularly vicious monk describes the effects of hunger on young lovers: "One physical want, one severe and abrupt lesson from the shrivelled lip of necessity, is worth all the logic of the empty wretches who have presumed to prate it . . . It silences in a second all the feeble sophistry of *conventional* life." His contention is, of course, that human nature is basically selfish, that comfort is a condition of love, and that the young couple's dying bitterly and apart proves it. Maturin himself is not satisfied with so simple a theory and, in fact, presents other examples of love which strengthens under duress. But that pain provides a release from conventional life he appears to acknowledge. It frees the artist from having to portray his characters in terms of their orientation to external custom, but it challenges him too, because it tests whether or not he has the power to portray anything else.

Periods of suffering can reveal a new kind of being who is dominated not by learned behavior or cool reason but by the simple immediacy of physical feeling. To those characters who have settled into dull routines of living death, the first hints of pain come as a promise of positive good. Thus, an old monk on his death bed expresses a perfect willingness to die, come heaven or hell: "I am a clock that has struck the same minutes and hours for sixty years . . . The monotony of my existence would make a transition, even to pain, desirable." Candor, a certain vigor of response, and integrity of being are associated with the state of heightened physical sensitivity brought about by actual or imagined pain. While trying to escape a monastery by crawling through its labyrinth of vaults, the young Monçada keeps remembering and recounting the horrible fate of others who had risked their lives before him:

All this detail, that takes many words to tell, rushed on my soul in a moment; — on my soul? — no, on my body. I was all physical feeling, — all intense corporeal agony, and God only knows, and man only can feel, how that agony can absorb and annihilate all other feeling within us.

Again and again, Maturin brings his characters into focus by showing them in an almost bestial state. And, in so doing, he not only separates them from social convention and abstract concepts, like the soul, but he shows them in a moment of intense and undivided vitality. For the artist, then, pain becomes an instrument by which life at an uncomplicated but nonetheless real level can be reached. The creature which the romantic novelist wanted to reach was the one who reacts to sight and sound and touch before it reacts to reason and custom. If Maturin assumed that it existed somewhere in everyone, it also seemed to him, writing in the second decade of the nineteenth century, that only a very sharp edge would bring it out.

2

But Maturin was not a romantic primitivist nor a mere sadist content to reduce his characters to palpitating flesh. The emergence of the purely physical character, like the shattering of conventions, is a preparatory phase in the experiment with pain. As the victim's suffering is prolonged, he becomes, once again, a thinking and complicated being, but his mind is no longer a register filled with approved and familiar ideas, but a new world shaped by and shaping the misery it encounters. As he traces in each of the narratives the history of a mind newly made by misery, Maturin illustrates a whole phase of romantic psychology and the creative process. After being forced into a state of keen sensuous awareness, the victim begins to defend himself from the full impact of the painful stimulus by automatically breaking it down into minute details. He thus becomes a sharp if not rationally selective observer, giving emphasis to particles not because of their relevance to a preconceived pattern, but because of their physical proximity to him at a certain moment and in a certain place. When the young Monçada is imprisoned in the monastery dungeon, he notices exactly how the cell is shaped and furnished, reflecting, "Thus it is that misery always breaks down the mind into petty details. We have not strength to comprehend the whole of our calamity. We feel not the mountain which is heaped on us, but the nearest grains press on and grind us." To continue the metaphor, the image of the external world is one molded to the shape of the observer, the concrete details noted become the elements of a self-portrait.

By means of first person narratives, Maturin attempts to explore the minds of his victimized characters, tracing their course from a state of physical sensation, to a keen but highly subjective observation of detail, to an increasingly distorted sense of external reality, and finally to a point of inventiveness which recreates an imaginary world more distinct and affective than the world of objective reality. Shut away from the light of day and the routine of men, Monçada tries to invent his own time in order to escape the seemingly eternal blankness of his confinement:

So I sat and counted sixty; a doubt always occurred to me, that I was counting them faster than the clock. Then I wished to be the clock that I might have no feeling, no motive for hurrying on the approach of time. Then I reckoned slower.

Monçada's problem is the opposite of that of the dying old monk who compares himself with a clock. Confined and suffering, even on the verge of lunacy, Monçada is the least mechanical of beings, sharply aware of himself, all the more painfully human in his incapacity to attain mathematical regularity. Through the perceptions of his imprisoned, isolated, or exiled narrators — as well as by means of the peculiar structure of the whole novel — Maturin unhinges fiction from clock and calendar chronology and makes time another projection of the individual imagination. "Minutes are hours in the *noctuary* of terror, — terror has no diary."

In terms of physical action, *Melmoth the Wanderer* is a surprisingly static novel, though it gives an impression of continuous and frantic movement. One character is trapped in a madhouse, another in a monastery, another left ashore on an uninhabited island. A Protestant family is immobilized by poverty, religion and language in Spain; an orphaned English girl lives a life of quiet retirement in a country castle. There are, of course, attempts at escape, but it is perfectly true that chronological time has almost stopped for most of these characters and has given way to the less regular, more interesting rhythm of their emotions and imaginings. One character might be speaking for all when he explains that "events which would make a life-lasting impression on others, pass like shadows before me, while thoughts appear like substances. *Emotions are my events.*" And it is just at this point in the victim's suffering, physically immobilized but mentally and emotionally excited, that he becomes inventive, even artistic, spinning out anecdotes, constructing scenery, describing gestures, remembering the past, anticipating the future, giving shape even to darkness.

3

For Maturin, as for Lewis, the artist is associated with the victim who unexpectedly finds himself inflicting confinement and deprivation on others. He sacrifices physical movement in time to the intense emotion of a moment. The fact that Maturin was called the "Fuseli of novelists" shortly after the appearance of *Melmoth the Wanderer* suggests more than a recognition of his special taste for the terrific. Fuseli's mannered drawings display a curious struggle with his subject matter which gives point to his exclamation, "Damn Nature! — she always puts me out." [4] It is a comment Maturin would have understood.

As one who imposes his own limits on the fluidity of life, the artist is, in Maturin's view, like an agent of death. Moreover, when the artist is most nearly the pure aesthetician — concerned with his response to composition, color, shape — he is least the compassionate man who is able to enter into the joys and sufferings of those he observes. However much they may have suffered themselves, Maturin's narrators can rarely resist expressing the peculiar aesthetic pleasure derived from watching the suffering of others. For all but the most depraved, this is not a prolonged form of sadism, but a momentary response usually followed by an onrush of sympathy and occasionally an attempt to be of help. Yet the instant exists when emotion has no moral consequence, but is an artistic medium which traces the outline of beauty. Beautiful objects, in the world of Maturin do not derive their beauty primarily from proportion but from their strange milieu. They are the early buds of *les fleurs du mal*, forms emerging from or receding into darkness and filth.

Beauty is best recognized when placed against that which it is not. Thus the painters Maturin invokes are those best known for their treatment of light and shade, and the scenes during which he calls them forth are often the most gruesome or melancholy in the book. A novice tormented by his superiors provides Monçada with a typical analogy:

I turned, and saw a group worthy of Murillo. A more perfect human form never existed than that of this unfortunate youth. He stood in an attitude of despair — he was streaming with blood. The monks with their lights, their scourges, and their dark habits, seemed like a group of demons who had made prey of a wandering angel, — the group resembled the infernal furies pursuing a mad Orestes. And, indeed, no ancient sculptor ever designed a figure more exquisite and perfect than they had so barbarously mangled.

It is obvious that Maturin is writing about and repudiating the perversion of human feelings in the name of religion. What complicates the scene is that the narrator relishes, with an artist's eye, precisely what the monks seem to enjoy doing to the beautiful novice. As Douglas Grant puts it, this is "the projection of a Protestant imagination tantalizing itself with scarlet notions of Rome."[5] As artist, the speaker is with the victimizers, even if, as moralist, he disapproves of them. Maturin demonstrates how moments of vivid pleasure mixed with pain can explode in lives of habitual repression. But who, one might ask, has been repressed and who is supposed to be pleased? Heterosexuality is treated as repressively in the novel as homosexuality. In fact, most sensual pleasure is shown somehow as blighted or obscured, not merely transient but inhibited and damaged at the core.

Maturin blames much repression on particular religious and political

195

institutions, but a distrust of the senses seems to be so deeply rooted in his own mind as to color his entire concept of beauty. In *The Milesian Chief*, an expedition to visit an island with a ruined abbey is discussed; one character suggests going at sunset. The hero, however, prefers a night journey by pale moonlight:

> "I would rather bring my mind than my senses; a mind that when it visits the place of wonders, will not, like Aladdin in the tale, be content with the gems that sparkle there; but will seek the genius of the place, and learn his secret, and dwell with him afterwards in the power and darkness of him that has mastered the spell." [6]

Maturin takes it for granted that some pleasures — perhaps the deepest sort — can be experienced only if the senses are curbed. The feeling of mystery, the straining to see what cannot be fully seen, contribute to the "power" of the moment. The island nearly overwhelmed by darkness or the flesh struggling against the inhibitions of the mind suggest the conditions of a peculiar beauty. Hence, one kind of "realistic" artist must dwell on that which his eye can never fully illuminate.

The burning of the prisons of the Inquisition, flames lighting up the night and playing against the dark towers, are described as "worthy of the pencil of Salvator Rosa, or of Murillo." The burial of a woman at night surrounded by her family, whose faces are dimly lighted by a single torch, is called worthy of "the pencil of the first of painters" and is looked upon by the youngest child "as a pageant got up for his amusement." The discovery "by moonlight" of a youth who has attempted suicide again prompts a comparison with Murillo or Rosa or "any of those painters, who, inspired by the genius of suffering delight in representing the most exquisite of human forms in the extremity of human agony." Finally, Elinor Mortimer, the Calvinist beauty, derives most of her charm from her retiring and melancholy manner. "No head of Rembrandt's, amid its contrasted luxuries of light and shade, — no form of Guido's, hovering in exquisite and speechful undulation between earth and heaven, could vie with the tint and character of Elinor's countenance and form."

Such scenes seem deliberately posed, deliberately bathed in shadow, so that, although classically proportioned forms are suggested, they are not fully revealed. Completeness of outline is replaced by an intense

196

highlighting of parts the perfection of which must be half-guessed at by the viewer since it is not provided by the artist. Beauty becomes, then, an unfulfilled promise, a hint of something beyond man's power to embody or the artist's power to convey. In most of the "picturesque" scenes in the novel, the characters portrayed are literally threatened by death as well as half-obscured by shadow; the central figures are what Maturin calls "heroes of submission," shown in helpless confrontation with a force stronger than they.

4

Maturin's carefully grouped portraits are not the mere whims of a warped aesthete, but a romantic vision of man's fallen state as emblemized by his incapacity to maintain stability and proportion in a life encircled by pain and death. If Maturin created new images of beauty in his dark art, they were images created in sorrow and longing for a beauty classically defined; an ideal lost, not rejected.

There is never any serious doubt in Maturin's works that the highly subjective and inventive state of mind brought about by extreme suffering is a form of insanity. Maturin projects, in the phrase of William F. Axton, a "madhouse world," and he knows it.[7] In Bertram, Imogine nearly goes mad by closing her senses to immediate reality and indulging her mind with images of her absent lover:

> The thoughts of other days are rushing on me,
> The loved, the lost, the distant, and the dead,
> Are with me now, and I will mingle with them
> 'Till my sense fails, and my raised heart is wrapt
> In secret suspension of mortality.[8]

Such madness may have its own compensations, even its own pleasures, but it is nonetheless a deviation from a remembered norm, a state of being in which man could still reach outside himself for communication, balance, support. The lovely Imalee, living alone on a tropical island, with only the trees and birds as friends, embodies life in perfect harmony with Edenic nature: "She lived like a flower, amid sun and storm, blooming in the light, and bending to the shower, and drawing the elements of her sweet and wild existence from both." But Maturin's other characters, having been deprived of innocent nature by original

197

sin and alienated from one another by the corruptions of civilization, spin myths in their isolation, tell incoherent tales nourished by imperfect memory, myopic vision, and a sensation of chronic pain. The novelist who writes of misery in fragmented episodes, like the artist who paints figures half-swallowed by shadow, is not on a romantic holiday from classical restraint. He sees himself in the same dilemma as his subjects, confronted by a hostile obscurity which he has not the vision to penetrate or the power to change.

Man's disjunction from nature, his inability to communicate with other men, and his weakness of vision are all depicted with a nightmarish logic in an early scene during which the young John Melmoth rushes to the Irish coast during a storm. It is known that a ship founders not far away, but in the darkness of night it can be seen only in brief and sudden appearances of the moon, which sheds just enough light to show that members of the crew are being swept violently into the sea. Though the rocky shore is crowded with observers trying to shout encouragement to the victims, the point emphasized is that they can be of no help and that even their voices are lost in the wind. The sympathetic young Melmoth is tormented by his own uselessness in the sight of so much suffering:

There is something so very horrible in the sight of human beings perishing so near us, that we feel one firm step rightly planted, one arm steadily held out, might save at least one, — yet feel we know not where to fix that step, and cannot stretch that arm, that Melmoth's senses reeled under the shock, and for a moment he echoed the storm with yells of actual insanity.

Once again, as in *The Monk,* we find the rational, even sympathetic, observer inadvertently imitating chaos. Compassion without power, which is the definition of the good man in Maturin's novel, places almost unbearable strain on individual sanity, to say nothing of morale, when confronted with the spectacle of human suffering. The young Melmoth's temptation comes, then, as it does in critical moments to all the major characters in the novel, in the form of self-defensive despair. He catches a glimpse of a dark figure standing high upon a rock, observing the spectacle in a state so literally unmoved that not even a thread of his "garments seemed ruffled by the blast." It is the young man's legendary wandering ancestor — a psychic double for John Melmoth and all characters with similar compassion — offering the ap-

198

parent serenity of a mind which always expects the worst, a heart which feels nothing, and a soul which has given up all hope. Bewildered, almost possessed, the young Melmoth climbs toward the "calm and dark" figure, but at the very moment before he reaches it, he falls from the rocks and wakes several days later in bed.

In the details of this scene the outline of the whole novel is sketched, for in it the setting, characters, and problems of the episodes which follow are all prefigured. Nature appears to mirror man's own depravity and confusion rather than providing a refuge from them. Nature is all darkness and chaos, destroying some while it keeps others helplessly waiting their turn as members of a great and terrified audience. Both the compassionate Melmoth and the cynical Melmoth are nothing more than spectators; neither caused the storm, neither can stop it, and neither can save so much as one of its victims. The difference between them, then, cannot be described in terms of action, but only in terms of attitude. One feels and hopes and therefore suffers mentally from the physical suffering he witnesses; the other feels and expects nothing, rejoices in his isolation from other men, and even asserts an indifference to nature, which gives him a kind of superiority over it. The struggle thus depicted is an internal one between two aspects of the self which can never be reconciled, yet which pursue and define one another as surely as night and day, death and life.

5

In *The Marriage of Heaven and Hell*, Blake speaks of the necessity of "Contraries" to human existence: "Attraction and Repulsion, Reason and Energy, Love and Hate . . . From these contraries spring what the religious call Good and Evil. Good is the passive that obeys Reason. Evil is the active springing from Energy." The pairing of opposites was not a practice peculiar to romantic writers, but a tendency to place them in a new and, above all, *closer* relationship with one another was. The Romantics did not invent the story that Lucifer was the most beautiful of the angels before his fall, but they were peculiarly fascinated by the nature of that beauty as it appeared after the blight.[9] Even the Christian Romantic, like Maturin, conceives of the traditional aesthetic and moral contrarities as bound in a marriage. The devil's beauty is no cheap disguise but the result of interwoven realities.

Melmoth, the "destroyer," is not a mad rapist or a frivolous seducer, but a constant husband united in an unholy matrimony with his victims. Most often, Melmoth's union with a character is spoken of in figurative terms. But, in the case of the innocent Imalee, there is a literal wooing, courtship, and wedding ceremony, all of which lead to the birth and death of an infant and the death of the mother caught between the temptations of the devil and the persecution of the Church. Marriage, the traditional symbol of order, expectation, and continuity, is transformed into an inevitable but unregenerative alliance. Maturin's counterpart to the Ancient Mariner does not wait outside the church talking to a guest, but goes in and weds the bride.

The mood of suspense and expectation — so common in the conventional courtship and marriage novel of the period — seems to have been deliberately avoided by Maturin. Before the "ceremony" in the deserted church, Imalee is already bound in an essential way to Melmoth. There are at least two preparatory "marriages" before the formal exchange of vows. During a storm which the two witness from the shore of Imalee's island, Melmoth cries, "Amid thunder I wed thee — bride of perdition!" Later in Spain, Melmoth asks Imalee to die to the world and preserve herself for him alone — "the single, pulseless, eyeless, heartless embracer of an unfertile bride." Finally, in the novel's most Gothic scene, the two are wed at night in a ruined chapel: "All was mist and darkness with her, — she knew not what was muttered, — she felt not that the hand of Melmoth grasped hers, — but she felt that the hand that united them, and clasped their palms within his own, was as *cold as that of death*." The italics are Maturin's and they serve as a partial explication of the passage. With or without them, the death symbolism is easy enough to see.

What is particularly important is that the marriage to death is a repeated and static performance. It is not presented as a matter of choice or subtle judgment for Imalee; it is not a moral or psychological option, but an event imposed on her externally and one which recurs figuratively countless times. Her life, after a certain point, becomes a series of dull and repetitious vows to death.

For all the expressions of grand passion and despite the *Romeo and Juliet* touches — the nightly visits beneath the balcony, the impending marriage to another "Paris," the secret wedding — the relationship between Imalee and Melmoth is without basis in physical reality, not contrary to nature but without nature. The substance of their intercourse is a "torrent of words" and its issue a dead child and a dying mother crazily proclaiming that she must love her "destroyer" and wondering with her last breath whether he will pursue her to paradise.

Imalee marries a fleshless phantom. She is a Juliet gone mad for the lack of a Romeo. She was perfectly content on her tropical island as long as it was innocent of human society. Her encounter with Melmoth and her sudden, almost miraculous transfer to Spain symbolize her passage to maturity, her recognition of a need for human contact. Whether that need is conceived of in sexual or more generally emotional terms is less important than the fact that, in the context of the novel, it cannot under any circumstances be fulfilled. The difference between Imalee's isolation on her island paradise and in her ancestral Spanish home is that in the first she does not know anything outside of her own world and therefore does not yearn to be out of it, while in Spain she feels a prisoner because she imagines a better world where human rapport is possible and remembers a simpler one where it was not necessary. Anticipation and memory expand as the realities of the present grow more and more disappointing and painful. Ultimately, because of their expansion, that reality diminishes. Imalee, like the young Melmoth, has a generous and loving heart, but even these models of Christian virtue cannot reach out of their isolation to other mortals.

They too become prisoners of subjective time which makes isolation seem the only constant and the struggle for release a certain form of self-defeat. If subjective time is an internal measure defined by fear, objective time, in Maturin's world, points to the source of that fear, death itself. For all but a very few characters, life is a struggle out of isolation into oblivion. In a world where time is ruin, positive change cannot exist, birth is only a repetition, growth an illusion, and marriage the fatal exposure to external reality.

In this long narrative of horror and perversity, nothing is treated with such consistent and sudden violence as the physical union of a robust young man with a beautiful young woman. The first two episodes noted in the manuscript of Stanton, the Restoration Englishman traveling in Spain, concern the fates of young lovers. First he sees the body of a beautiful girl who had been struck by lightning being carried

201

by mourners and followed by two more bearers with "the blasted and blackened figure of what had once been a man, comely and graceful . . . They were lovers, and he had been consumed by the flash that had destroyed her, while in the act of endeavouring to defend her." Almost immediately, Stanton proceeds to a large house where an old woman tells him the story of a marriage which had taken place there many years ago amid much pomp and rejoicing. But at a feast which followed a few days later, the strange Melmoth appears, the priest who had celebrated the nuptials dies suddenly, and the bride is discovered in the bridal chamber "a coarse in the arms of her husband."

In the Spaniard's Tale, a Superior discovers that one of his monks has a mistress in his cell and he reacts like Carathis discovering Vathek in the arms of Nouronihar. In a world where flagellation, starvation fasts, and imprisonment are the norm, heterosexual union appears as a freakish abomination:

The Superior . . . had no more idea of the intercourse between the sexes, than between two beings of a different species. The scene he beheld could not have revolted him more than if he had seen the horrible loves of the baboons and the Hottentot women . . . Love was a thing he always believed connected with sin, even though consecrated by the name of a sacrament, and called marriage, as it is in our church.

These lovers pay for their moment of natural union by being walled up in a vault and left to starve, but though the agent of their destruction is human, the general pattern of their fate is much the same as that of other young lovers in the novel. It would seem that what is not accomplished by Church or State, will be taken care of by fire, flood, lightning, or plague.

The only durable — though hardly blissful — marriages are those without basis in physical reality, that is, in which the partner is acceptable precisely because he has no concrete identity, sexual or otherwise, distinct from what already exists within the original character. He may be the mirror reflection of an appalling self or, like Melmoth, he may be a negation of self. He can fascinate and terrify by his presence but he cannot, by his own power, change anything. He has no seminal power to breed good or evil, but can only cast a shadow of doubt, despair, and death. The marriage of Melmoth and Imalee is the novel's central image of this indissoluble duality in man's nature, but there are at least two other relationships which repeat the theme and embody it.

When the young Monçada decides to escape from the monastery where his family has forced him to take vows, he puts himself in the hands of the basest member of the convent, a parricide who has taken refuge from the law by joining a religious order. In every way the ugly and corrupt monk is the apparent opposite of the virtuous and handsome Monçada, yet the narrator himself suggests the parallels to a strange courtship and marriage. When the parricide first attracts the attention of Monçada in the monastery garden, it is by touching his habit:

How is it that crime thus seizes us in life with a fearless grasp, while the touch of conscience trembles on the verge of our garment. One would almost . . . say that guilt is masculine, and innocence feminine. I grasped his wrist with a trembling hand, and whispered — "Juan," in the same breath. He answered — "Alonzo," and passed me onward in a moment.

When the two are crawling through the labyrinthine recesses of the convent vaults, Monçada continually thinks of his guide in extreme and contradictory terms: "Crime gave him a kind of heroic immunity in my eyes"; "I dreaded him as a demon, yet I invoked him as a god"; "His presence was at once an irrepealable curse and an invincible necessity." Circumstances have made them more alike than Monçada would like to admit: "We hear the throb of each others hearts, and yet dare not say, 'My heart beats in unison with yours.'" When Monçada can no longer stand the blasphemies and gruesome tales of his companion, he curses him and calls their association an "unnatural coalition . . . which must cease at the moment of my escape from the convent and from you." The immediate issue of this attempted escape is the death of Monçada's real brother, waiting outside the convent, at the hands of the treacherous parricide. Monçada is consigned to the Inquisition, and there are later escapades of torment and escape, but symbolically the dark self has usurped the role of the good brother, has cast the victim deeper into a subjective universe sealed off from contact with society and concrete nature.

Another "unnatural coalition" occurs in one of the last narratives in the novel, between Elinor Mortimer and John Sandal. Full of tender-

CHARLES ROBERT MATURIN

ness and admiration for her handsome kinsman, the devout young lady cannot reconcile the stories of his valor in battle with his apparent gentleness of manner:

Her health, her rest, and her imagination, became the prey of indefinable fantasies. The cherished images of the past, – the lovely visions of her golden childhood – seemed fearfully and insanely contrasted in her imagination with the ideas of slaughter and blood – of decks strewed with corses – and of a young and terrible conqueror bestriding them . . . Her mind, vacillating between contrasts so strongly opposed, began to feel its moorings give way.

When John Sandal returns from the wars, however, he wins his cousin's heart again with his graceful manners and almost feminine beauty. After a certain time, a wedding is planned, but the groom fails to appear and Elinor is left bereft and brooding. Eventually, John returns, marries another cousin who dies with her infant twins in childbirth, and it is later explained that though he had always loved Elinor, he had deserted her upon being informed (erroneously) that they were brother and sister. As a result of these misfortunes and confusions, John sinks into dumb idiocy, in which state he is nursed for the remainder of his years by the loyal and forgiving Elinor.

The psychological pattern is not unlike that worked out in the conclusion of *Jane Eyre*: once the aggressive, energetic, and masculine characteristics of the man have been subdued, he becomes a partner suitable to the ministrations of the heroine. There is "union" only where there can be no natural marriage. The idea of a physically potent John Sandal almost drives his beloved to distraction. In fact, her incapacity to cope with masculine sexuality except in morbid fantasies is a madness which is eventually personified in the addled being of John Sandal. In nursing him, Elinor nurses herself. At the moment he conforms to the peculiar shape of her mind, he becomes as much of a husband as she will ever have — that is to say, no husband at all.

6

Thus Maturin, the Christian minister, provides narrative within narrative, layer within layer, probing always deeper and deeper, and coming up with a rearrangement of the same basic phenomena: isolation, the brief pain of knowledge, and the long, long madness which separates memory from oblivion. The lesson he tries to teach — which is not to

204

despair — is all the more moving because his vision of man and nature gives so much to despair about. Maturin's Christian hope in God's mercy is shaped and intensified by his Calvinistic disbelief in man's ability to help himself. The most positive thing one can do is to keep faith in the Lord. That is the way to avoid ultimate despair, but it is based upon an attitude toward man and nature which leaves hope nowhere to go but heavenward.

Along with his institutional quarrel with Roman Catholicism, Maturin had serious theological objections to what he considered the Church's cavalier attitude toward human nature and especially its insistence on man's ability to participate, through good works, in his own redemption. *Melmoth the Wanderer* is filled with satirical jibes at the Catholic preoccupation with active charity and the competitive means by which Catholics try to attain heaven. Priests and pious ladies compare the wretchedness of the beggars they have helped and keep count of the sick they have visited. Maturin's point — certainly a familiar Protestant one — is that, even in his acts of apparent charity, man shows himself to be a corrupt creature motivated by self-interest.

The reformist's wish for a purging of worldly distractions is one of the controlling ideas of the novel. When the innocent Imalee comes to Spain from her tropical island, she speaks of hearing of a religion "so beautiful and pure" that in a Christian land she expected to find all Christians and was disappointed instead to find "only Catholics." Her idea of perfection is Christian virtue practiced in a natural, uncivilized setting like that of her island. The world of Catholic Spain is all restraint and contortion, "intelligence and luxury," while her natural paradise with its shores of "beauty and blessedness," is a place where birds fly freely and do not "break their bills against gilded wires."

If the scenes of monastery life narrated by Monçada show the perversity of Catholic asceticism, the long section in the Spanish household of Imalee's (Isadora's) parents demonstrates the hypocrisy of Catholic worldliness. Some of Maturin's best satire is directed against Imalee's mother, Donna Clara, who can shift her attention from a fine point of conscience to the dressing of her hair without a pause:

She [would] fret about the family clock not chiming synchronically with the bells of the neighboring church where she performed her devotions . . .

205

CHARLES ROBERT MATURIN

She fretted about everything, from the fattening of the 'pullen,' and the preparation for the olio, up to the increasing feuds between the Molinists and Jansenists . . . and the deadly dispute between the Dominican and Franciscan orders, relative to the habit in which it was most effective to salvation for the dying body of the sinner to be wrapped. So between her kitchen and her oratory, – her prayers to the saints, and her scoldings to her servants, – her devotion and her anger, – Donna Clara continued to keep herself and domestics in a perpetual state of interesting occupation and gentle excitement.

One can imagine the benevolent gusto with which Chaucer might have drawn such a character, or the stinging wit with which Pope would have coupled these incongruities. In the context of *Melmoth the Wanderer,* however, there is no gusto, and wit quickly gives way to wrath. The elements of this portrait are shown to be the vicious traits of a self-indulgent, superstitious, and arrogant bigot who disgusts the artist who has created her. For Maturin, the oratory and the kitchen do not belong together, and to mingle them in one's thoughts is not merely silly but sinful. In fact, man's tendency to think so much of things — whether food or shrouds — diverts him from the one true object of hope, the spirit of God.

Despite Imalee's dreams of a natural, almost primitive, Christianity, most of the evidence in *Melmoth the Wanderer* suggests that Maturin found the natural world as much of an obstacle to salvation as man's fallen human nature. Storms, lightning blasts, turbulent seas, and black nights may force man to turn in fear to God, but they are hardly the emanations of his benevolent power or the direct channels through which he may be reached. God is not in nature, he provides an alternative to it. In his religious poem, *The Universe,* Maturin depicts man as "most impotent," "an insect atom, on its fluttering leaf" tossed in a storm, capable of being "preserved" by God alone.[10] Man's only hope is to escape the turbulence of the natural world and the corruption of his own human nature by trusting in the goodness of God.

But goodness is defined by Maturin in an almost totally negative way as that which is purified of physical life. "Pure spirit," "pure devotion," "affection pure" and "earthless purity" are phrases repeated throughout *The Universe* to suggest the highest good. It follows that God would be conceived of as purity itself, an alternative to man just as he is an alternative to nature. The Incarnation, with its insistence on flesh and blood, must have been unpalatable to Maturin since he often writes as though it never occurred. His characteristic image of God is not the loving Christ, the son and brother of man, but "the great Contriver." Despite his earnest and holy war against despair, Maturin's peculiar combination of Calvinism and Deism is very like a religious system which undoes the work of the Nativity. It places man beneath contempt and God beyond human reach.

At the end of Part I of *The Universe*, Maturin describes the rise and fall of civilizations and the God who watches from heaven:

> . . . . beyond all,
> The spirit of creation sits, unmoved,
> Presiding.[11]

If that is Imalee's heavenly reward, one can hardly help thinking that she would have been better off making friends with some of the grosser impurities of earth while she had the chance. It would be inaccurate and overly simple to say that this is Maturin's hidden message to the reader of *Melmoth the Wanderer*. It might well be said, however, that it was Maturin-the-artist's message to Maturin-the-minister. But Maturin-the-minister did not like the earth and, therefore, though the message was continuously being sent, it appears not to have been received. The reader of *Melmoth the Wanderer* is witness to a tormented debate which seems to be taking place across a canyon. Empty space absorbs arguments and images before they ever reach the other side. The worst of all possible worlds and the most barren of pure heavens drift together into incoherence and, like the echoes in Forster's Marabar caves, give equal cause to despair.

XI

THE PRIVATE MEMOIRS AND CONFESSIONS OF A JUSTIFIED SINNER

James Hogg

1824

James Hogg was born of poor parents, he received almost no formal education, he was neither well-known nor highly esteemed by most of his contemporaries, and today he is remembered for a few poems and one extraordinary novel. Upon reading *The Private Memoirs and Confessions of a Justified Sinner*, originally published in 1824, André Gide wrote, "It is long since I can remember being so taken hold of, so voluptuously tormented by any book." [1] In his own lifetime Hogg was referred to as "the greatest hog in all Apollo's herd," but Wordsworth and De Quincey recognized a peculiar genius in the Ettrick Shepherd; and his fondness for border ballads, the rhythms of country dialects, and folk tales with supernatural turns endeared him to Scott.

Like Scott's best fiction, Hogg's novel is "Scotch to its very marrow." [2] While other romantic writers sought inspiration (or, at least, atmosphere) from the Black Forest, the Alps, or the Pyrenees, Scott and Hogg were able to find it at home. One might almost say that they were unable to find it anywhere else. Early in *Waverley* the young hero expresses the same disbelief articulated by Henry Tilney when confronted with the possibility of violence "as falling within the common order of things, and happening daily in the immediate vicinity, without his having crossed the seas, and while he was yet in the otherwise well-ordered island of Great Britain." Both Scott and Austen treat the righteous complacency of their English heroes with irony, but the difference is that Scott thrusts his hero into the Highlands and temporarily disturbs his tranquillity, while Jane Austen merely raises an eyebrow.

Scotland, for Scott and Hogg, was at the same time a source of the sublime and the familiar. Surely, its mountains, lochs, and rocky coasts were as wild and haunting as any that could be found on the continent; Edinburgh and its brooding castle could hardly be bettered by a Bavarian schloss or a Spanish cloister. But for the native Scottish writer, these picturesque elements were not items in a book of travel sketches nor "sites" visited on a grand tour, but the natural contours of a world known since childhood. As important as the physical landscape of Scotland — and firmly bound up with it — was the spirit of the common people, their relations with one another and with foreigners, their attachment to family and to land, and, of particular importance, their attitude toward the supernatural. When writing about Scotland, Scott and Hogg could endow their characters with authentic Presbyterian habits and views rather than with a false Catholicism, though Scott, of course, made use of both. Moreover, each had an interest in the ways in which ancient and regional superstitions blended with Christian doctrine.

Hogg's first novel, or novella, was *The Brownie of Bodsbeck*, a tale of the Royalist suppression of the Covenanters near the end of the seventeenth century. Though Hogg wrote his book first, it was published after Scott's *Old Mortality*, and the similarity of theme caused many, including Scott, to take it as an imitation. The very existence of the book made Scott uncomfortable, but, what was worse, he felt that his friend's treatment of the religious and political issues showed him to be a careless historian. "I like it very ill — very ill indeed . . . it is a distorted, a prejudiced and untrue picture of the Royal party." Hogg is said to have replied, "It is a devilish deal truer than yours though." [3]

The exchange strikes at the center of one of the most important differences between the two writers. Hogg, as Scott pointed out, was "profoundly ignorant of history." He had little of Scott's antiquarian curiosity; his collection of ballads and tales was unsystematic, his sources were friends and relatives, and very often, his own fertile imagination. While Scott's aim in Old Mortality was to recreate in credible terms a historical period filled with inflammatory contention, Hogg's interest, even at this early date, was to explore the effects of unusual events on individual sensibilities. Most of the sensibilities in The Brownie of Bodsbeck are rather too susceptible and superstitious to make for much variety of characterization, though they probably are a fairly accurate reflection of the reactions of simple country folk to "history." What is important to notice is that Hogg does not pretend to take a historian's interest in public event, factual detail, or chronology. In one of his rare references to a date, he rather casually notes that "the incidents here recorded took place . . . I believe, in the autumn of 1685." [4] The narrative tone is not that of a scholar writing a book, but of a countryman telling a story, eager to hurry past the trivialities and get on to the "good parts."

Public event — in this case, the Royalist persecution of the Covenanters — serves as the catalyst to private reaction. There is a sense, then, in which Hogg's tale might be considered "truer" than Scott's, not because it provides a balanced assessment of the larger issues, but because it attempts to explore the effects of great events on the inner lives of a few simple people. Hogg's narrative is, as Scott says, most certainly "distorted" and "prejudiced"; it is a loosely connected series of anecdotes, legends, dream-visions, and downright lies which were passed about by country people in the south of Scotland in this period in reaction to the sudden and terrifying appearances of Royalist troops on the lookout for "psalm-singers" and to the equally terrifying and mysterious appearances of the hunted fanatics. Hogg does, of course, explain at the end that the "brownie" and other "spirits" and "demons" spotted by various people at odd times of night are really Covenanters, made shaggy and thin by months of hiding in caves.

But the point of the narrative does not lie in the explanation at the end; it is in the telling of the parts along the way. Whatever the ultimate rational explanation may be, the people have had their frights and nightmares; no explanation can go back and eradicate them. They are true experiences, however little they are grounded in reason. Hogg's method anticipates Yeats's justification of his own interest in folklore: "Folk imagination . . . creates endless images of which there are no

210

ideas. Its stories ignore the moral law and every other law, they are successions of pictures like those seen by children in the fire . . . Everything seems possible to [country folk], and because they can never be surprised, they imagine the most surprising things." [5]

Throughout *The Brownie of Bodsbeck,* Hogg is preoccupied with the ways of telling a story and with the extent to which these ways invariably reveal something about the teller, whether or not they are suited to other kinds of truth. A shepherd's gossipy wife tends to conclude her most far-fetched stories with the emphatic statement that "this is a plain and positive truth"; the narrator apologizes at the beginning of chapter two for interrupting his story in order to provide background "before proceeding with the incidents as they occurred, which is the common way of telling a story in the country" (but not, he implies, the only way); a hypocritical curate tells an old woman a story "fitted admirably to suit her weak and superstitious mind"; a righteous young woman calls her mother's frightened complaints "words of delirium (which) I will not set down in my memory as spoken by you." One young man, evidently so distressed by the stories of demons in the region, dreams while lying naked in bed that a beautiful queen of the faeries comes to him and tries to lure him into following her; when he refuses, she turns into a horrible monster and grabs hold of his wrists; he reaches for a knife, but in cutting off her fingers, severs his own thumb. With its combination of erotic fantasy and pathological repression, the incident has great psychological possibilities. Indeed, the dream bears some resemblance to Lockwood's nightmare of Catherine clutching at him through the bedroom window until he finds himself rubbing her wrist against the broken glass. Hogg's dreamer is neither a main character nor a narrator whose story goes beyond the telling of his own dream, yet the intensity of his vision and the vitality of his language hint at a symbolic potentiality which Hogg would put to more effective use in *The Confessions of a Justified Sinner.*

2

Though Hogg had not yet learned at the time of the writing of *The Brownie of Bodsbeck* how to turn his interest in "dreamy stories about ghosts and apparitions and persecutions" into a coherent narrative, he had begun to place an emphasis on each teller and *his* truth (as distinct from the disinterested historian and *the* truth) which would develop in his later years into something like a romantic creed. Though his *Lay Sermons on Good Principles and Good Breeding* are, on the whole, fairly conventional reflections on Christian prudence, there are several recurring themes which are, in their origin, more romantic than Christian. In distinguishing between reason and instinct, Hogg begins with the traditional distinction between men and animals, discusses the value of memory, language, the ability to ask questions — those rational faculties which lead man to understand himself and recognize his dependence upon a supreme being. But as soon as Hogg tries to link reason with the divine, the less he sounds like a Christian rationalist and the more like Shelley on the poetic imagination. "I know and feel that there is an intelligent principle within me striving to burst the slender and corporeal boundaries within which it has pleased God to imprison and confine it." [6] He speaks of the "sublime faculty" by which man is "capable of contemplating the effects of . . . Divine perfections" and by means of which he can "soar above his own feelings."

Even these sentiments might be taken as unexceptional expressions of Christian enthusiasm if it were not for the way Hogg eventually applies them to art. His insistence upon the unique, sublime, almost sacred quality of human "reason" — a term which seems to include all the faculties of the mind — leads him to an equally forceful insistence on the artist's independence from and superiority to regulative convention. In a sermon on *Reviewers*, he appears almost obsessed by the need to proclaim the artist's right to find justification only in himself and in the terms of his own work: "Never allow any person to persuade you that criticism is a science, and that an author must go astray unless he follows certain rules . . . No rules ever devised by man can make a poet . . . The rule ought to be in every man's breast." If a writer is to learn from other writers, let him not imitate but take inspiration from the greatest and least imitative geniuses: "Take the simplicity of Moses, the splendour of Job, David and Isaiah. Take Homer and, if you like, Hesiod, Pindar, and Ossian; and by all means William Shakespeare. In short, borrow the fire and vigour of an early period of society, when a nation is verging from barbarism to civilisation; and then you will imbibe the force of genius from its original source. Nourish the inspiration, and despise the cold rules of criticism."

Hogg's claims for art and the artist's inspiration are, in some ways, analogous to his claims for the Christian's reliance on revelation. In a sermon on *Deism*, he rejects as futile and insensitive all efforts to arrive logically at a natural religion, arguing that the divine would not be divine if it were capable of being measured, analyzed, and thoroughly understood. "I think it is best, in supporting the doctrines of the Christian religion, always to avoid any attempt to explain mysteries. The necessity and belief of a mystery is one thing, but the explanation is another." The argument is not new with Hogg, but what it says about his attitude toward mystery and explanation is significant, especially in light of the disagreement with Scott on the nature of "truth."

Hogg states here and he demonstrates in his later fiction — as Scott never could bring himself to do — a belief in a realm of reality different from that which can be profitably subjected to rational inquiry. In this sermon he is talking about religious revelation, but elsewhere the same attitude is adopted toward the artist's imaginative vision, the sleeper's dream, and the psychopath's projections. A "mystery," for Hogg, is not a challenge for a solution; that only means that it will be deprived of its essence and converted into the terms of a different reality. The challenge for the artist is not to produce respectability by means of translation, but to enter into strange places and tell what they are like. Flannery O'Connor once commented on a remark of St. Gregory's in a way that Hogg would have understood: "Every time the sacred text describes a fact, it reveals a mystery. That is what the fiction writer, on his lesser level, hopes to do." [7]

3

The first and most obvious thing a reader notices about *The Private Memoirs and Confessions of a Justified Sinner* is that it is two books in one — two separate accounts written by different hands about the same characters and, superficially, the same events. As he proceeds with the second account, the reader finds himself making more and more frequent and complicated comparisons. The broken structure of the work, usually taken as an ingenious reinforcement of the theme of human duality, is more radical an innovation than any other single element of the work. It forces the reader to confront two kinds of reality, each of which is compelling and consistent within itself, yet neither of which altogether explains the other. Each has hints, nuances, and details which enrich the other. The two accounts interact, but they do not fully correspond; they may be — indeed, they must be — compared, but neither serves as the key, the solution, the answer to the other.

The very fact that the more distinctly subjective account, the memoir, *follows* the narrative which a disinterested "editor" has patched together from "tradition" and "parish registers" indicates that Hogg was departing from — or, more precisely, reversing — one of the major conventions of the Gothic mystery. When a story is told twice in a novel by Radcliffe or Clara Reeve, it is first told, whether or not the first person is employed, as if through the eyes of a terrified, confused, and highly excitable heroine and only at the end retold "as it really was" by a sensible, all-knowing narrator or a wise family friend. Hogg is clearly doing something altogether different and more serious in *The Confessions of a Justified Sinner.* He takes his nightmares *and* his common sense more seriously than Mrs. Radcliffe does, but he is not nearly as sure as she seems to be of what they have to do with one another.

On first reading, it would seem obvious that the Editor's Narrative is, as advertised, an impartial account, derived largely from country tradition, of the Colwan family: the Laird of Dalcastle, his wife, and their sons, George and Robert, the former of whom is handsome, athletic, outgoing, the latter a pale, sickly, and fanatic Calvinist, driven by envy to fratricide. But even before we come to the second narrative, Robert's Memoir, several basic "facts" are placed in doubt. For one thing, it is suggested, though never proved, that the two are only half-brothers, born to the same mother, George sired by the lusty old laird and Robert by his mother's chaplain, the self-righteous and hypocritical Reverend Mr. Wringhim. Secondly, and more important, though the circumstances appear to weigh most heavily against Robert, the testimony of witnesses to George's murder is sufficiently confused to allow for suspicion of a second and even a third villain. Finally, and most disturbing of all, it is not absolutely certain that George is dead, for if

214

there were witnesses to the "murder," there are also witnesses to George — or some unholy image of him — walking arm in arm with his brother after the event. Thus, before we come to the second narrative, we are faced with sufficiently contradictory versions of the truth to cause us to wonder about the events, but perhaps even more than that, about the witnesses.

Nearly all of the critical episodes related in the Editor's Narrative, whether or not there is a confusion about details, involve observers and participants, and the concurrent image of a game or sport in which some are players and others spectators. The narrative opens with a description of the wedding feast of the Laird of Dalcastle who "danced . . . snapped his fingers . . . clapped his hands . . . [and] saluted every girl in the hall" while his puritanical bride watched disapprovingly "absolutely refusing to tread a single measure." [8] Later in the bridal chamber, it is the groom's turn to watch without participating while his bride insists upon praying and reading Scripture late into the night until, out of boredom and fatigue, the old man falls asleep, and she takes refuge with one of her bridesmaids. In the morning, when the bride is found, each accuses the other of "playing":

"You sly and malevolent imp," said the laird; "you have played me such a trick when I was fast asleep! I have not known a frolic so clever, and, at the same time, so severe. Come along, you baggage, you!"
"Sir, I will let you know that I detest your principles and your person alike," said she. "It shall never be said, Sir, that my person was at the control of a heathenish man of Belial — a dangler among the daughters of women — a promiscuous dancer — and a player of unlawful games."

The entire episode and dialogue would not have been out of place in a novel of Fielding's or Smollett's, but what might have remained a static situation of comic incongruity is used by Hogg as a preamble, an unobtrusive warning of darker developments to come. The relationship between the laird and his wife does not progress much beyond this conventionally comic stage largely because they have little to do with one another even while living under the same roof. "The upper, or third story of the old mansion-house was awarded to the lady for her residence. She had a separate door, a separate stair, a separate garden." So long as they agree to keep themselves, their habits, and their ways of seeing things separate, there is little likelihood of complication or danger. The reader can laugh because he sees that each speech is a fair representation of the feelings of the speaker and, at the same time, a misrepresentation or, at least, an extreme exaggeration of the character being addressed. The integrity of each, however limited, is preserved and the comedy maintained so long as there is no serious effort on either side to impose terms on the other. We see that neither the laird nor his wife is changed or affected by the speech or behavior of the other, and, therefore, though we might ultimately find them monotonous, we are amused and untroubled by them. It is only when the mentality or language of one intrudes upon and mingles with that of another that order and identity are threatened. As the old laird tries to explain to his wife when she insists upon praying when he prefers to make love: "It would be like reading the Bible and the jest-book, verse about, and would render the life of man a medley of absurdity and confusion."

4

The remainder of the Editor's Narrative, dealing as it does with collisions of temperament, philosophy, and theological systems, is indeed a "medley of absurdity and confusion." What is so interesting, however, is not simply Hogg's presentation of emotional and intellectual conflict, as reflected in the hatred of one brother for another, but the way in which Robert strikes at the basis of his brother's reality, threatening his sanity and finally his very identity. The demonic brother disturbs the "normal" and conventional George with the kinds of questions which Hogg himself, more gently and subtly, makes his reader ask: Who am I? What is real?

The two brothers who have been raised and educated separately have their first important encounter at a tennis match. The scene is one of the most striking and symbolically telling in the novel. Handsome, fair-haired, blue-eyed George is the agile winner, the "hero," the "king of the game." The dark, "devilish-looking," shadow-like figure is Robert, the "onlooker," not playing, but watching, sneering, standing in his brother's way, and eventually spoiling the game. Unlike their parents, the old laird and his puritanical wife, the brothers, once they meet in Edinburgh, do not go their separate ways, though clearly George would prefer it. Robert's intention is to depose the "king of the game," obviously not by defeating him at tennis, but by changing the terms of the contest altogether. The disagreement is more basic than that presented in most narratives in which the characters, however they may differ morally and socially, exist in the same context of reality. George, like his father, is a carefree and sporting man; he thinks life is to be enjoyed as a test of skill and wit; he is good-natured, he would not intentionally harm another, but he is not obsessively scrupulous. The tennis game is as serious to him as most things are in his life, and when the "party played for considerable stakes — namely a dinner and wine at the Black Bull tavern . . . George, as the hero and head of his party, was much interested in its honour."

Robert, too, likes a contest: we are told that "he knew no other pleasure but what consisted in opposition." Yet for him the opposition is not a matter of physical dexterity — in which even the "hero" may occasionally lose — but a predetermined and absolute spiritual righteousness against the damned. He projects a supernatural environment which is at war with the natural environment inhabited by his brother. It is not merely that he disapproves of his brother's playing tennis — which, of course, he does — but, what is psychologically much more disturbing, he attempts to redefine the "game" in mid-play, to transform himself from witness to major participant, to render ridiculous all rules and regulations but his own. Under the circumstances, it is not surprising that the reader is given no information about George's tennis opponent. We simply must take for granted that someone is there hitting the ball back to him. But his spiritual and psychological opponent demands so much attention from the crowd, from the reader, and finally from George himself that the "game" cannot continue under the aspect of a well-regulated sport. The system — George's "kingdom" — breaks down amidst laughter, cursing, and general confusion.

The scene is a small masterpiece of ominous humor and absurdity. By choosing an innocuous and highly formalized athletic contest as his "event," Hogg demonstrates the formative power of viewpoint. We first see the match as the crowd sees it and then as George himself sees it — an exhilarating test of skill in which there is little room for misunderstanding. It appears to be clear who is winning. The disruption comes not because of a disagreement about scoring, but because of an unstated challenge to the conventional roles of spectator and player.

Robert who, according to one system of things, is an onlooker, is, according to another, *the* major player, God's warrior doing battle against the personification of corruption. Without debating the point, but by simply acting upon it, he forces the other participants, quite against their will, to *watch* him and, in doing so, to become confused about their previous roles and allow the game to turn into chaos.

Largely because of the impersonal tone of the Editor's Narrative the reader is not forced to choose the point of view of the clubby tennis players or of the fanatic Calvinist. Both viewpoints have obvious limitations which the reader may not wish to claim for his own, yet in combination they possess a curious tension and life. The reader, as always in this book, is encouraged to weigh and to compare but discouraged from drawing conclusions. He senses early in the narrative that to adopt one system or one vocabulary — whether the old laird's or his wife's, George's or Robert's — is to ignore or to annihilate the others. Hogg's intention, it would seem, is to keep several views alive and to keep his reader alive to them. Hence, when Robert takes up the cry of one of the players, "That's a damned fine blow, George!", and tosses it back mockingly at his brother, we can respond to it in a variety of ways. We may be amused, with Robert, at the parroting of the self-consciously virile and hearty language of the sportsmen; we may be irritated, like George, at the envious little spoilsport who cannot bear to see others enjoy themselves, and we may be vaguely disturbed by the way the word "damned" is loosened from its colloquial and metaphysical contexts and left suspended somewhere between the two.

The next time Robert intrudes upon a game, George and his friends are playing cricket, and this time the interruptions are so bold that the other players cry out to "kick him out of the play-ground! Knock down the scoundrel." But George, having been maddened into hitting Robert with his tennis racket the last time, realizes that "he wants nothing else" since, of course, to strike back is to submit to the rules of *his* game. With this warning, George anticipates one of the major dilemmas of the novel: how do you combat an irrational enemy without becoming like him?

For a time, George tries to remove himself from view in the hope that his brother will give up his malicious intentions and go away. But this, of course, is no solution, and the first morning that George dares to take a walk in the country, a monstrous apparition of his brother appears in a cloud before him. Terrified, he runs from it and stumbles into Robert, who had been standing nearby. Though this is later "explained" as a shadow or reflection, the basic point is clear enough. George's game has been permanently ruined. Without wishing it, or even understanding it, he is gradually forced to behave as though Robert's way is the only one. What begins as a reflex develops into a habitual reaction too strong for self-discipline and withdrawal. The reaction is a mirror image of the initial act of hostility and of the viewpoint which justified it. After each of the intrusions upon his games, George had tried to become reconciled to his brother, and though each time he failed, he tries again when he stumbles into him on his morning walk. But there is a new tone in the voice of the carefree sportsman who calls his brother "wretch" and demands to know whether "the devil was that friend who told you I was here." Robert denies it and pulls free, saying that his reconciliation with his brother is as complete as "the lark's is with the adder." We are accustomed to this kind of language from Robert, but what comes as a chilling mark of his success is George's joining the "holy war" and calling out after him, "If thou are not a limb of Satan, I never saw one." The confusion of roles is nearly complete. The two brothers who were introduced as conventional opposites, are beginning to act and sound alike.

5

The major and climactic scene of the Editor's Narrative is the duel in which George is slain. To attempt even a brief and neutral summary of the episode is to falsify it in a more seriously damaging way than plot summaries of novels usually do. For the questions raised by the scene are not merely, "Who killed George?" and "Why?" but, "Who was there?" and "Was George really killed at all?" The reader finds himself entangled in a mystery which bears a closer resemblance to the fictional world of Alain Robbe-Grillet than to that of Ann Radcliffe. We are not simply invited to look for a villain, we are asked to reconsider the nature of reality and the relationship of the human witness to "external" event. We can hardly ask, "Who did it?" when we are far from sure what "it" is.

Hogg has moved steadily in his Editor's Narrative from clarity to obscurity, from the neat and comic contrast of the laird and his wife, through the less comic but still relatively distinct contrast between George and Robert, to a blurring of the brothers' roles which in the climactic duel scene produces a profoundly disturbing confusion of identity and event. It has already been noted that Hogg reversed the Gothic mystery-story order of narration by placing the "subjective" account after the narrative of the disinterested editor. But even within the Editor's Narrative, we find the same pattern of regression. Hogg has acted upon the fixed and reassuring conventions of the Gothic novel as Robert has acted upon the rules of tennis. Hogg is his own marplot, intruding upon the clichés of fiction and shattering the reader's expectations by raising questions so sweeping as to make conventional solutions and conventional questions seem irrelevant.

Events grow stranger as the narrative progresses, and when the crucial moment of the duel arrives, the "editor" removes himself and presents as his major witness, Bell Calvert, a whore, reputed to be "a swindler and impostor." As in the characterizations of the laird and his wife, Hogg looked to the eighteenth century for the prototype of this character and called upon the tradition of the talkative, good-hearted prostitute who is more entertaining than accurate as a historian. Nonetheless, Bell Calvert is all we have for the moment, and we are forced to consider the events as she reports them. We know from other sources that George Colwan, who has been drinking in a tavern with some friends, has had a falling out with Thomas Drummond, a hot-tempered Scotsman. Drummond leaves the party in anger, and a short time later George is sent a message by a man *presumed* to be Drummond to meet him outside in the alley. George's friends try to dissuade him from going, but once he leaves,

the inadvertent party, left within, thought no more of the circumstance till the morning, [when] the report had spread over the city that a young gentleman had been slain, on a little washing-green at the side of the North Loch, and at the very bottom of the close where his thoughtless party had been assembled.

The "inadvertence" and "thoughtlessness" of George's friends do not connote disloyalty or cowardice, for in an affair of honor it would have

220

been necessary for him to face the challenge on his own and, in any case, neither the nature of the dispute nor the character of Drummond indicated a duel to the death. The point that Hogg seems to be making — and here again he departs from the formula of melodrama — is that the hero, the idol and leader of a group of young men, faces the great challenge of his life alone and dies without the knowledge or consolation of sympathetic witnesses. Hogg's first mention of George's death is reported to the reader, without urgency or passion, as George's friends would have heard the next morning the news which "had spread over the city that a young gentleman had been slain." The irony lies in an exposure of the peculiar untheatricality of life in which "great" events can occur without the benefit of an observant and judicious chorus. It is the same point made by Auden in *Musée des Beaux Arts* when the poet speaks of how suffering occurs "While someone else is eating or opening a window or just walking dully along." What is stressed is not the limitation of human virtue but the even greater limitation of human awareness. There is no reason to doubt that George's friends would have cared had they *seen* what was taking place. The irony is that despite their affection for their friend and their physical proximity to him at the moment of his death, *they do not see him suffer.* Hogg challenges one of the basic conventions of fiction: the major — and, particularly, the painful — events in a life should be reported as though witnessed by a trustworthy observer who can fit each episode into a coherent pattern. Nobody, he unsportingly implies, sees that much of anyone but himself.

Thus, the alternative to a first-person narrative is not an omniscient narrative, but a disinterested patching together of reports by a variety of witnesses. The result is like a trial presided over by an absent-minded judge. Bell Calvert's story takes up at the point where Drummond is said to have left the tavern. She persuades him to join her in her room and when he leaves, watches him from her window as he passes two other men, one dressed in tartans very much like Drummond's and the other in black. Meanwhile, Bell has been joined by a new client, and she points out to him that the companion of the man in black looks exactly like Drummond, though she has just seen Drummond heading in the opposite direction. The Drummond-like man, described

221

by Bell as a spirit or demon or apparition, conceals his companion in a doorway, knocks on the tavern door, is joined by George Colwan whom he challenges to a duel. George is willing, but he wants "to have friends with us to see fair play." This is George's last effort to re-establish the order of a sportsmanlike contest.

The other stormed at these words. "You are a braggart, Sir," cried he, "a wretch — a blot on the cheek of nature — a blight on the Christian world — a reprobate — I'll have your soul, Sir. You must play at tennis, and put down elect brethren in another world tomorrow."

Once again the vocabulary of the athlete and that of the religious zealot vie absurdly with one another, each trying to assess, define, and ultimately to control the situation. But as there appears to be no common ground, no experiential link through which communication and compromise might be established, language breaks down and gives way to violence. To add to the confusion and madness of the duel, Bell includes in her terrified account the reactions of her client, watching with her from the window, who takes the whole episode as entertainment and cannot keep from exclaiming, "That's grand! That's excellent!" whenever an artful thrust is made. Just as George appears to have gotten the best of his opponent, the figure in black emerges from the dark entry and stabs him in the back. George's dying words — "Oh, dog of hell, it is you who has done this!" — suggest to the reader, though obviously not to Bell since she is unacquainted with the Colwans, that Robert is his brother's murderer.

Bell's narrative draws to a close with her pondering over the extraordinary resemblance between Drummond and George's challenger, yet since she had seen Drummond walk past the man, she is certain it cannot be he: "We have nothing on earth but our senses to depend upon: if these deceive us, what are we to do?" After she tells her story to Mrs. Logan, the old laird's good-natured mistress, the two women decide to spy on Robert at home in Dalcastle. They see him walking arm in arm with a companion who looks and acts like George, though Bell saw him killed and Mrs. Logan laid him in his coffin.

"It cannot be in nature, that is quite clear," said Mrs. Logan. "Yet how should it be that I should *think* so — I who knew him and nursed him from infancy — there lies the paradox. As you said once before, we have nothing but our senses to depend on, and, if you and I believe we see a person, why, we do see him. Whose word, or whose reasoning can convince us against our own senses?"

Soon after this, the Editor's Narrative comes to a close. We learn little more except that Robert disappears mysteriously and that Thomas Drummond, accused of the murder of George Colwan, "was outlawed and obliged to fly his country," and eventually became a distinguished officer in the Austrian army.

Before proceeding with the second account, Robert's Memoir, the reader is left with no solution and a variety of possibilities. We may entertain the possibility that something unnatural has occurred, that the devil's hand has been responsible for the strange events, particularly the appearance of Thomas Drummond's and George Colwan's doubles. We may also presume that Bell is crazy or, in an effort to protect one of her own clients and benefactors, dishonest. Further, we may suppose that Bell's impressive and bizarre tale plunges Mrs. Logan into a state of hysteria so that she too believes she is seeing ghosts. The problem is that, though the discrediting of the two ladies may rid us of one kind of ghost and devil, it by no means clarifies the case. We are still left wondering what went on that night, who was there, and who did what to whom. And if we cannot take anthropomorphic devils seriously, we are forced to reconsider the minds that can. As Robert's Memoir will demonstrate, that is hardly a reassuring exercise.

"*Like* is an ill mark," says an old servant when asked to swear in court that a gown which resembles one belonging to her mistress is in fact the same gown. Yet "like" is nearly all we have to rely upon in this novel. It is a book of resemblances, some inexplicably close, some incongruously distant. In the Editor's Narrative, most of the resemblances are noted and described by witnesses, like the old servant, or Bell Calvert, or Mrs. Logan, who are only tangentially involved in the action and who see in the central characters not reflections of themselves but of other major characters. However serious, even brutal the events become, there is always the detached tone of a spectator watching a game he does not fully understand, though he can see that the opponents tend to resemble one another and mirror each other's actions.

223

6

Robert's Private Memoir, as the opening paragraph illustrates, is an inside view. In the Editor's Narrative, the witnesses were describing things which were usually not happening to them, while in the second narrative, everything worth noting at all is worth noting because Robert sees it as happening to or because of him. The language is personal, overwrought, and prophetic:

My life has been a life of trouble and turmoil; of change and vicissitude; of anger and exultation; of sorrow and of vengeance. My sorrows have all been for a slighted gospel, and my vengeance has been wreaked on its adversaries. Therefore, in the might of Heaven, I will sit down and write.

Robert's subject is not, like that of the editor, a chain of curious events, but "my life." His rhetoric — repetitious, alliterative, hyperbolic — is like that of an enthusiastic preacher who begins his sermon at a high pitch of fervor. If the witnesses in the first narrative were not always sure of their emotions — whether or not to laugh or cry, whether to cheer for the underdog or run screaming out of the stadium — Robert, on the contrary, seems to have struck his single emotional note: the outrage of a wronged man.

Early in Robert's Memoir, the subject of resemblance is brought up when an old servant hints that Robert is "so like" the Reverend Mr. Wringhim that the minister, rather than the Laird of Dalcastle, must be the boy's father. More important, in the symbolic development of the novel, than the boy's physical resemblance to Wringhim is his inheritance of the minister's self-righteousness, his belief in justification, and his habit of identifying himself with Old Testament figures. Wringhim likes to think of himself as Melchizedek, and the young Robert imagines himself as David, "the sinful king of Israel," who repents and becomes the Lord's favorite. The reader may at first be amused by this kind of talk which, as Scott and Hogg had shown in earlier works, was common among zealous Scots Calvinists. But what humor there is in this language must stem from the reader's sense of the disparity between it and the true nature of the characters who employ it. Wringhim, for example, is a literary stereotype, the ludicrous religious hypocrite, a cross between Thwackum and Tartuffe. But Robert is not nearly so easy to assess. Because of the fact that he tells the story and because of the *way* he tells it, we find it all but impossible to separate him from his language. Indeed, the further we read into his memoir, the more convinced we become that his language — however hyperbolic and typological — does, in a sense, define him. To put it in another way, we see him *become* as excessive and rigidified as his words.

In the first narrative, because of the changes and uncertainties of narrative voice, the possibility of irony is always kept open. But in Robert's Memoir, detachment, even of the wavering and confused sort encountered in the earlier narrative, is absent. Wringhim, and the easily detected disparity between behavior and language which he represents, quickly ceases to be an important element in Robert's "life" story. With the loss of perspective comes the loss of irony and with the loss irony, not simply an insensitivity to hypocrisy, but an ignorance of a life beyond language. For Robert, language becomes a closed system which imposes on life rather than a loose organization of signs which shift, fuse, and alter meaning according to circumstance. If the reader of the Editor's Narrative had been made to feel the discomfort of following a narrative in which each speaker admits the inadequacy of his testimony, he is made to feel the opposite and greater discomfort in the Memoir, whose author claims to have the perfect and only true testimony. The Editor's Narrative makes too few claims, Robert's Memoir too many; the Editor's Narrative appears too artless and life-like in its confusions; Robert's Memoir is so artful that life, especially that of the speaker, can hardly survive it.

Hogg places us in the mind of a man damned or mad, or both. And the sign of his condition is his inability to allow life and his own human nature qualities and dimensions beyond those circumscribed by his religious and linguistic systems. He does not see his scheme as an approximation of truth but as the truth itself — whole and unchangeable. Everything must be fitted into his preconceived pattern. But life, deprived of potentiality, is deprived of itself. Robert's Memoir is not, therefore, the history of a troubled life, but of a living death — an existence stopped and settled, a condition without a future. The doctrine of justification provides the theological basis for the state of mind Hogg attempts to recreate in the memoir. If a man is justified or saved once and forever by God's grace, nothing he does — however vicious

225

— can ever remove him from that divinely endowed state. Thus, Robert's life, even as he himself sees it, is a finished matter; the conclusion precedes and, in a sense, makes superfluous the telling of the tale.

Why is it, then, that Robert's Private Memoir makes such fascinating reading? Surely we do not wonder, as readers of *Faust* once may have, whether Robert will be damned or saved. His salvation and damnation amount to the same thing — the elimination of doubt, the arresting of flux — and the predetermined solution is offered at the beginning of the mystery rather than at the end. In terms of the conventional moral allegory, as well as in those of the Gothic terror tale, there is no mystery to be resolved in conclusion. And this, after all, is a terrible thing.

According to Robert's inflexible fanaticism, where there is life there is heresy. His early "conversion" is instead his giving himself up to the devil, the personification of all beings, principles, and systems which deny life to others in order to preserve themselves. Once Robert has encountered his satanic double — "What was my astonishment on perceiving that he was the same being as myself!" — everything becomes crystal-clear to him. He is God's instrument against the wicked — and, of course, his companion will tell him who is or is not wicked. So far as the Memoir is concerned, this is the climax and denouement. When Robert returns home from the meeting with his double, his mother finds his voice and manner "changed" and hardly recognizes him; she presumes him to be "either dying or translated," and Wringhim admits, "I could not have known you for the same person." Robert is, with most of the Memoir still to go, *lost.* One does not read on to see whether that decision can somehow be reversed. Given what we have learned so far from the book, that is unthinkable. We do not read on to see whether hell can be avoided but to see what it is like.

Hell is like the mind of a madman. But if we have been attentive readers of Hogg we ought to remember that "like" — even at best — is an "ill mark." Hogg's work is not allegory or an ingenuous form of autobiography; it is an early form of symbolist fiction in which various configurations of imagery *suggest* several things at once and "stand for" nothing but themselves. It is out of keeping with the spirit of the book to speak of such words as "soul," "devil," or "hell" as though they were elements of a cumbersome vocabulary, pointing toward, but not yet ready to serve the sophisticated purposes of psychological analysis. Robert's damnation and his intercourse with a diabolical double are not metaphors for his madness, they are its complements. To address oneself to the psychological aspects of Robert's Memoir is not a way of solving the mystery but a way of describing one of its manifestations. A pattern of schizophrenia can be detected, but whether it is the symptom of an individual malady or the condition of the universe remains uncertain.

Robert's metaphysical and moral system is so arbitrarily rigid that human nature cannot survive it. Viewed psychologically, those aspects of himself which cannot be reconciled to the scheme split off from his consciousness and take on, in his eyes, identities distinct from his own being. The devil, described by Robert, as a chameleon figure, may assume his own shape, that of his brother, or even an absence of shape and consciousness as during the periods when Robert acts the seducer without being aware of it. Certainly as interesting, and even more appalling than the various shapes and non-shapes of the devil, is the spectacle of Robert undergoing a shrinkage and ultimately a disintegration of his own conscious personality. The more populated Robert's world becomes with "external" guardians and enemies, the less there is for him to do but react to their initiative. Confusing the flux, contradiction, and complexity of life with sin, Robert attributes more and more energy to forces beyond his own conscious knowledge and control. Thus, natural enough feelings of rivalry and envy for a stronger and handsomer brother, rather than being acknowledged as a commonplace and potentially manageable weakness in himself, is gradually converted into the extraordinary simplicity of his metaphysical scheme. Since he considers himself to be justified by God, his hatred of his brother must be the righteous hatred of one of the elect for one of the damned. If one grants the premise, it may be said that the reasoning, like most forms of deduction, is consistent within its own terms. Thus, Robert's madness is not by any means the erratic "medley" of "absurdity and confusion" the reader has heard about and encountered in the Editor's Narrative. Quite the contrary; though the tone is emotional, the reasoning is cool, neat, and clear. All of his crimes, including his self-murder, are predictable and schematically coherent. And still the disturbing question remains: is Robert's version of things an appalling deviation from nature or is it a reflection of an even more appalling, because general, truth?

7

Once finished with both the Editor's Narrative and Robert's Memoir, the reader may well wonder where, in all of this, is the artist? Is there a controlling hand or has Hogg once again assembled an intriguing but disconnected series of episodes? The answer takes us back to the disagreement between Scott and Hogg on the nature of truth in fiction. If one takes as Hogg's main subjects, murder, insanity, demonic possession, and suicide, it would be difficult to claim originality or unusual artistic merit on that count. If these have been the subjects of great tragic drama of the past, they have also been the standard fare of the worst Gothic fiction. To be reminded of the conventionality of Hogg's "bizarre" material is to be reminded of the extraordinary way in which he presents it. Rather than give too refined and Jamesian an air to the achievement, it might be better to avoid the term "point of view," and say that the originality and a good measure of the aesthetic integrity of Hogg's novel derive from his preoccupation with the number of "true" ways in which a story can be told.

One has the impression, upon completing the book, of having witnessed and imaginatively participated in an event, though by no means of having "grasped" it. And this would seem to be one of Hogg's significant accomplishments: to have told the story in a variety of ways without having destroyed the life and the mystery of it in the process. Hogg's novel is closer to the new *romans noirs* referred to by Robbe-Grillet in his essay on Raymond Roussel than to the detective novel in the Victorian tradition of Dickens, Wilkie Collins, and Conan Doyle. As in the earliest Gothic fiction, surfaces must be taken seriously because they are all one has. In Robbe-Grillet's words, "the too transparent explanation becomes itself a form of opacity." [9] The "new novel" is not an answer but a question, not a theory but an investigation; one does not read it in order to discover the solution offered on the last page, but in order to witness the convergence of different realities and to participate in the formulation of questions about them.

CONFESSIONS OF A JUSTIFIED SINNER

Though not nearly so self-conscious as most twentieth-century novelists, Hogg does occasionally hint at his sense of the artist's function in his book. The emphasis on games and systems and the seriousness with which they are applied to life has a relevance for the artist constantly confronted with the necessity of choosing structures, patterns, plots, through which to express himself. Many of Hogg's stories are "borrowed" from folklore, and some of his best poems are the imitations which were collected in *The Poetic Mirror*. The repeated references to resemblances, reflections, images, and analogies in *Justified Sinner* are reminders of the standard devices of the literary artist. Indeed, the fact that Robert's loss of soul and sanity — ultimately, the loss of his self — is marked by his giving way to a highly stylized, at times almost hypnotic rhetoric, indicates something of Hogg's misgivings about the deadening powers of formalistic convention — literary as well as theological.

Hogg employs the familiar image of Satan as a marplot, stepping in and spoiling harmless human games, but he also reminds us that Satan is as often a skilled artist, seeking to break down one kind of order so that he can establish a far stricter and more burdensome one of his own. Robert notes in his Memoir that his strange companion's "art" is "without a parallel," which, if true, would make it the only thing in the book of which that could be said. It is not quite true, however; in this book of parallels, it could not be. The devil's art has a host of likenesses: the quick maneuver, the too subtle argument, the seductive smile. The object of his craft is to create hell — which, like its maker, can be found almost anywhere. Near the end of the narrative Robert tries to escape from his strange companion as well as from the civil authorities. As he races from place to place, he begins to realize that there is no real movement or change; every inn, farmhouse, stable — even the very earth — is a prison and a torment so that wherever he turns, he must say, like Marlowe's Mephistopheles, "Why this is hell, nor am I out of it!"

At one point he takes refuge in a weaver's cottage and finds himself locked for the night in a tiny room filled with looms. The episode has the mixture of absurdity and sense, humor and pathos, symbolic potential and concrete reality, which characterize the best sections of both narratives:

229

At first I thought I was in a dream, and felt the weaver's beam, web, and treadle-strings with my hands to convince myself that I was awake . . . I trembled . . . and . . . went doiting in amongst the weaver's looms, till I entangled myself, and could not get out again without working great deray amongst the coarse linen threads that stood in warp from one end of the apartment to the other. I had no knife to cut the cords of this wicked man, and therefore was obliged to call out lustily for assistance. The weaver came half naked . . .

"What now, Mr. Satan? What for are ye roaring that gate? Are you fawn inna little hell, instead o' the big muckil ane?" . . .

My feet had slipped down through the double warpings of a web, and not being able to reach the ground with them (there being a small pit below) I rode upon a number of yielding threads, and, there being nothing else that I could reach, to extricate myself was impossible. I was utterly powerless; and, besides, the yarn and cords hurt me very much. For all that, the destructive weaver seized a loom-spoke, and began a-beating me most unmercifully, while, entangled as I was, I could do nothing but shout aloud for mercy, or assistance, whichever chanced to be within hearing.

The scene has the grotesque humor of some medieval illuminations or of the paintings of Hieronymous Bosch, where the sinner looks silly even in his suffering, where the imp with a prod may as well be a circus clown with a pandy-bat, where, in short, sadism and farce are inexplicably linked. One's reaction is likely to be the unhappy combination of "This is too ridiculous to be true" and "This is too true to be funny." Hogg's use of humor is in no sense a case of "comic relief," nor is it inconsistent with the essential seriousness of his work. His portrait of Robert as a man possessed is first of all a portrait of a silly person, one who fits Bergson's description of the mechanical hence comic character who behaves in such rigid and predictable ways as to be laughable. Robert's exaggerated verbal attacks on his brother, couched in the most pompous of scriptural terms, never altogether lose their comic note as established in the early scene when the laird's bride accuses him of being "a heathenish man of Belial — a dangler among the daughters of women." But Hogg adds to this slight comic portrait two crucial elements: pain and death. By the time we reach the scene in the weaver's cottage, we are as certain as we can be about anything in this novel that Robert has brought about the death of his brother and mother and, very probably, two other people. Secondly, in reading Robert's Memoir, we have seen, amidst all the raving and righteous moralizing, a man suffering terribly. Thus, in the loom episode, lines of the simplest sort — perhaps because, by way of contrast, they *are* so straightforward and plain — can be unexpectedly moving: "I was utterly powerless; and, besides, the yarn and cords hurt me very much." What these lines express specifically and literally has been so obvious to the reader in a general way for such a long time that it comes as a kind of satisfying, if pathetic, reminder of Robert's last remnant of humanity. We needed to hear him say it at least once, simply, without rationalization, without defense. Hogg chooses a scene which might have been treated as farce — in which Robert might have been seen as a thing, a mere object of laughter — to remind us that Robert has enough life left in him to be able to say, "It hurts." And by doing this, he provides something better than a rational explanation to the mysteries, wild visions, and coincidences of the story; he provides a bond of human vulnerability between his protagonist and his reader.

The episode in the weaver's cottage reinforces several other themes of the novel which are closely related to Robert's psychological, spiritual, and physical dilemma. His sin and his madness are expressed in terms of his moral righteousness and religious fanaticism, which *confine* his entire mind and being in a "network" of the rigidly simple doctrines of justification and predestination. The temptation is legalistic reductionism and, as a Scotsman still living among people who tended to be zealous in their literal application of dogma, Hogg obviously knew his subject.[10]

Hogg's distrust of rules, reflected in his lay sermons on religion and literature, may be responsible to some extent for his curious and rather undisciplined career as an artist. The trouble with most of his longer prose and verse narratives is that they are too loosely episodic, too diffuse, too negligent of the slightest conventions of unity. Only once — in *The Private Memoirs and Confessions of a Justified Sinner* — does he balance his unruly taste for life's curiosities with a sense of coherent form. The coherence itself is of a peculiar sort, not chronologically consecutive as one expects in realistic narratives, but constructed out of a series of analogues and resemblances. The reader is not expected to "follow a thread"; if he reads in the way that that metaphor suggests, he is likely to become extremely confused. Instead, Hogg states or embodies a basic theme as early as the marriage scene of the Laird and Lady of Dalcastle and proceeds to repeat it with an extraordinary number of moral, religious, and psychological variations. The theme — the unending war between freedom and restraint — does not change, but is deepened, enriched, enlarged upon, until it penetrates well beneath that level of the reader's consciousness which demands dates and facts.

Like most other writers of romantic fiction, Hogg was not altogether happy with the novel as a literary genre, even though it made relatively few formalistic demands. One can hardly read the diatribes against literary rules in the lay sermons without wondering whether the spectacle of Robert caught in the loom, as well as suggesting the fate of man caught in the snares of the devil or tangled in religious dogma or trapped by his own anxieties, might also be Hogg's half-comic image of a character bound in literary convention and battered by an overactive author, a "destructive weaver." Hogg wanted only enough art to express his awe of life. More than that was too much. His neoclassical predecessors and Calvinist neighbors seem to have stimulated in him a passion for freedom. He was a Christian and a Scotsman, but something in him would have responded to Thoreau's belief that "the wisest man preaches no doctrines; he has no scheme; he sees no rafter, not even a cobweb, against the heavens. It is clear sky." [11]

XII

WUTHERING HEIGHTS

Emily Brontë

1847

Wuthering Heights is the masterpiece of English romantic fiction. A study of earlier experiments in narrative technique and subject matter shows, as a number of critics have demonstrated, that it does not stand quite alone in the history of the English novel.[1] It is part of a tradition or, more accurately, a counter-tradition, since, at its most radical and vigorous, the impulse behind it is precisely that which resists congealing into standard and easily imitable shapes. And yet, *Wuthering Heights* does stand apart from the rest. It is so much better than any other attempt at romantic fiction; indeed, along with *Emma* it is one of the few perfect novels in nineteenth-century English. Others may be more complex, more expansive, but *Wuthering Heights* belongs to that small group of books which convey the impression of an utterly self-sufficient world where style and content really are the same and where the reader can think of nothing useful to add nor superfluous to delete.[2]

It is part of the distinction of *Wuthering Heights* that it has no "literary" aura about it. Emily Brontë does not quote Shakespeare like Walpole and Mrs. Radcliffe; she does not have her characters recite poetry like Lewis; she does not allude to ancient epic or chivalric romance like Scott; and she does not "discover" old documents, letters, or confessions like nearly all of her predecessors. Emily Brontë does not go out of her way to call attention to the fact that what she is presenting has been written down and must necessarily be comparable to other things which have been written down.

There is an appropriateness to the fact that the original manuscript of *Wuthering Heights* has been lost. It is a book which defies many of the usual methods of scholarship and, the little we know of Emily Brontë's life discourages comparison with other writers. "Perhaps not since Sappho has there been such a person," wrote John Cowper Powys. "Certainly she makes the ghosts of de Stael and Georges Sand, of Eliot and Mrs. Browning, look singularly homely and sentimental." [3] It *can* be said — and, of course, has been — that Heathcliff is Byronic, that Catherine is Shelleyan, that the storms are Shakespearian. It can, in other words, be said that Emily Brontë read books, certainly the Bible and Shakespeare, Austen and Scott, and the romantic poets and, it would appear, even Bulwer-Lytton and Sheridan Le Fanu.

Emily Brontë, like any other writer, had to depend on some literary conventions. Her novel does have a beginning and an end; there are dramatically realized scenes, speeches, descriptions of place; there is also, as C. P. Sanger has shown, an extraordinary precision and balance in the presentation of the genealogies of the Earnshaws and Lintons.[4] Even some of the social conventions familiar to Jane Austen are still visible. What makes certain literary and social forms appear so distinctive in *Wuthering Heights* is that they are forced to mingle on equal terms with the deeply subjective perceptions of individual memory and dream. Brontë attempts to eradicate the subject-object distinction by refusing to write a new Battle of the Books in which the historical register and the private memoir collide in midfield. In *Confessions of a Justified Sinner* Hogg had ingeniously armed the two sides for warfare and then permanently postponed the encounter. But it was Scott who provided an allegory of the literary conflict inherent in English romantic fiction before *Wuthering Heights*.

On the battlefield of Culloden, young Waverley's private dream of glory comes into conflict with historical "reality." Reality triumphs, and the subdued hero begins his trip homeward to marriage, maturity, and the recognition that "the romance of his life was ended, and that its real history had now commenced." Scott had indicated several times earlier in his novel that private dreams and memories are not to be taken as reliable or meaningful reflections of human experience. After all, the character in *Waverley* with the most "prodigious memory" is Davie Gellatley, a loyal and entertaining servant, but half-crazy. Young Edward himself loved to daydream, but when he did, he was "like a child among his toys" and the stuff of his dreams was "splendid yet useless."

Emily Brontë's approach to memory and dream could hardly be more dissimilar. Early in her novel she has Nelly Dean commence her narrative to Lockwood with all the ease and simplicity of a nurse telling a fairy tale to a child: "One fine summer morning — it was the beginning of harvest, I remember — Mr. Earnshaw, the old master, came downstairs." [5] Without apology or explanation, in fact, without calling any attention to it at all, the main narrator and most dependable witness we have, casually admits that what she is saying — and nearly everything to follow — is told from memory. The point about Davie Gellatley was that his good memory got him nowhere, that, on the contrary, it kept him isolated from the present by too much dwelling in the past. If Nelly's memory does not get her everywhere, it does get her and us about as far into the lives of Catherine and Heathcliff as any outsider could hope to go. Also, rather than trapping her in the past, Nelly's memory is essentially an instrument for enlarging the present. She tells the story in order to "explain" to Lockwood how Heathcliff and the others living at Wuthering Heights came to be as they are.

The introduction of dream in *Wuthering Heights* also provides a striking contrast to the way Scott first takes it up in *Waverley*. Lockwood, on his second visit to Heathcliff, is forced by a storm to remain overnight. He is put into a room which had belonged to Catherine Earnshaw, glances at some of her books, including a girlhood diary, and then falls asleep and immediately begins dreaming. His first dream, which could be one of Hogg's comic-grotesque anecdotes, places him in a chapel where he listens to a seemingly interminable sermon, hears himself accused of some unspeakable sin, and is beaten by the other members of the congregation without being able to defend himself because he has no pilgrim's staff of his own. The second dream begins with a tapping at the window and ends with Lockwood scraping the wrist of a childlike Catherine Linton against the broken pane because she refuses to let go of his arm.

Lockwood's dreams are not described in a vocabulary different from that used to describe his waking experiences. There is no shift in tone or emphasis. Without needing to know the rest of the story, we can see that the dream is no childish "toy" but a vivid embodiment of adult feelings of guilt and impotence. We are made to witness the interpenetration of waking and dreaming perceptions. Lockwood has read Catherine's diary and noticed a book containing a sermon before falling asleep, but the influence is not only in one direction. When Heathcliff hears Lockwood's cries, he comes to the room, listens to the account of the nightmare, and, after sending Lockwood away, rushes to the window and addresses the specter of Lockwood's dream. The distinction between waking and dreaming is not nearly so clear as one might suppose. Or, to put it another way, life in *Wuthering Heights* is often like a dream, not, as the conventional analogy would have it, because of its sweet brevity, but because of its indifference to reason and its capacity to bring together the incompatible in a single figure or event.

In attempting to say something about *Wuthering Heights,* one is constantly forced to resort to categories, distinctions, and oppositions which the novel either ignores or unites. The subject of narrative technique, so fascinating to some novelists, seemed not to interest Emily Brontë, at least not in the abstract way it interested Scott and Hogg. She did not attempt to oppose or contrast different versions of truth to one another; she made a new truth out of old fragments. To argue that her book is not dreamlike because Yorkshire looks just like that or that it is not unhistorical because the seasons and dates are worked out down to the last hour is to miss one of the major aspects of her achievement. *Wuthering Heights* is like dream *and* like life *and* like history *and* like other works of literature precisely because Brontë rejects the exclusiveness of these categories. They continually inform and define one another.

Nelly Dean is the perfect vehicle for the inside-outside view. As nurse and housekeeper, she has access to the most intimate aspects of family life, to births and deaths, to love scenes and quarrels; she is like a mother to Catherine and the young Heathcliff. Yet, she is not literally a member of the family and, given the English class system of the period, she would have been well aware of her "place" in the household. It is pointless to argue about whether Nelly Dean is a "good" or "bad" character, whether she is sympathetic, genuinely close to the families she serves, or whether she is selfishly detached, even jealous, and therefore hypocritical in her protestations of loyalty. She is detached enough to be able to articulate what might be impossible for Catherine or Heathcliff to put into words, and yet she is involved enough to engage our compassion and, occasionally, to inspire awe. As Carl Woodring has put it, "Firm at the center, her character seems conveniently amorphous at the periphery." [6]

Through the memory of Nelly Dean, Brontë unobtrusively reconciles the extremes of viewpoint represented by Lockwood and Heathcliff. It is one of the early ironies of the novel that the passionless Lockwood pretends to have "a sympathetic chord" which tells him how Heathcliff feels. The fact is that neither Lockwood nor Heathcliff could possibly tell the story without focusing almost exclusively on himself. Nelly can do otherwise. Unlike the governess in James's *Turn of the Screw*, Nelly Dean is not the most interesting figure in the book and, in fact, there are long and important sections in which the reader is hardly aware of her.

2

Wuthering Heights is filled with transformations, the fusion of opposites or the interchange of aspects, until there are fewer and fewer clear distinctions and more and more newly realized continuities. In calling the work "a poem in the fullest and most positive sense of the term," Swinburne pointed to its stylistic and thematic integrity. "There is no monotony, there is no repetition, but there is no discord." [7] What is most impressive is the exactness with which Brontë's artistic method corresponds to her subject: the choice of narrators, the coupling of the inaccuracies of memory with the precision of history, the joining of the vague illogic of dream with the concrete intensity of waking consciousness. Even the creation of individual characters reflects the process. Heathcliff derives his being from a variety of literary, natural, psychological, and biographical sources. He is Byronic, even Gothic, and goes about threatening, like Manfred, Montini, and Falkland, to "smash people to atoms." But he is also a creature of nature, a wild horse or an untamed mongrel. And he is, in his obsessive need to possess Catherine, a personification of a deep sexual urge.[8] He may also be — though this is the most difficult to demonstrate — some compilation of men in Emily Brontë's life. But any one of these designations, if stressed too much, undoes Brontë's work, for it is the character in his wholeness

237

that she makes us see. Brontë's work is a perfect illustration of Coleridge's secondary imagination at work: "It dissolves, diffuses, dissipates, in order to recreate; or where this process is rendered impossible, yet at all events it struggles to idealize and unify. It is essentially vital." The reader is able to respond to the originality of the recreation partly because Brontë makes him a witness to the dissolution of the old patterns out of which the new vision is formed. Inga-Stina Ewbank puts it well when she says, "The weakness of the writing of much nineteenth century fiction is that it takes the situation for granted and indulges in the emotion; Emily Brontë lets her words explore and define the situation itself." [9] To read *Wuthering Heights* is not, as in reading *Emma*, for example, to experience a "finished" work, the end product of a brilliant mind, but to experience a process much like that described by Coleridge in which disintegration precedes unification. Coleridge's verbs, as always, are significant: "dissolve," "diffuse," "dissipate," all connote the separation of parts, the loosening or weakening of whatever element has bound them together. Preconception must be broken down in order that new perception may occur.

Brontë allows us the stability of our preconceptions in the first pages of the novel; the opening paragraphs of *Wuthering Heights* could not have had the effect on readers of the nineteenth century that the opening of *Mrs. Dalloway* or *Portrait of the Artist as a Young Man* had on readers of the twentieth. The first sentences of the book narrated by Lockwood are fictional commonplaces both in construction and in substance:

I have just returned from a visit to my landlord — the solitary neighbour that I shall be troubled with. This is certainly a beautiful country! In all England, I do not believe I could have fixed on a situation so completely removed from the stir of society. A perfect misanthropist's Heaven.

If one has already read the book, it is difficult not to see something ominous in the references to trouble, solitude, and misanthropy. But to approach these sentences on a first reading is hardly to be unnerved. Everything appears to be in order — which is to say in much the same order encountered in dozens of other novels of the period. The narrator is in England, he has just returned from that standard pastime of characters in polite novels, a visit to his neighbor. The relationship of the neighbors is the standard one of tenant and landlord. The spot is isolated but the country is "beautiful" in an, as yet, unspecified way, and it appears likely that the narrator is a man on holiday from the city since he draws the conventional comparison between his quiet retreat and "the stir of society." Even the comment about the place being a "misanthropist's Heaven" is cheerfully made. We do not expect that we are meant to take either expression literally; the narrator has, after all, just visited his neighbor. And as for Heaven, we realize that that is merely a manner of speaking about a place that is restful and pretty.

Once one has read through *Wuthering Heights*, these opening lines take on a pungent irony. But it is important to see that the irony is not inherent in the lines themselves (as it is in the first paragraph of *Pride and Prejudice*) but is a function of the insights we gain later in the book. It is a measure, in other words, of the distance we travel from the familiar world introduced on page one to the strange world, latent in the familiar, but not made explicit until some of the conventional solidity has been undermined. The early pages of *Wuthering Heights* are filled with instances of Brontë's imagination "dissolving" the preconceptions with which Lockwood comes to Wuthering Heights and which the reader, simultaneously, brings to the book. The prospects of polite neighborly intercourse are almost immediately shattered by Heathcliff's unfriendliness and the strangeness of his household. The formalities of a tenant toward his landlord are made to appear irrelevant when Lockwood sees that Heathcliff, despite his gentlemanly bearing, lives in squalor, and grotesquely absurd when he finds himself, during his "social" call, set upon by a pack of ferocious mongrels in his landlord's sitting room. The reader, like Lockwood, loses his bearings at this point. He realizes that this is not to be a novel of manners or even a social novel in the manner of *Caleb Williams*. Heathcliff is not like Tyrell, a tyrannical landlord; he is perfectly indifferent toward his new tenant. It is becoming clear which preconceptions will not do, but it is not at all clear yet what will take their place.

Immediately following Lockwood's mention of his visit to his landlord comes the bland reflection that he is certainly in "beautiful country." This innocuous reference to nature is even more radically undermined than the comment about his neighbor. Two things that city people are expected to say when they come to the country — especially in novels — is that it is "beautiful" and far from the "stir" of society. The Yorkshire countryside of Brontë's novel is doubtless "beautiful" at certain seasons, though it is often ugly and occasionally downright terrifying as presented in the book. The main point is that it is constantly changing, constantly "astir," the furthest thing possible from what is usually called setting (as though static) or background (as though distant). Brontë thus presents and then immediately undercuts the familiar distinction between city and country: one need know very little of Lockwood's former life to realize that no place and no society in his past could have been more furiously agitated than nature and society in the region of Wuthering Heights.

Despite the reception he receives on his first visit, Lockwood returns for a second time to Heathcliff's house and is forced to remain overnight because of a snowstorm. The next morning he finds the face of nature changed:

The whole hill-back was one billowy, white ocean; the swells and falls not indicating corresponding rises and depressions in the ground — many pits, at least, were filled to a level; and entire ranges of mounds, the refuse of the quarries, blotted out from the chart which my yesterday's walk left pictured in my mind.

Certainly this is another kind of nature from the one found in the novels of Ann Radcliffe. For though Emily St. Aubert also suffers the discomforts of stormy weather, her storms are intermittent and ultimately harmless blemishes on the essentially placid, unchanging face of nature. Since nature is a reflection of a benevolent God, it is, despite minor signs to the contrary, a reminder to faithful men and women of his majesty and constancy. But Brontë's nature is not Wordsworth's wise teacher either, for Lockwood, with the "chart" of yesterday's walk in his mind, would still have lost his way. It is true that Heathcliff is able to guide his unwelcome guest home, but his own easy association with nature only serves to underline the difference between Brontë and Wordsworth. Heathcliff has not learned from nature to be patient, charitable, or serene. Quite to the contrary, he is Brontë's natural man largely because he is as changeable and deceptive, as liable to sudden shifts, as the northern climate.

3

Dante Gabriel Rossetti said that *Wuthering Heights* was "laid in hell, — only it seems places and people have English names there." [10] It might have been more accurate to say that the novel is laid where hell and heaven meet. Of Lockwood's "harmless" opening lines, none proves to be more ominous than his remark about the location being "a perfect misanthropist's Heaven." From the Christian point of view, the concept is a bald contradiction since, for a man who cannot love other men, there is not likely to be a heaven. But even taken more broadly as signifying any place of relative peace and contentment, "heaven" hardly seems the word to describe Heathcliff's situation at Wuthering Heights. Brontë relies upon and, at the same time, undercuts both the religious meaning of the term and its casual figurative connotation. As always in the book, standard forms and concepts are visible, but constantly subject to revision and transformation, as though they were being seen through clear but agitated water.

Perhaps the only characteristic that all the varied attempts to describe heaven have in common is their inadequacy before the task. The place seems to dissolve or change locations upon being touched by words. It turns into a hope, a dread, a dream, or, without warning, into hell. And it is a typical paradox of the novel that its elusiveness, its resistance to definition, is its prime claim to reailty. Like all the other realities of this novel — love and hatred, death and life itself — heaven demands boundaries if it is to remain in the realm of human comprehensibility, and yet ultimately it must reject rationally imposed boundaries if it is to be itself.

At least twice Nelly Dean reveals her view of heaven as a place of repose, an end to the dangers and pains of life. When Mr. Earnshaw dies, she observes young Catherine and Heathcliff comforting each other: "No parson in the world ever pictured heaven so beautifully as they did, in their innocent talk; and, while I sobbed, and listened, I could not help wishing we were all there safe together." Beauty and innocence and, above all, safety, are stressed. It is one of the milder statements of the death-wish in the novel but nonetheless one that reminds the reader that even the seemingly stable and sensible housekeeper is sometimes sufficiently frightened and puzzled by life to be willing to exchange it for another existence. When Catherine Earnshaw dies in childbirth, Nelly attends her and watches over her corpse:

No angel in heaven could be more beautiful than she appeared; and I partook of the infinite calm in which she lay. My mind was never in a holier frame, than while I gazed on the untroubled image of Divine rest. I instinctively echoed the words she had uttered a few hours before. "Incomparably beyond and above us all! Whether still on earth or now in heaven, her spirit is at home with God!"

After more pious reflections on the safe repose of the "endless and shadowless hereafter," and death's tranquilizing effect on her mind, Nelly proceeds to unravel her own neat stitches:

To be sure, one might have doubted, after the wayward and impatient existence she had led, whether she merited a haven of peace at last. One might doubt in seasons of cold reflection, but not then, in the presence of her corpse. It asserted its own tranquillity, which seemed a pledge of equal quiet to its former inhabitant.

Immediately following this apparently calm meditation on death and heaven, Nelly addresses Lockwood directly: "Do you believe such people *are* happy in the other world, sir?" The "season of cold reflection" is upon her even as she has been recalling a moment of unusual serenity. Life in the form of a question intrudes upon the static picture of death and, simultaneously, the substance of the question raises the opposite possibility of death or the dead encroaching upon life. Nelly Dean's image of heaven as a place of perpetual slumber is neither original nor complex; it cannot satisfy even her for more than a short time largely because the metaphors traditionally associated with death awaken in her anything but tranquil associations. She speaks of Catherine's "release" into an "endless," "shadowless," "boundless" eternity, yet side by side with these abstractions are stock phrases which associate death with confinement. Nelly refers to her holy "frame" of mind while watching in the "chamber of death" and meditating on Catherine's spirit being "at home" with God since the still corpse "seemed a pledge of equal quiet to its former inhabitant." Nelly's images of "Divine rest" are made on earth and therefore necessarily introduce boundaries even when seeking to portray infinity.

But the problem is not merely one of the limitations of stock language. Remembering an earlier speech of Catherine, the reader suspects that even a Dante or a Milton would be incapable of creating a paradise acceptable to Catherine Earnshaw without Heathcliff. Before her marriage to Edgar she tells Nelly of a dream in which she saw herself in heaven and was "extremely miserable."

"Heaven did not seem to be my home; and I broke my heart with weeping to come back to earth; and the angels were so angry that they flung me out, into the middle of the heath on the top of Wuthering Heights, where I woke sobbing for joy. That will do to explain my secret . . . I've no more business to marry Edgar Linton than I have to be in heaven."

Without Heathcliff, heaven is not a "home," not in any sense a place of repose for Catherine. And since Heathcliff is identified with Catherine's being or, perhaps more accurately, her consciousness of being, it is really that consciousness which she refuses to lose. In a sense, she is the opposite of Hogg's Robert Colwan who, in believing himself to be justified, consigns himself to an existence bounded by rule without possibility of change. In rejecting heaven, Catherine is not, as Nelly suggests, revealing her sinful nature; she is not rejecting good in favor of evil, but rather making a characteristically romantic gesture toward a liberation of the self. Like the heroes and heroines of earlier romantic fiction, Catherine is perpetually "in flight." Though her flight is more often figurative than literal, it too is a flight from confinement, from that which restricts and oppresses. And just as Emily St. Aubert, Caleb Williams, and Maturin's young Spanish novice repeatedly "escape" from one prison only to find themselves in another even darker than the first, Catherine discovers that the haven at the end of each flight must in turn be abandoned. Even "paradise" is a misery for those who are in it because to be contained is to be in hell. True release cannot, therefore, be conceived of, even metaphorically, in terms of place but rather in terms of movement away from one place and toward another.

The central location of *Wuthering Heights* is not the Earnshaw house or Thrushcross Grange, but the ever-changing ground (or billowing sea) between them. Emily Brontë does not represent good and evil or heaven and hell as static phenomena in these houses; both places are capable of temporarily housing either extreme. When Heathcliff and Catherine are still children, they peer into the windows of Thrushcross Grange, admiring the splendid furnishings of the place and envying the Linton children:

"We should have thought ourselves in heaven! And now, guess what your good children were doing? Isabella . . . lay screaming at the farther end of the room, shrieking as if witches were running red-hot needles into her. Edgar stood on the hearth weeping silently."

Once again, what looks like heaven to those outside is hell for the inhabitants. When Catherine marries Edgar and moves to Thrushcross Grange, she tells Nelly that she felt as if she were groveling in an "abyss." Later, in her illness, she "burns" and feels herself to be in a "hell of tumult," wishing only to get out and run free on the open moors.

But even nature, as we have already seen from Lockwood's adventure, provides poor material with which to construct a heaven. Long after Catherine's death, her daughter and the sickly Linton compare their ideas of a perfect summer's day.

"He wanted all to lie in an ecstasy of peace; I wanted all to sparkle, and dance in a glorious jubilee. I said his heaven would be only half alive, and he said mine would be drunk; I said I should fall asleep in his, and he said he could not breathe in mine."

The characters, in describing heaven, are, of course, describing themselves. But more than that, the traditional boundaries between heaven and earth and heaven and hell are eradicated. Each picture of heaven is a condition of nature rather than an alternative to it; and each is a hell from the point of view of the other. Although Linton's picture is more tranquil than Catherine's, both suggest a continuing process, "humming," "shining," "singing," "blowing," "flitting," "pouring," and "undulating." The closest we can come in this book to a definition of heaven is in terms of movement or becoming, a place only insofar as it can suggest other places, a polarity which implies and contains its opposite extreme.

Brontë's characters absorb and embody their own ideals and thus it become all but impossible to define those ideals separately. The standard distinctions between heaven and hell, life and death, are dissolved and reabsorbed into a new organic form which tends toward a new unity in multiplicity. When, at the end of the novel, Heathcliff appears to be near death, Nelly Dean advises him to call a minister who can talk to him about the Bible and explain "how unfit you will be for its heaven, unless a change takes place before you die." Heathcliff replies: "I have nearly attained *my* heaven; and that of others is altogether unvalued, and uncoveted by me!" Heathcliff refers to his burial next to Catherine, and we have come full circle to what Lockwood referred to as the "perfect misanthropist's Heaven." In death he mingles his flesh with Catherine's as he never could do in life. The details of the burial have been called grotesque and morbid, yet they are in keeping with Heathcliff's character and the mood of the entire novel. For sex and marriage are as inadequate to the needs of Heathcliff and Catherine as the heaven of others is.

4

By way of contrast to the vital operation of the secondary imagination, Coleridge describes the lesser faculty of fancy as having nothing to play with but "fixities and definites." As we have seen, little remains fixed or definite for long in *Wuthering Heights*. It is therefore futile to argue about whether Brontë's work is a novel of character or of action. Character is motion and gesture in the novel, and Catherine and Heathcliff are inconceivable except in terms of their passion. We are told that they read books, write letters, and drink tea, but these quiet moments which so often provide an Austen or an Eliot with the opportunity to analyze their characters, appear in *Wuthering Heights* as faded, almost unreal appendages from some vague and irrelevant world. As we become more deeply engrossed in Catherine's nightmares, her temperamental outbursts, and nervous movements, it becomes increasingly difficult to imagine her sitting quietly for an hour over her embroidery. She has no life of any significance or credibility outside of her passion for Heathcliff. Character is no more "fixed" than heaven; nor is it, in George Eliot's words, a gradual "process and an unfolding," but rather energy or power seeking total release.

Brontë's dynamic conception of character and place is sustained by and reflected in her imagery.[11] Nature, savage and gentle, turbulent and calm, is consistently associated with every human mood and action in the book. The language is highly metaphorical, but it is also highly analogical. And the difference between a verbal equation and a verbal comparison is more than merely rhetorical. Metaphor may be so deeply rooted as to be unobtrusive as a manifestation of the kind of synthesis the novel treats on a great many levels. Analogy always calls attention to itself, and, in doing so, calls attention to the essential difference between the two phenomena being compared. Thus when we read that Heathcliff looked "like a savage beast" and "almost as if he came from the devil"; and that his hair is "like a colt's mane"; or that Hareton moves "exactly as a spaniel might"; or that the younger Catherine "trembles like a reed"; has a face "just like the landscape"; and sometimes behaves "as chill as an icicle and as high as a princess," we are reminded that, despite suggestive points of similarity, we are dealing with human nature *distinct* from brute nature and the supernatural. There is the consolation — if that is what it can be called — that heaven is "above," hell "below," and nature "out there," on levels parallel to human experience but not coincident with it.

By employing simile so often and so well, Brontë intensifies the energy of her metaphors because the reader is permitted to *see* — as he does when the landscape is covered with snow — the distinguishing marks "blotted out" to make way for metamorphosis. (Even the prosaic Lockwood notes that the "hill-back *was* one billowy, white ocean" not just "like" one.) The most famous speech in the novel is the one in which Catherine tries to explain to Nelly Dean her feelings for Edgar Linton and Heathcliff. From the beginning, she adopts analogical constructions in reference to Edgar and direct equations between herself and Heathcliff:

"He's more myself than I am. Whatever our souls are made of, his and mine are the same, and Linton's is as different as a moonbeam from lightning, or frost from fire."

When Nelly seems not to understand her meaning, Catherine searches for more similes and even attempts one to describe her love for Heathcliff:

"My love for Linton is like the foliage in the woods. Time will change it, I'm well aware, as winter changes the trees. My love for Heathcliff resembles the eternal rocks beneath — a source of little visible delight, but

necessary. Nelly, I *am* Heathcliff . . . so, don't talk of our separation again
— it is impracticable; and — "

The abrupt transition from analogy to absolute identification is a
powerful piece of drama. Catherine attempts and then rejects comparisons, and finally makes a simple assertion which, on the face of it, is a
logical absurdity. The equation once made, her words break off into
silence, for there is no other or better way to say it. If Catherine had
been made to go about repeatedly through the book making such statements, she could only have appeared a kind of zany parody of the divine
("I am who am," "I am the resurrection," "I am the bread of life") of
the sort one finds in the Victorian Gothic of Bulwer-Lytton and
H. Rider Haggard, whose Ayesha regularly refers to herself as "I the
Mighty and Undying." But the whole point is that Catherine does not
ordinarily speak this way, she is straining the conventions of language
and logic in a moment of great emotional intensity. As readers, we are
witnesses, therefore, not to an *ab extra* implanting of supernatural attributes into human characters, of the sort attempted by Walpole, but
of a movement, indeed a rush, toward what Catherine calls "an existence
of yours beyond you."

"Like is an ill-mark," says one of Hogg's characters. And Hogg, while
acknowledging the limitation of language as analogy, uses that limitation in order to probe the depths of reality. Emily Brontë also knows
how to make use of words as approximations. Indeed, it is her skill and
restraint in conventional linguistic discipline that make her occasional
outbursts so powerful. When Nelly recalls Catherine's phrase, "incomparably beyond and above us all," we are moved not merely by a harmonious arrangement of words, but by a context of mortality and frustrat-
ing verbal limits which gives the expression its meaning. To rail against
restraint, like some of the early Gothic novelists, without demonstrating
the least aesthetic or existential acquaintance with it was, by contrast, to
invoke isolated formulas with no power to move.

Heathcliff's language shows much the same kind of strain as Catherine's. When speaking of Catherine's marriage to Edgar, he draws
scornful comparisons: "He couldn't love as much in eighty years as I
could in a day"; "You might as well try to fill a horse-trough with the
sea" or "plant an oak in a flowerpot" as expect Catherine's passion to

247

be matched by Edgar's. But when Catherine dies, his cynicism and maliciousness turn into a kind of madness, a monomania in which all experience is equated with or, better, absorbed by "one universal idea," his union with Catherine. In speaking of this union, Heathcliff too rejects comparisons and insists upon a literal conjunction. Upon first hearing that Catherine has died peacefully, Heathcliff begs her to haunt him:

"The murdered *do* haunt their murderers. I believe — I know that ghosts *have* wandered on earth. Be with me always — take any form — drive me mad! only *do* not leave me in this abyss, where I cannot find you! Oh God! it is unutterable! I *cannot* live without my life! I *cannot* live without my soul!" (The emphases are Brontë's.)

Heathcliff prays to be haunted by a real ghost, even if it means madness, rather than to be separated from Catherine. Once again we witness a character literally straining against reason in order to express what he is in terms of what he wishes to be, as Beckford would put it, filling himself with "futurity." Catherine's wish results in an early death, but Heathcliff lives long enough to suffer the consequences of what he has prayed for. We are reminded of the delicate balance Brontë has maintained between the world of orderly distinctions and that of irrational fusion when we read one of Heathcliff's last speeches. His universe *is* Catherine:

"What does not recall her? I cannot look down to this floor, but her features are shaped on the flags! In every cloud, in every tree — filling the air at night, and caught by glimpses in every object, by day I am surrounded by her image! The most ordinary faces of men and women — my own features mock me with a resemblance. The entire world is a dreadful collection of memoranda that she did exist, and that I have lost her!"

It is the kind of speech which, with slightly different wording and in another context, might easily seem sentimental, even maudlin. That is, if we could interpret it as "a manner of speaking." But we have come to see that Heathcliff's manner of speaking, as he himself says earlier, is not figurative but actual. It is, in other words, his manner of being. His passion has, at least temporarily, subdued nature, for the universe he describes here is not one in which fire and wind and wild animals contribute to the definition of man, but one in which the image of a single woman obliterates all else.

5

Though there is general agreement among critics that *Wuthering Heights* is a great work of art, there has never been anything like a consensus about its moral significance. A number of hypotheses have been proposed which tend to collect around two distinct viewpoints. David Cecil and Dorothy Van Ghent, among others, argue that the novel is essentially amoral and point to the fact that Catherine and Heathcliff are treated as natural phenomena, no more subject to moral categories than a mountain or a storm.[12] According to this argument, the presence of conventionally moral characters like Edgar and Nelly Dean only emphasizes Brontë's amorality because these characters are so much less interesting and alive than Heathcliff and Catherine. To those who hold to the opposite view, among them, Arnold Kettle, Brontë makes a firm and clear moral judgment of all her characters.[13] Catherine, like a great many other young women in nineteenth-century novels, betrays her own feelings, marries out of a desire for social respectability, and suffers wretchedly because of it. Heathcliff, like the demonic protagonist of a revenge play, eventually destroys himself with his own passion. And finally, the union of the younger Cathy and Hareton reestablishes a tranquil social order and asserts the civilized value of self-discipline.

Both views have merit, yet if taken to the extreme, both are inadequate. It is difficult, in the face of the cyclical structure of the novel and its ironic last words, to insist upon "conclusive" evidence. There seems little doubt that Brontë sees man as in part a moral being, but it is equally clear that this is not all she sees. One of the reasons the moral elements in the novel are weak is that the will is shown to be effective only when it cooperates with circumstances which it did not create. Catherine and Heathcliff are both "willful" characters, yet there is no evidence that they caused the mysterious bond which develops between them. Catherine appears to want a life with Edgar, but her effort to live happily without Heathcliff is a failure. Heathcliff's attempted revenge on the Earnshaw family is a display of a cruelly strong will, but stronger still is the attraction of Catherine even from beyond the grave.

249

As Heathcliff's control over the Earnshaws and Lintons increases, his hold on himself diminishes. He speaks of himself more and more frequently in passive terms, and near the end of the narrative confesses to Nelly that the thought of being with Catherine "has devoured my existence — I am swallowed in the anticipation of its fulfillment." The language may remind us of Faust but the situation does not. Heathcliff's demon is not intellectual pride or lust or even love; nor can it be fully characterized by any moral abstraction. His obsession is with a specific human person and it does not yield easily to generalization. To say that he has behaved improperly may be correct without being adequate.

Swinburne once observed flippantly of Catherine and Heathcliff that their manners "are quite other than Belgravian." [14] But, good or bad, neither manners nor morals are the main issue in *Wuthering Heights*. All the characters have them and therefore it would not be appropriate to ignore them altogether. But our most serious attention is attracted by forces which manners cannot conceal or morals control and by the unique reactions of particular individuals to those forces. As Jane Austen so often and so well demonstrated, the writer concerned with "conduct" is concerned with the community and the general principles which apply to its life. There is a community of sorts in *Wuthering Heights*, just as there are morals and manners, but the extraordinary originality and power of the novel come from its presentation of the private life which communal rules cannot touch. In this, Emily Brontë achieved with unmatched success the aim of every romantic novelist.

Heathcliff is not Everyman, and he and Catherine do not, by any means, represent "all young lovers everywhere." Their experience of one another, Brontë appears to be saying, is ultimately unknowable to anyone but themselves. An appropriate observation, then, is not that it defies morality but that it obscures perception and *therefore* makes external moral judgment uncertain. We are, in a curious way, once again facing the problem posed by Ann Radcliffe when she separated Emily St. Aubert from her clear vistas in the dark corridors of Udolpho. In Radcliffe there is always the sense that the traditional moral categories would apply if only the heroines could figure out where they are — as, in each case, they eventually do.

Brontë offers no solution to the sublime. The "secret" of the relationship between Catherine and Heathcliff cannot be divulged, and that may be why we can take it so seriously. Only religion, psychology, and art are able to subsume the paradoxes inherent in a work like *Wuthering Heights* because they too are grounded in the deficiencies of reason. Brontë does not repudiate moral order any more than she does social order, but she sees them as tenuous and fragile constructs in constant need of reshaping and repair in the aftermath of the storm that is over and in preparation for the one that is always coming. To put it another way, it is not the *value* of order that she questions but its durability, its capaciousness, its power. Her own habit of mind is neither syllogistic nor empirical. She does not seek conclusions but rather looks for ways of freeing herself from them in order to be able to ask new questions.

The last paragraph of *Wuthering Heights* has been much discussed, and little can be added to what has already been said about the imagery of serene nature and the ironic tepidity of Lockwood's "conclusion" as he stands at the headstones over the graves of Catherine, Edgar, and Heathcliff:

> I lingered round them, under that benign sky; watched the moths fluttering among the heath and hare-bells; listened to the soft wind breathing through the grass; and wondered how anyone could ever imagine unquiet slumbers, for the sleepers in that quiet earth.

As in the opening lines of the book, there is much in what Brontë says about Lockwood which is suggestive of the method and theme of the entire novel. Reducing the sentence to its subject and verbs, we have as good an epigraph to *Wuthering Heights* as we are likely to find anywhere: "I lingered . . . watched . . . listened . . . and wondered." Still, the "meaning" of this conclusion, like the question of the novel's morality and structural perfection, continues to provoke debate. Are there ghosts in this book or not? Is Lockwood a blind fool or is his the voice of sanity and reason? It is natural to want to answer these questions once and for all and to be done with them. But it seems more appropriate to the spirit of the book that the debate should not end.

251

EPILOGUE

We have seen over and over again that romantic novels have troubled and unsatisfactory endings. One might say that a resistance to conclusiveness is one of the distinguishing characteristics of romantic fiction. The memorable scenes and original insights come not in climaxes, which often tend to be melodramatic and unconvincing, but in the prolonged preparation for and ingenious prevention of climax—Emily St. Aubert about to be raped, Caleb Williams about to be caught, Edward Waverley on the verge of treason, young Frankenstein in pursuit of his own destruction, Melmoth's victims at the edge of despair, the Colwan brothers in a seemingly perpetual contest.

In its broadest meaning, resistance to conclusiveness is an extension (or an attempted extension) of the ego beyond the limits imposed on it by time and place. As we have seen, this temporal and spatial restlessness motivates the dominant gestures of romantic fiction — the breaking out and running free and the continuous dreaming and remembering of other times and places. Though romantic novelists learned much from the epic and picaresque traditions, the wanderings of their heroes and heroines are neither serious quests nor aimless meanderings. Romantic characters are not unconscious of goals; goals are, in fact, what they are fleeing from. Caleb Williams and Frankenstein may be said to have achieved their "aims" as their stories begin; the central concern of each narrative is flight from the consequences of consummation. Emily St.

Aubert is the mistress of evasion, but Ambrosio, Waverley, and Melmoth are also characters who are defined in terms of escape and pursuit.

Only the Caliph Vathek appears to be on a fixed course toward a place which he reaches and which the reader watches him enter. If the Hall of Eblis scene in *Vathek* is read as a moral commentary on the rest of the book, the reader is likely to rebel, just as he does at the strong moral overtones at the endings of *The Monk*, *Waverley*, *Frankenstein*, and *Melmoth the Wanderer*. The difficulty is not necessarily that the moral commentary is without its own wisdom, but that it does not address itself to and certainly does not "solve" the psychological problems which have been so impressively raised earlier in each narrative.

If, on the other hand, the Hall of Eblis scene is taken not as a moral frame but as a saturation point, an exhaustion of desire and diffusion of the will, then it can be seen not as a punishment or reward, but as a recurring dread seeping into the vitals of the living, undermining their faith in reason and reality, loosening their hold on fixed forms and conclusive findings. The Hall of Eblis may be a "place" where Vathek finally goes, but it is also a *tendency* which has been growing inside him from the beginning.

The treatment of "place" is curious in romantic fiction. One is tempted to say that with Radcliffe the English novel moved outdoors. But despite the increasing importance of vistas and shady groves, Gothic novels, as their titles often suggest, are particularly concerned with buildings. In fact, the abbeys and castles of early romantic fiction appear to be designed to keep nature out. *The Castle of Otranto* and *The Mysteries of Udolpho* are embarrassed by household trappings — servants, meals, furniture — as they are by the conventions of the domestic novel. The interiors in these novels can assume an aura of mystery, but too often they are an assemblage of homely details which form an awkward context for extraordinary events. They encompass much activity but little believable life, and therefore, despite duels, assassinations, and suicides, nothing ever seems to change.

Those novels in which the stability and order of a household are left behind go further in developing the sensibilities of individual characters, but the norms of civilization, though geographically distant, are never very far away. Vathek, Caleb Williams, Waverley, Frankenstein, and Melmoth are not associated with one particular place. In fact, their separation from a place of relative comfort and security is an essential element in their history. But their gestures of self-liberation are necessarily affected, if not wholly determined, by the restraints which they have "abandoned."

Similarly, the most daring thematic innovations of the romantic novelists — the uses of the supernatural and of wild nature, of dream and madness, of physical violence and perverse sexuality — are played ironically or melodramatically against the conventions which they impugn. In terms of setting, tone, and character grouping, romantic novelists often seem to be writing two books in one. Even Emily Brontë, by presenting both Wuthering Heights and Thrushcross Grange, appears at first to be doing this. But through much of her novel the opposition is shown to be an illusion. The households intertwine. Brontë subverts domestic tranquillity without leaving home, but then "home" in her novel does not connote insulation. Wuthering Heights and its inhabitants are accessible to the natural and the supernatural — to ferocious dogs and a strange orphan boy, to a phantom girl thrusting her hand through a window, to the socially correct Lockwood and the uncultivated Hareton, to the fanatic Joseph and the conventionally pious Nelly. Despite its apparent sturdiness, its walls are a thin envelope with little capacity to contain or protect. Static and restricted identity, whether of a household or a person, is an impossibility in the world of *Wuthering Heights*. Individuality, in this most individualistic of novels, is shown to be synonymous with vulnerability. Death and new life are continually intruding.

We so often dismiss the ghosts and apparitions of romantic fiction as silly and insipid that we overlook the extent to which romantic novelists introduced death into fiction as a serious psychological concern. There are deaths in Defoe and Fielding, and Clarissa's death scene must be the longest in English fiction. But in most early realistic and sentimental fiction, death is treated as an event. It is something that happens to people. As a structural device, it is of great use to the novelist. Because of it, fortunes are made or lost, children are confined or released, feuds are initiated or resolved, families separated or united, and stories started or stopped.

For the romantic novelist, death, as an event, is an anticlimax. Death begins as a figment of the imagination, becomes a tendency of mind, and often turns into an obsession. As such, it is not merely a character's worst dream but, from the point of view of story and structure, a novelist's nightmare as well. It is a tow away from achievement and social accommodation, away from symmetry and decorum, away from clarity, meaning, method, and morality, and away from any idea of endings as "accomplishments" or "resolutions." Death, thus conceived, is a marplot. Once allowed into the mind of a major character, it begins its work of unfastening hinges almost before the author has had the chance to put the parts together.

What distinguishes the romantic egoist from most classically tragic heroes is that his ambition is not a temporary or isolated violation of a firm moral or social order, but a mania more powerful than the frail semblances of order which it defies. Lust, curiosity, intellectual pride, envy, and fanaticism are the names given to the dominant tendencies of romantic protagonists, but the moral connotations of these terms are misleading. For though the limits of conventional morality are exceeded, the romantic novelist is more interested in the extent to which the individual tries to bypass the boundaries of the flesh. The strange preoccupation with physical violation in romantic fiction is not so much a matter of breaking laws as it is of breaking life itself. Paradoxical though it may seem, the only permanent escape from climax is death, which has no plot, no beginning, middle, or end. The longings of a Frankenstein, or an Ambrosio, or a Heathcliff cannot be realized in life and, least of all, in the kind of life which was supposed to be the domain of novelists — even Edward Waverley recognizes that his drift is toward death. And so the endings are retreats or explosions, except, of course, the ending of *Wuthering Heights*, which is, magnificently, neither.

After *Wuthering Heights*, it is difficult to find any work which carries the possibilities of intuition, subjectivity, or lyricism further in the novel without losing the old-fashioned outlines of the form altogether. Similarly, it is all but impossible to find any great nineteenth-century fiction, however realistic its total conception, which does not contain somewhere deep in its texture the provocative, unsettling, irrational descendants of the ghosts which Walpole had half-jestingly aroused in his modern romance.

NOTES

INDEX

NOTES

INTRODUCTION

1. Harry Levin, *The Gates of Horn: A Study of Five French Realists* (New York: Oxford University Press, 1963), p. 47.

2. Clara Reeve, *The Progress of Romance* (Dublin, 1785), p. 111.

3. George F. Whicher, *The Life and Romances of Mrs. Eliza Haywood* (New York: Columbia University Press, 1915), p. 20.

4. Quotations are taken from *Constable's Edition of The Castle of Otranto* ed. Montague Summers (London: Constable and Co., 1924). The text of *The Castle of Otranto* is based on the first edition of 1765.

5. *Yale Edition of Horace Walpole's Correspondence*, ed. W. S. Lewis, 34 vols. (New Haven: Yale University Press, 1937–1965), XVI, 44. Hereafter cited as *Yale Walpole*.

6. *The Letters of Horace Walpole*, ed. Peter Cunningham, 9 vols. (Edinburgh: Grant, 1906), II, 364.

7. *Yale Walpole*, XVI, 270.

8. Ian Watt, *The Rise of the Novel* (Berkeley: University of California Press, 1957), p. 28.

9. John Berryman, Introduction to *The Monk* (New York: Grove Press, 1952), p. 27.

10. For a discussion of realism and its relation to the concept of the "thing," see Levin, *The Gates of Horn*, pp. 33–35.

11. *The Works of Tobias Smollett, M.D.*, 8 vols. (London, 1797), II, vi.

12. Watt, *Rise of the Novel*, p. 32.

13. Ibid., p. 301.

14. Edmund Burke, A *Philosophical Enquiry into the Origin of Our Ideas of the Sublime and the Beautiful*, 6th ed. (London, 1770), p. 108.

15. Ibid., p. 332.

16. Ibid., p. 213.

17. Ibid., p. 287.

18. Ibid., p. 212.

19. Ibid., p. 216.

20. Ibid., p. 212.

21. *Hurd's Letters on Chivalry and Romance*, ed. Edith J. Morley (London: H. Frowde, 1911), p. 118.

22. Samuel Taylor Coleridge, *The Table Talk and Omniana*, ed. H. N. Coleridge (London: G. Bell and Sons, 1923), p. 231.

23. Immanuel Kant, *The Critique of Judgment*, trans. J. H. Bernard (New York: Hafner, 1951), p. 88.

24. Ibid., p. 89.

25. Ibid., p. 98.

26. Ibid., p. 99.

27. *Letters of Horace Walpole*, ed. Peter Cunningham, IV, 333.

28. Robert Alan Donovan, *The Shaping Vision: Imagination in the English Novel from Defoe to Dickens* (Ithaca: Cornell University Press, 1966), p. 252.

29. E. M. Forster, *Aspects of the Novel* (London: Arnold, 1928), p. 49.

30. For an interesting discussion of this character type, see Karl Kroeber, *Romantic Narrative Art* (Madison: University of Wisconsin Press, 1960), chap. 7 and pp. 190–191.

31. J. J. Rousseau, *Eloisa*, 3 vols. (Philadelphia, 1796), I, xvi.

32. Ibid., p. xvi.

33. Frank Norris, *The Responsibilities of the Novelist* (New York: Doubleday, Doran & Co., 1928), p. 148.

34. D. H. Lawrence, *Studies in Classic American Literature*, reprinted in *The Shock of Recognition*, ed. Edmund Wilson (New York: Farrar, Straus and Cudahy, 1955), p. 949. *Studies* was first published in 1923.

35. Newton Arvin, *Herman Melville* (New York: Viking Press, 1950), p. 79.

36. Nathaniel Hawthorne, *The Marble Faun*, in *The Writings of Nathaniel Hawthorne*, 22 vols. (Boston: The Riverside Press, 1900), IX, xxiii–xxiv.

37. *Yale Walpole*, II, 110.

38. *Letters of Horace Walpole*, ed. Peter Cunningham, IV, 333.

I. THE CASTLE OF OTRANTO

1. *Yale Walpole*, I, 88.
2. *The Works of John Dryden*, ed. Sir Walter Scott, rev. George Saintsbury, 18 vols. (London, 1881–1892), XVII, 327.
3. *The Spectator*, ed. Donald F. Bond, 5 vols. (Oxford: Clarendon Press, 1965), I, 269, 297.
4. *Hurd's Letters*, p. 114.
5. Ibid., p. 138.
6. *Coleridge's Miscellaneous Criticism*, ed. Thomas M. Raysor (London: Constable and Co., 1936), p. 148.
7. Ibid., p. 7.
8. *Letters of Horace Walpole*, ed. Peter Cunningham, III, 205.
9. *Yale Walpole*, X, 192.
10. *Letters of Horace Walpole*, ed. Peter Cunningham, IV, 333.
11. Northrop Frye, *A Study of English Romanticism* (New York: Random House, 1968), p. 64.
12. Quotations are taken from *Constable's Edition* of *The Castle of Otranto* and *The Mysterious Mother*, ed. Montague Summers (London: Constable and Co., 1924). The text of *The Mysterious Mother* is based on the first edition published at Strawberry Hill in 1768.
13. *The Works of Tobias Smollett, M.D.*, V, 186.
14. *The Works of Alexander Pope, Esq.*, ed. William Warburton, 9 vols. (London, 1770), IV, 166–167n.
15. *Yale Walpole*, XXVIII, 160.

II. VATHEK

1. *Life at Fonthill, 1807–1822*, ed. Boyd Alexander (London: Rupert Hart-Davis, 1957), p. 143.
2. Howard B. Gotlieb, *William Beckford of Fonthill* (New Haven: Yale University Press, 1960), p. 64.
3. Fatma Moussa Mahmoud, "Beckford, *Vathek* and the Oriental Tale," *William Beckford of Fonthill, 1760–1844, Bicentenary Essays* (Cairo: Tsoumas, 1960), pp. 63–121.
4. Lewis Melville, *The Life and Letters of William Beckford of Fonthill* (London: William Heinemann, 1910), p. 143.
5. Ibid., pp. 65–66.
6. Ibid., p. 106.
7. William Beckford, *Biographical Memoirs of Extraordinary Painters* (London, 1834), pp. 123–124, 134.
8. *The Journal of William Beckford in Portugal and Spain*, ed. Boyd Alexander (London: Rupert Hart-Davis, 1954), p. 160.

9. Ibid., p. 201.
10. Ibid., p. 41.
11. Ibid., p. 229.
12. William Beckford, *The Vision* and *Liber Veritatis*, ed. Guy Chapman (Cambridge: Cambridge University Press, 1930), p. 9.
13. *Journal in Portugal and Spain*, p. 46.
14. Ibid., p. 280.
15. Ibid., p. 81.
16. Ibid., p. 213.
17. Ibid., p. 127.
18. Melville, *Beckford*, p. 143
19. Stéphane Mallarmé, Introduction to *Vathek* (Paris, 1876), quoted in William Beckford, *Vathek, with the Episodes of Vathek*, ed. Guy Chapman, 2 vols. (Cambridge: Cambridge University Press, 1929), I, xxv.
20. Sacheverell Sitwell, *Beckford and Beckfordism* (London: Duckworth, 1930), pp. 21, 34.
21. Quotations are taken from William Beckford, *Vathek*, ed. Roger Lonsdale (London: Oxford University Press, 1970). The text is based on the third English edition of 1816 which contains Beckford's corrections of the first English edition, the Samuel Henley translation of 1786. The second English edition was a reissue of the 1786 translation. There are three French editions: the Lausanne edition of 1786 upon which the Henley translation is based, the slightly modified Paris edition of 1787, and the substantially revised Paris edition of 1815.
22. For an excellent discussion of humor and irony in *Vathek*, see James Henry Rieger, "Au pied de la lettre, Stylistic Uncertainty in *Vathek*," *Criticism*, 4:4 (Fall 1962), 302–312.
23. Wayne Booth, *The Rhetoric of Fiction* (Chicago: University of Chicago Press, 1961), p. 85.
24. Beckford, *The Vision*, ed. Chapman, p. 9.
25. Ibid., p. 9.
26. Algernon C. Swinburne to Stéphane Mallarmé, quoted in Mallarmé's *Oeuvres completes* (Paris: Gallimard, 1951), p. 1599, translated and reprinted by Boyd Alexander in "The Decay of Beckford's Genius," *William Beckford of Fonthill, Bicentenary Essays*, ed. Fatma Moussa Mahmoud, pp. 27–28.

III. THE MYSTERIES OF UDOLPHO

1. For a discussion of Mrs. Radcliffe's influence on contemporary literature, see Aline Grant, *Ann Radcliffe* (Denver, Colo.: Swallow, 1951), pp. 112, 142.
2. Virginia Woolf, "Phases of Fiction," *Granite and Rainbow* (London: Hogarth Press, 1958), p. 108.

3. Quotations are taken from Ann Radcliffe, *The Mysteries of Udolpho* 2 vols. (London: J. M. Dent, 1931). The text is based on the 1794 edition.
4. Grant, *Ann Radcliffe*, p. 84.
5. Ann Radcliffe, *Gaston de Blondeville, St. Alban's Abbey, and A Memoir of the Author with Extracts from her Journals*, 1st ed., 4 vols. (London: Henry Colburn, 1826), I, 54.
6. *Coleridge's Miscellaneous Criticism*, ed. Raysor, p. 357.
7. Ann Radcliffe, *Gaston de Blondeville* . . . , I, 39.
8. Frye, *A Study of English Romanticism*, p. 29.
9. Grant, *Ann Radcliffe*, p. 145.
10. Woolf, *Granite and Rainbow*, p. 108.
11. *Coleridge's Miscellaneous Criticism*, ed. Raysor, p. 357.
12. T. N. Talfourd, "Memoir of the Life and Writings of Mrs. Radcliffe," *Gaston de Blondeville*, . . . , I, 106.

IV. CALEB WILLIAMS

1. William Hazlitt, *The Spirit of the Age* (London: J. M. Dent, 1910), p. 184.
2. Quotations are taken from William Godwin, *The Adventures of Caleb Williams or Things As They Are*, ed. David McCracken (London: Oxford University Press, 1970). The text is based on the corrected second edition of 1796. The first edition was published in 1794.
3. William Godwin, *Imogen: A Pastoral Romance* (New York: New York Public Library, 1963), pp. 21–23.
4. William Godwin, *St. Leon: A Tale of the Sixteenth Century*, 4 vols. (London, 1816), I, 1.
5. William Godwin, *Memoirs of the Author of a Vindication of the Rights of Women*, 1st ed. (London, 1798), pp. 200–206.
6. William Godwin, "Letter of Advice to a Young American," *Uncollected Writings by William Godwin*, ed. Jack W. Marken and Burton R. Pollin (Gainesville, Florida: Scholars' Facsimiles & Reprints, 1968), pp. 429–444.
7. William Godwin, Preface to *St. Leon*, I, viii.
8. William Godwin, Preface to *Fleetwood; or The New Man of Feeling*, 2 vols. (New York, 1805), I, vii.
9. William Godwin, *Memoirs of the Author of a Vindication of the Rights of Women*, pp. 202–203.
10. Quoted in William Godwin, "Thoughts Occasioned by the Perusal of Dr. Parr's Spital Sermon," *Uncollected Writings by William Godwin*, ed. Marken and Pollin, p. 319.
11. Ibid., p. 300.
12. William Hazlitt, *The Spirit of the Age*, p. 183.

NOTES TO PAGES 84–103

13. Herbert Read, Foreword to George Woodcock, *William Godwin* (London: Porcupine Press, 1946), p. vii.

14. William Hazlitt, *The Spirit of the Age*, p. 183.

15. For a discussion of Swift's influence on Godwin, see James A. Preu, *The Dean and the Anarchist* (Tallahassee: Florida State University Press, 1959). Other literary influences and parallels are explored in Eric Rothstein, "Allusion and Analogy in the Romance of *Caleb Williams*," *University of Toronto Quarterly*, 37 (October 1967), 18–30.

16. Quotations are taken from William Godwin, *Enquiry Concerning Political Justice*, ed. Raymond A. Preston, 2 vols. (New York: Alfred Knopf, 1926). The text is based on the corrected edition of 1796. The first edition was published in 1793.

17. The original ending of *Caleb Williams*, which Godwin never published, appears as Appendix I in David McCracken's edition of the novel. In that version, Caleb's testimony is not believed and the book concludes with him raving in a prison cell.

18. See Leslie Stephen, *Studies of a Biographer*, "William Godwin's Novels," 4 vols. (London: Smith, Elder & Co., 1907) III, 111–143.

19. David McCracken, ed., Introduction to *The Adventures of Caleb Williams*, p. xxii.

20. Quoted in *Uncollected Writings by William Godwin*, p. xxix.

21. Ibid., p. 300.

22. Edward Baldwin (pseudonym for William Godwin), *Fables, Ancient and Modern* (London, 1812), p. 204.

V. THE MONK

1. *The Life and Correspondence of M. G. Lewis*, ed. M. Baron-Wilson, 2 vols. (London, 1839), I, 80.

2. Ibid., I, 128.

3. Quoted in Louis Peck, *A Life of M. G. Lewis* (Cambridge, Mass.: Harvard University Press, 1961), p. 164.

4. *The Journal of Sir Walter Scott, 1825–1832*, ed. D. Douglas (Edinburgh, 1891), p. 7.

5. Ibid., p. 7.

6. Louis Peck, *A Life of M. G. Lewis*, p. 14.

7. For a discussion of German influences on *The Monk*, see André Parreaux, *The Publication of The Monk* (Paris: Librairie Marcel Didier, 1960), pp. 26–31.

8. Sir Walter Scott, "Essay on Imitations of the Ancient Ballad," *The Poetical Works of Sir Walter Scott, Bart.*, 11 vols. (Edinburgh, 1830), XI, 48.

9. D.A.F. de Sade, *Idée sur les Romans* (Paris, 1878), pp. 31–32.

10. Ibid., pp. 32–33.

11. *Coleridge's Miscellaneous Criticism*, ed. Raysor, p. 370.

12. Elenore Lester reporting on a lecture by Jan Kott, *The New York Times*, June 30, 1968, sect. II, p. 3.

13. D.A.F. de Sade, *Idée sur les Romans*, p. 44.

14. Marquis de Sade, *Oeuvres*, ed. Maurice Nadeau (Paris: Éditions du Seuil, 1947), p. 48.

15. Ibid., p. 52.

16. Quotations are taken from Matthew G. Lewis, *The Monk* (New York: Grove Press, 1952). The text is based on the first edition of 1795.

17. Louis Peck, *A Life of M. G. Lewis*, p. 113.

18. Ibid., p. 36.

19. Ibid., p. 37.

20. Jean Genêt, *Our Lady of the Flowers*, tr. Bernard Frechtman (New York: Grove Press, 1963), p. 221.

VI. NORTHANGER ABBEY

1. Louis Peck, *A Life of M. G. Lewis*, p. 175.

2. David Rives, *Literary Memoirs of Living Authors of Great Britain*, 2 vols. (London, 1798), I, 372–373, quoted in André Parreaux, *The Publication of The Monk*, p. 88.

3. T. J. Mathias, *The Pursuits of Literature* (London, 1798), p. 239.

4. Anonymous, "Review of *Prometheus Unbound*," *The Literary Gazette*, no. 190 (September 9, 1820), 581.

5. John Styles, *Lord Byron's Work Viewed in Connexion with Christianity and the Obligations of Social Life* (London, 1824), p. 22.

6. Francis Jeffrey, "Review of *The White Doe of Rylstone*," *The Edinburgh Review*, no. 25 (October 1815), 355–356.

7. Anonymous, "Review of *Adonais*," *The Literary Gazette*, no. 255 (December 8, 1821), 772.

8. John Styles, *Lord Byron's Work*, p. 22.

9. Quoted from Dr. Parr's "Spital Sermon" in *Uncollected Writings by William Godwin*, pp. 312–313.

10. T. J. Mathias, *The Pursuits of Literature*, p. 345.

11. Francis Jeffrey, "Review of *The Excursion*," *The Edinburgh Review*, no. 24 (November 1814), 3.

12. Jane Austen, *Northanger Abbey* and *Persuasion* in *The Novels of Jane Austen*, ed. R. W. Chapman, 5 vols. (London: Oxford University Press, 1959), chap. V. Quotations from *Northanger Abbey* are taken from this edition.

13. Excellent discussions of the dual aspect of *Northanger Abbey* may be found in Marvin Mudrick, *Jane Austen, Irony as Defense and Discovery*

(Princeton, N.J.: Princeton University Press, 1952); Howard Babb, *Jane Austen's Novels, The Fabric of Dialogue* (Columbus: Ohio State University Press, 1962); Henrietta Ten Harmsel, *Jane Austen, A Study in Fictional Conventions* (The Hague: Mouton & Co., 1964); A. Walton Litz, *Jane Austen, A Study of Her Artistic Development* (New York: Oxford University Press, 1965); and Frank J. Kearful, "Satire and the Form of the Novel: The Problem of Aesthetic Unity in *Northanger Abbey*," *Journal of English Literary History*, 32 (December 1965), 511–527. Mudrick argues that parody prevails over realism, while Babb takes the reverse position. Litz, Ten Harmsel, and Kearful show the two conventions in balance, each informing and qualifying the other.

14. An interesting discussion of the importance of words in *Northanger Abbey* may be found in Joseph Wiesenforth, *The Errand of Form, An Assay of Jane Austen's Art* (New York: Fordham University Press, 1967). Despite the merits of his general argument, I think Wiesenforth overstresses Henry Tilney's hold on reality.

15. It is at this point that I disagree with Wiesenforth's assertion that "when Henry is looked at with respect to his concern for language, he is seen to be totally aware of reality" (*The Errand of Form*, p. 15). In my opinion, the critic who has examined Henry's reproach most sensitively is Frank J. Kearful ("Satire and the Form of the Novel," pp. 523–524) who argues that the speech "takes advantage of our false psychological security." My view is that it does not change the basic situation except insofar as it removes Henry from his pedestal and shows that even good sense and reason have their limits.

VII. WAVERLEY

1. Sir Walter Scott, "Essay on Imitations of the Ancient Ballad," *The Poetical Works of Sir Walter Scott, Bart.*, 11 vols. (Edinburgh, 1830), XI, 39–55.

2. *The Journal of Sir Walter Scott, 1825–1832* (Edinburgh, 1891), p. 155.

3. *Northanger Abbey* is discussed in "Miss Austen's Novels," *Quarterly Review* (January 1821), reprinted in *Critical and Miscellaneous Essays of Sir Walter Scott*, 3 vols. (Philadelphia, 1841), I, 408–435.

4. Quotations from *Waverley* are taken from *Waverley Novels*, 25 vols. (Edinburgh, 1852–53), vol. I. Known as the "Library Edition," this is based on Scott's last revised edition of 1829–33.

5. *The Prose Works of William Wordsworth*, ed. Rev. Alexander B. Grosart, 3 vols. (London, 1876), II, 89.

6. *The Letters of Percy Bysshe Shelley*, ed. Frederick L. Jones, 2 vols. (London: Oxford University Press, 1964), II, 277.

7. William Hazlitt, *The Spirit of the Age*, p. 224.

8. The comments on Scott and Romanticism are from Georg Lukács, *The Historical Novel*, trans. H. and S. Mitchell (London: Merlin Press, 1962), pp. 31–63; David Daiches, "Scott's Achievement as a Novelist," *Scott's Mind and Art*, ed. A. Norman Jeffares (Edinburgh: Oliver and Boyd, 1969), p. 21; Edgar Johnson, *Sir Walter Scott: The Great Unknown*, 2 vols. (New York: Macmillan, 1970), I, 524–530; and Francis R. Hart, *Scott's Novels: The Plotting of Historical Survival* (Charlottesville: University Press of Virginia, 1966), p. 4.

9. *The Journal of Sir Walter Scott*, p. 119.

10. Ibid., p. 66

11. *The Works of John Ruskin*, ed. E. T. Cook and A. Wedderburn, 39 vols. (London: G. Allen, 1904), V, 336.

12. As Francis R. Hart says, Waverley's "experience and its world are dreamlike, but all too real; he is experiencing the disintegrating interpenetration of romance and reality" (*Scott's Novels*, p. 27).

13. Daiches, "Scott's Achievement as a Novelist," *Scott's Mind and Art*, p. 33.

14. Levin, *The Gates of Horn*, p. 45.

15. Kroeber, *Romantic Narrative Art*, pp. 181–182.

16. Walter Pater, *Appreciations* (London: MacMillan, 1924), pp. 8–10.

17. Samuel Butler, *The Way of All Flesh* (New York: Random House, 1950), pp. 417–418.

VIII. *FRANKENSTEIN*

1. Sir Walter Scott, "Remarks on *Frankenstein*," *Blackwood's* (March 1818), reprinted in *Critical and Miscellaneous Essays of Sir Walter Scott*, I, 448.

2. Quoted in Howard B. Gotlieb, *William Beckford of Fonthill*, p. 61.

3. For a discussion of the genesis of *Frankenstein*, see James Rieger, *The Mutiny Within* (New York: G. Braziller, 1967), pp. 237–247.

4. *Mary Shelley's Journal*, ed. Frederick L. Jones (Norman: University of Oklahoma Press, 1947), pp. 32–33.

5. Quotations are taken from Mary W. Shelley, *Frankenstein, or The Modern Prometheus*, ed. M. K. Joseph (London: Oxford University Press, 1969). The text is based on the third edition of 1831, Mary Shelley's revision of the 1818 first edition.

6. M. K. Joseph, Introduction to *Frankenstein*, p. xiv.

7. *Mary Shelley's Journal*, p. 183.

8. *The Letters of Mary W. Shelley*, ed. Frederick L. Jones, 2 vols. (Norman: University of Oklahoma Press, 1944), I, 281.

9. Mary Shelley, *The Last Man*, ed. Hugh J. Luke, Jr. (Lincoln: University of Nebraska Press, 1965), p. 5.

10. Ibid., p. 18.

11. Quoted in *Mary Shelley's Journal,* p. 20.

12. Thomas Macaulay, "Review of Thomas Moore's *Letters and Journals of Lord Byron,*" *Edinburgh Review,* no. 53 (June 1831), 544.

13. Elizabeth Nitchie, *Mary Shelley* (New Brunswick, N.J.: Rutgers University Press, 1953), p. 219. For a fascinating account of the stage history of *Frankenstein,* see pp. 218–231.

14. William Hazlitt, "Review of Shelley's *Posthumous Poems,*" *The Edinburgh Review,* no. 40 (July 1824), 494.

15. Percy Bysshe Shelley, "A Discourse on the Manners of the Ancients, relative to the Subject of Love," *Essays and Letters by Percy Bysshe Shelley,* ed. Ernest Rhys (London, 1886), p. 48.

16. For a discussion of the polar symbolism in *Frankenstein,* see James Rieger, *The Mutiny Within,* pp. 79–89.

17. *The Complete Works of Samuel Taylor Coleridge,* ed. W. G. T. Shedd, 7 vols. (New York, 1884), III, 326.

18. Ibid., II, 449.

19. Quoted in Ford K. Brown, *The Life of William Godwin* (London: J. M. Dent, 1926), p. 375.

IX. NIGHTMARE ABBEY

1. Thomas Love Peacock, "Memoirs of Percy Bysshe Shelley," *The Halliford Edition of the Works of Thomas Love Peacock,* ed. H. F. B. Brett-Smith and C. E. Jones, 10 vols. (London: Constable, and Co. 1934), VIII, 112.

2. Ibid., p. 74.

3. Ibid., p. 101.

4. Ibid., p. 113.

5. Thomas Love Peacock, "The Four Ages of Poetry," *The Halliford Peacock,* VIII, 19–20.

6. *The Letters of Percy Bysshe Shelley,* II, 98.

7. Ibid., p. 6.

8. "The Four Ages of Poetry," *The Halliford Peacock,* VIII, 20.

9. "Letters," *The Halliford Peacock,* VIII, 204.

10. Quotations from *Nightmare Abbey* are taken from *The Halliford Peacock,* vol. III.

11. *The Halliford Peacock,* V, 2.

12. *The Complete Works of S. T. Coleridge,* III, 567.

13. William Hazlitt, *The Spirit of the Age,* p. 194.

14. *The Halliford Peacock,* V, 67.

15. *The Letters of P. B. Shelley,* II, 8, 26.

16. Ibid., p. 363.

X. MELMOTH THE WANDERER

1. Quotations are taken from Charles Robert Maturin, *Melmoth the Wanderer*, ed. Douglas Grant (London: Oxford University Press, 1968). The text is based on the first edition of 1820.
2. Douglas Grant, Introduction to *Melmoth the Wanderer*, p. xi.
3. C. R. Maturin, *The Milesian Chief*, 4 vols. (London, 1812), I, iv.
4. Quoted by Nicolas Powell in his Introduction to *The Drawings of Henry Fuseli* (London: Faber and Faber, 1951), p. 21.
5. Douglas Grant, Introduction to *Melmoth the Wanderer*, p. xi.
6. Maturin, *The Milesian Chief*, I, 179.
7. William F. Axton, Introduction to *Melmoth the Wanderer* (Lincoln: University of Nebraska Press, 1961), p. xviii.
8. C. R. Maturin, *Bertram, or The Castle of St. Aldobrand* (London, 1816), p. 23.
9. Axton, Introduction to *Melmoth the Wanderer*, p. xi: "In his moral ambiguities of character, the hero-villain exemplifies the relativism and the fascination with moral paradox which typify his age."
10. C. R. Maturin, *The Universe: A Poem* (London, 1821), p. 11. Although Maturin's name appears on the title page, authorship was claimed by James Wills, a young friend of the novelist's. For a fair analysis of the dispute, see Niilo Idman, *Charles Maturin, His Life and Work* (London: Constable and Co., 1923), pp. 271–276. It is my opinion that the poem is probably a collaboration and that the religious views expressed in it are identical with those expressed by Maturin in his other writings.
11. Ibid., p. 34.

XI. THE PRIVATE MEMOIRS AND CONFESSIONS OF A JUSTIFIED SINNER

1. André Gide, Introduction to *The Private Memoirs and Confessions of a Justified Sinner* (New York: Grove Press, 1959), p. x.
2. Quoted by Gide from a remark by Dorothy Bussy, ibid., p. x.
3. James Hogg, *Familiar Anecdotes of Sir Walter Scott* (New York, 1834), pp. 167–170.
4. Quotations from *The Brownie of Bodsbeck* are taken from *Tales and Sketches by the Ettrick Shepherd*, 2 vols. (Glasgow, 1837), vol. I.
5. From a conversation between Yeats and Joyce, quoted in Richard Ellmann, *The Identity of Yeats* (New York: Oxford University Press, 1954), pp. 86–89.
6. Quotations from Hogg's sermons are taken from *A Series of Lay Sermons on Good Principles and Good Breeding by the Ettrick Shepherd* (London, 1834).

7. Flannery O'Connor, *Mystery and Manners*, ed. Sally and Robert Fitzgerald (New York: Farrar, Straus & Giroux, 1970), p. 184.

8. Quotations are taken from James Hogg, *The Private Memoirs and Confessions of a Justified Sinner* (New York: Grove Press, 1959). The text is based on the first edition, which was published anonymously in 1824.

9. Alain Robbe-Grillet, *Pour un nouveau roman* (Paris: Les Éditions de Minuit, 1963), p. 90.

10. For a discussion of the Antinomian controversy in Scotland in the eighteenth century, see Louis Simpson, *James Hogg: A Critical Study* (Edinburgh: Oliver & Boyd, 1962), pp. 170–173.

11. Henry David Thoreau, *A Week on the Concord and Merrimac Rivers*, ed. Walter Harding (New York: Holt, Rinehart & Winston, 1963), p. 55

XII. WUTHERING HEIGHTS

1. Possible sources for *Wuthering Heights* are suggested in Chapter XIV of A. Mary F. Robinson, *Emily Brontë* (London, 1883); Leicester Bradner, "The Growth of *Wuthering Heights*," PMLA, 48 (March 1933); and Florence Swinton Dry, *The Sources of Wuthering Heights* (Cambridge, Eng.: W. Heffer & Sons, 1937). The best critical discussion of the relationship between *Wuthering Heights* and the Gothic tradition is in Inga-Stina Ewbank, *Their Proper Sphere: A Study of the Brontë Sisters as Early Female Novelists* (Göteborg: Akademiforlaget-Gumperts, 1966).

2. The perfection of construction in *Wuthering Heights* has been noted by a number of critics, including Mark Schorer in his Introduction to *Wuthering Heights* (New York: Rinehart Edition, 1950) and contested by Albert J. Guerard in his Preface to *Wuthering Heights* (New York: Washington Square Press, 1960).

3. John Cowper Powys, *Suspended Judgments* (New York: G. A. Shaw, 1916), p. 314.

4. C. P. Sanger, *The Structure of Wuthering Heights* (London: Hogarth Press, 1926).

5. Quotations from Emily Brontë's *Wuthering Heights* are taken from the 1847 text (New York: Rinehart, 1950).

6. Carl Woodring, "The Narrators of *Wuthering Heights*," *Nineteenth Century Fiction*, 11 (March 1957), p. 303.

7. *The Complete Works of Algernon Charles Swinburne*, ed. Sir Edmund Gosse and Thomas J. Wise, 20 vols. (London: W. Heinemann, 1926), IV, 47.

8. For a Freudian analysis of *Wuthering Heights*, see Thomas Moser,

"What is the Matter with Emily Jane? Conflicting Impulses in *Wuthering Heights*," *Nineteenth Century Fiction*, 17 (June 1962), pp. 1–19.

9. Ewbank, *Their Proper Sphere*, p. 153.

10. *Letters of Dante Gabriel Rossetti*, ed. Oswald Doughty and John Robert Wahl, 4 vols. (London: Oxford University Press, 1965), I, 224.

11. An exhaustive study of the imagery of *Wuthering Heights* may be found in Elisabeth T. M. Van De Laar, *The Inner Structure of Wuthering Heights: A Study of an Imaginative Field* (The Hague: Mouton, 1969).

12. Lord David Cecil, *Early Victorian Novelists* (London: Constable, 1934), pp. 147–159, and Dorothy Van Ghent, *Form and Function in the English Novel* (New York: Rinehart & Co., 1953), pp. 153–170.

13. Arnold Kettle, *An Introduction to the English Novel*, 2 vols. (New York: Harper & Row, 1960), I, 139–155.

14. *Swinburne*, IV, 49.

INDEX

Addison, Joseph, 27, 33
American Romanticism, 23–24
Aristophanes, 187
Arvin, Newton, 24
Auden, W. H., 221
Austen, Jane, 2, 79, 100, 118, 121, 137–
138, 144, 148, 175, 181–182, 187, 209,
234; *Northanger Abbey*, 118, 122–135,
136–137; *Love and Freindship*, 132;
Emma, 233, 238
Axton, William F., 197

Balzac, Honoré de, 189
Baudelaire, Charles, 189
Beckford, William, 2, 22, 81, 100, 104,
147, 155, 172, 188, 191; *Vathek*, 2,
44–45, 50–64, 253; *Modern Novel
Writing*, 43; *Dreams, Waking
Thoughts and Incidents*, 46; *Bio-
graphical Memoirs of Extraordinary
Painters*, 46; *The Vision*, 48, 63; *Por-
tuguese Journal*, 48
Beddoes, Thomas Lovell, 35
Behn, Aphra, 37
Berryman, John, 7
Blake, William, 29, 45–46, 52–53, 63,
100, 199
Booth, Wayne, 55
Brontë, Emily, 1, 7, 22–23; *Wuthering
Heights*, 233–251, 254–255
Bulwer-Lytton, Edward, 24, 234, 247
Burke, Edmund, 83, 185; *Philosophical
Enquiry into the Origin of Our Ideas
of the Sublime and the Beautiful*, 12–
17
Burney, Fanny, 22
Burton, Robert, 185
Butler, Samuel, 154
Byron, George Gordon, Lord, 7, 45, 51,
70, 99–100, 107, 119, 157–158, 177,
179, 189

Camus, Albert, 83, 96
Cecil, David, 249
Céline, Louis Ferdinand, 56
Coleridge, Samuel Taylor, 15, 19, 29–
30, 36, 69, 76, 96, 103, 120–121, 155,
169–171, 177, 179, 183–184, 238, 245
Collins, Wilkie, 228
Collins, William, 5, 66
Congreve, William, 3
Conrad, Joseph, 148
Cooper, James Fenimore, 24

Daiches, David, 139, 153
Dante, 58, 61
Defoe, Daniel, 4, 7, 9, 24, 34, 254
De Quincey, Thomas, 65, 208
Dickens, Charles, 20, 228
Diderot, Denis, 32
Donovan, Robert, 18
Dostoevsky, Feodor, 31, 190
Doyle, Arthur Conan, 228
Dryden, John, 6, 27, 30, 37

INDEX

INDEX